Managing Reproductive Life

Fertility, Reproduction and Sexuality

GENERAL EDITORS:

David Parkin, *Director of the Institute of Social and Cultural Anthropology, University of Oxford*

Soraya Tremayne, *Co-ordinating Director of the Fertility and Reproduction Studies Group at the Institute of Social and Cultural Anthropology, University of Oxford*

Volume 1
Managing Reproductive Life: Cross-Cultural Themes in Sexuality and Fertility
Edited by Soraya Tremayne

Volume 2
Modern Babylon? Prostituting Children in Thailand
Heather Montgomery

MANAGING REPRODUCTIVE LIFE

Cross-Cultural Themes in Sexuality and Fertility

Edited by
Soraya Tremayne

Berghahn Books
New York • Oxford

First published in 2001 by

Berghahn Books
www.BerghahnBooks.com

Editorial offices:
604 West 115th Street, New York, NY 10025, USA
3 NewTec Place, Magdalen Road, Oxford OX4 1RE, UK

Library of Congress Cataloging-in-Publication Data
Managing reproductive life : cross-cultural themes in sexuality and fertility / edited by Soraya Tremayne.
p. cm. -- (Fertility, reproduction, and sexuality ; v. 1)
Includes bibliographical references and index.
ISBN 1-57181-500-7 (cl. : alk. paper) --
ISBN 1-57181-317-9 (pb. : alk. paper)
1. Kinship. 2. Sex customs. 3. Human reproduction. 4. Fertility, Human. 5. Reproductive health. 6. Population policy. 7. Health policy. I. Tremayne, Soraya. II. Series.

GN487 .M36 2001
304.6'32--dc21 2001049935

British Library Cataloguing in Publication Data
A catalogue record for this book is available from the British Library.

Printed in the United States on acid-free paper.

ISBN 1-57181-500-7 (hardback)
1-57181-317-9 (paperback)

CONTENTS

List of Figures and Tables

FOREWORD

Re-cast, the analysis of kinship remains at the core of socio-cultural and biological anthropology. It sometimes takes the traditional form of the study of the marriage, descent and transmission rules by which groups perpetuate themselves over time. Less obviously, it is also often in the form of questions about gender. Gender itself can be unpacked. It may be studied as relational identities, with variations extending beyond the dualistic biological model of male and female to various socio-cultural and biological constructions of cross-sexual behaviour and transformation. Or, as in this volume, the study of gender focuses on the role of women's sexuality and reproductive capacity in a range of varying social contexts in which women's agency is pitted against other attempts to harness, exploit or alter that capacity. The key question is who and/or what actually manages women's sexuality and reproductive life. The earlier anthropological concern with kinship as being at the basis of social continuity drew on an array of distinctions such as that between paternal as against genitorial rights (social versus physical fatherhood) and spoke of men's rights in women's genetrix or procreative powers, and, less often, of women's own genetricial or reproductive rights. The view was of such rights being transacted along with the women in whom these rights were vested, sometimes in exchange for bridewealth or accompanying dowry in marriage, and as part of a system of alliances between inter-marrying groups. The glossary of terms was impressive but undeniably objectified women, often more so than the indigenous concepts of the societies being studied.

Later structuralist analyses depicted marriage as forming exchanges between groups rather than fulfilling the demands of descent. The approach eventually led the way to thinking of women as well as men playing a part in such exchanges. This was the so-called descent versus alliance debate. The image of descent groups exchanging their men and women in the present as against that of lineal descent groups perpetuating themselves over time through control over women's reproductive powers, certainly gave women more agency than under the old descent-based model. But it was agency still carried out within a framework of male reproductive control. The two perspectives also complement each other: people strategise for the best marriages and alliances; but they may also think of their ancestors and future lines of progeny in doing so. Either perspective invokes rules of marriage alliance or descent affiliation.

The remarkable cases that emerge from Amazonian societies suggest that neither alliance nor descent theory usefully explain the dynamics of fertility and reproduction in that part of the world. Belaunde's account of the Peruvian people, the Airo-Pai, is of a highly coherent blending of cosmological and inter-personal elements in the relationship of a woman and her husband, who, through the couvade and other kinds of behaviour, shares responsibility with his wife for the couple's success in producing children and in spacing them at intervals that their subsistence mode can tolerate. They are, moreover, culturally enjoined to express this sharing of responsibility as a common desire to have children and to talk about it in an appropriate language of emotions.

A quite different picture of the role of emotions is evident in Unnithan-Kumar's portrayal of rural Rajasthani women's experiences of reproduction in Jaipur, India. It is the women largely alone who see themselves as carrying the mental and physical burden of pregnancy and child-bearing, so much so that it is more to spiritual healers and or private gynaecologists that they turn rather than to the child delivery services provided by the state. There are here regularities and a pattern of reproductive behaviour, but the intervention of the state healthcare system, however little it may sometimes be used, inevitably modifies the role of kinship and family.

More generally, as this volume shows, rule-governed structures of the descent versus alliance kind sit uneasily with countervailing practices and events. Teenagers become pregnant not just before marriage but outside and even in defiance of the possibilities of any marriage being arranged; mothers turn to prostitution in order to make ends meet, cherishing their children but having also to provide for parents and a natal family of their own birth; or, prostitutes turn to motherhood in order to change their status and provide for a future; other women, having demonstrated to themselves and others that they can become pregnant, procure abortions on the premise that, at a later date, they can become a mother, as Day describes in her study of London sex workers, a decision that may later be precluded by the ever-present threat of infertility. Sometimes wider social changes do not directly bring about a change in the rules but threaten to do so indirectly. Hampshire's study of Fulani temporary male out-migration shows that it is the resultant increase in sterility rates that may induce change rather than actual decisions about fertility, and that women's worsening health is part of this change.

Can we say that new rules are being set up? At a micro-level there may be some consistencies in behaviour in the short-term, but there is also on-going alternation of expectations, norms and ideals. In her introductory analysis of recent shifts in the anthropological study of kinship, Tremayne shows how many earlier anthropological starting-points are no longer appropriate. The concern with reproductive rights remains important but, under the influence of feminism may now refer not to men's and local descent groups' control of women's fecundity, but to international questions of human rights, in which women's agency as choice-makers is expected to be central, as Harris and Smyth argue should be the case even in refugee reproductive policy. From this new perspective, reproduction now becomes a matter of women's health and not only the means of social continuity. While biomedicalised as never before, women's bodies here become means of protest, strategy and power as well as of subordination and passivity.

Such concerns are nowadays set against a wider concern in policy circles with rapid population growth, a tension made more acute when an increasing proportion of mothers are young teenagers and themselves regarded as children. Arranged child marriages have been customary in many societies, so that what appears distinctive nowadays is an alleged increase in teenage pregnancy out of wedlock, a kind of reversal. Increased urbanisation, poverty, tourism and population concentration may be cited as overarching causes and yet, within this, as Heather Montgomery shows, young Thai girls may not always seek to avoid pregnancy despite acknowledging its adverse effects, for it may mean a change in recognised status from child to adult, from dependent to carer and hence to one owed duties by others and not simply having to perform them for others. While some thereby accept it, other girls do reject motherhood if they can, with the result that motherhood is by no means the unambiguous status category an earlier anthropology might have depicted. Such ambivalence of views on the part of the girls and the ambiguity of the category of motherhood may, on the one hand, show how dangerous it is to assume that the young women are homogeneously and totally passive in the face of internationally driven prostitution, but it also indicates what are in reality a limited set of choices open to them. In Teesside, in the United Kingdom, also, teenage pregnancy is by no means always judged by members of the local population in the same way, as Russell demonstrates.

While motherhood here presupposes at least the fiction and even possibility of choice and some freedom of definition, writ large it is always a social category embedded in a chain of associations and practices, as Cornwall suggests. She shows how among the Ado-Odo of South-Western Nigeria women with and without children share in the collective construction of motherhood as referring not just to those who physically have children but also those who handle, hold, care, feed and foster them but do not always have children of their own. As in many African societies the handing round of children to hold reinforces a kind of communal conceptualisation of child-caring responsibility, quite unlike the western nuclear family focus on a single child-parent relationship. As a downside, however, such inclusive or comprehensive motherhood may extend blame for a child's death to the jealous witchcraft of one of the holders, especially if she lacks children.

Motherhood and teenage pregnancy may here then be ambiguous categories, or at least as comprising elements uncaptured by the English terms. But so also, as Boyden shows more generally, is that of childhood itself. English vocabulary distinctions such as child, youth, adolescent, teenager and young man or woman aim to essentialise stages of early human growth. This differs from even modern Hong Kong where, as Martin shows, a persisting traditional Chinese family model encourages parents to think of their children as future providers rather than as objects to be celebrated in the present, as if abstracted from their developing status as proto-adults. The English terms in fact do no more than hint at cross-cutting and usually subjective distinctions between pre- and post-pubertal, rebellious and responsible, promiscuous and chaste, and developing and developed, setting up a whole chain of negative stereotypes with, as Boyden says, urban street youth characterised as the most violent, sexually deviant and reviled social category. Nevertheless, selectively used, such terms may often be the basis of western-derived international symposia and recommendations. They Euro-centrically ignore alternative distinctions made in indigenous languages. Even in countries like Britain, as Russell describes, young people in Teesside have developed their own ways of making sense of and acting with regard to teenage pregnancy which do not always reflect those of planners. Add to this the fact that, as Price and Hawkins indicate, the health needs of young people in developing countries have only recently come to the attention of policy-makers, it is of even greater importance to bring to bear a more nuanced anthropological perspective to counter the 'policy discourse' employed by demographic technicians and others. Maturation stages, including what we translate as the transition from child to adult, may be (ritually) marked in all societies but in different ways and with different emphases and social consequences. Local ethnographic accounts are time-consuming to write and read, but global generalisations may become inaccurate or too broad to be useful.

What comes through strongly in this volume, the first of a new series, is the view that different socio-cultural constructions of maturation, sexuality and reproductive processes make sense in relation to each other on a comparative basis and are not simply mapped on to an assumed biologically universal distinction between child and adult. Evident also is the conflict between sexuality and reproduction for the purpose of social perpetuity and as means to personal ends, a conflict often only resolved or tolerated through transcendent ritual and/or belief. Viewed cross-culturally, the management of reproductive life is not just a matter of formal systems of authority, control and knowledge transmission, nor of following policy-makers' directives, nor even of integrating these with indigenous ones. It also extends to recognising the metaphysical and cosmological understandings and practices that everywhere accompany rules, plans and policies.

David Parkin
Oxford, March 2001

Preface

This volume is the result of a two-day workshop held in October 1999 organised by the Fertility and Reproduction Studies Group at the Institute of Social and Cultural Anthropology (ISCA), University of Oxford. The chapters were selected from twenty-four papers presented at ISCA's Fertility and Reproduction Seminars. The choice reflects the dynamics of the current issues in this field. Since this is the first in a series on Fertility, Reproduction and Sexuality, it also aims at setting the scene for future publications.

The book as a whole explores the social dynamics of human reproduction from a cross-cultural perspective. It examines the contextual nature of fertility and reproduction as it relates to people's lives today. A number of interrelated themes on fertility/infertility, reproduction, parenthood, vulnerable groups and policy issues are addressed, all of which are of increasing concern at a global scale. The 1994 Cairo International Conference on Population and Development (ICPD) highlighted the importance of understanding the complexities of the issues involved in human reproduction, and resulted in a universal agreement by the participating countries to place reproductive health and reproductive rights firmly in the context of human rights. Several of the countries which were signatories of the ICPD resolutions have subsequently shown a real commitment to adopt clear population policies, and a great deal of effort and resources have been allocated for this purpose. However, it is beyond the scope of this book to examine whether as a result of ICPD we have a better understanding and more effective policies towards improving the problems of reproductive health.

The book has two distinct objectives: first, it aims at demonstrating the diversity and complexity of the ways and means used by people to remain in control of their fertility. It examines what reproduction means to different people in very different communities, from the pastoral nomads of Burkina Faso to London sex workers, and what strategies each community uses to regulate its fertility and for what purpose. The second aim is to provide examples of some of the global issues concerning fertility and reproduction in contemporary societies. Included are: the problems of youth and vulnerable groups such as refugees; the importance of gender relations; the misconceptions of planners and their interventionist policies, and whether policies can go wrong if planners fail to take into account the specific combination of cultural factors as determinants of values in fertility and reproduction. The title reflects the active role people play in regulating their fertility. The contributors unanimously agree that, contrary to the recent tendency among planners to focus on women as the main decision-makers, and the popular image that associates fertility and reproduction predominantly with women, human reproduction goes beyond women. The complex web of social relations and institutions surrounding human reproduction means that it takes at least two people, and frequently the wider social group, to determine and manage fertility in a community.

One of the common themes of the authors is the resourcefulness and adaptability of human societies in the way they alter their strategies to adapt to change. With the exception of two chapters, all address the dynamics of human reproduction in contemporary societies. However, the book is divided into parts largely on the basis of the emphasis put on a particular topic:

Part One addresses agency and identity. Four case studies reflect the key issues of the role of human agency, and of the various strategies people adopt in their communities to retain their social status and to preserve themselves or their community from what they perceive as outside threats – including those of planners and policy makers. The case studies cover small communities, but the size and statistical relevance of the examples are not of importance here. Rather, the aim is to highlight the less visible aspects which play a crucial role in decision making by communities, and which are often overlooked by modern states and their policy makers.

Part Two explores the meaning of parenthood, fertility and infertility, and how these are used by individuals to ensure reproductive continuity, or to reinforce or restore their respectability in the community. It starts with a chapter on the mechanism involved in fertility regulation among the pastoral nomads in Burkina Faso. The two following chapters address the implications of being childless, the meaning of being a parent in cases of infertility in Nigeria, and the meaning of children to Chinese parents. The last chapter discusses the importance of gender complementarity in the regulation of fertility in ensuring safe and healthy reproduction among a small Amazonian community of Peru.

Part Three concentrates on what is becoming increasingly an issue of widespread concern, namely the reproductive health of vulnerable people. Two major groups in this category are young people and refugees. They are both growing in numbers and have become the target of attention on the global scene. The reproductive health of young people, especially in the developing world has become a top priority. The first chapter clarifies what is meant by childhood and youth, and describes the wide range of definitions of these concepts. It provides a historical and sociological perspective, and highlights the areas where this understanding can help the success of implementing policies. This is followed by a chapter on the sexual and reproductive health of young people in developing countries and the meeting ground of global policies with local issues. The third chapter is a case study of teenage pregnancies in the UK, which challenges several of the assumptions made by health officials on teenage sexuality and pregnancy. The last chapter is concerned with policy towards refugees' reproductive health; a much under-researched area. Refugees are one of the largest vulnerable groups in the world and yet very little is known of their sexual and reproductive needs once they are displaced.

I wish to thank the ESRC for generously funding the workshop, and Rolla Khadduri for her excellent report on the workshop. I owe particular gratitude to Anna Enayat for her help in the preparation of this manuscript at its various stage and to David Parkin for his Foreword and for the unfailing support he has given to this project.

Notes on the Contributors

Luisa Elvira Belaunde is a lecturer at the Department of Anthropology, University of Durham. She has carried out fieldwork amongst several indigenous Amazonian peoples, about whom she has published several articles. She has also conducted applied development and health research in Latin America and Africa.

Jo Boyden is a social anthropologist and presently a senior research officer at the Refugee Studies Centre, University of Oxford. She has for many years been involved in research, writing, training, policy development and advocacy in relation to especially disadvantaged children. Her main interests include child development, social integration and socalisation in the context of armed conflict and forced migration, research ethics, methods and methodology and cultural constructions of childhood.

Andrea Cornwall is a Fellow of the Institute of Development Studies at the University of Sussex, where she works on participation in development, gender and sexual and reproductive health. She has published on a range of development, gender and health-related themes and is co-editor, with Alice Welbourn, of *Realising Rights: Transforming Approaches to Sexual and Reproductive Wellbeing* (Zed, forthcoming).

Sophie Day is Senior Lecturer in Anthropology at Goldsmiths College, London. She has published extensively on her work with prostitutes in London, and is currently involved in a Wellcome Trust supported project looking at changes in the sex industry 1985–2000 and a European Union supported network for HIV/STI prevention among prostitutes across Europe.

Kate Hampshire is Lecturer in the Department of Anthropology, University of Durham. Her main research interests are in the health and demography of African pastoralists, and in the interface between anthropology and demography. She has carried out extensive fieldwork among Fulani agropastoralists in Northern Burkina Faso and is currently involved in research on delivering health services to nomadic pastoralists in Chad.

Colette Harris is presently Director of the Women in International Development Programme at Virginia Tech University, USA. A specialist in the field of gender and development, from 1996–2001 she implemented a community-based development project together with a local NGO in Tajikistan, CIS. She was formerly a research associate at the University of Amsterdam.

Kirstan Hawkins was formerly a Lecturer in Anthropology and Health at the Centre for Development Studies, University of Wales, Swansea and is currently an independent researcher and consultant. She specialises in the anthropology of sexual and reproductive health, and has undertaken ethnographic fieldwork in Bolivia and Zambia. Her commissioned activities include providing social development expertise for the design and monitoring of sexual and reproductive health programmes, social analysis of health sectors, and participatory social monitoring of health interventions.

Diana Martin took her first degree in Chinese. She subsequently spent twenty years in Hong Kong and wrote her doctoral thesis on pregnancy and childbirth among the Chinese of Hong Kong. She now teaches part-time at the Department of Social Anthropology, Oxford University and at Oxford Brookes University. She is a member of the Fertility and Reproduction Studies Group at the Institute of Social and Cultural Anthropology, University of Oxford.

Heather Montgomery is Lecturer in Childhood Studies at the Open University and a member of the Fertility and Reproduction Studies Group at the Institute of Social and Cultural Anthropology, University of Oxford. Her book, *Modern Babylon? Prostituting Children in Thailand* will be published in this series by Berghahn in 2001. She writes on issues of children's rights and the anthropology of childhood.

Neil Price is Subject Leader in Population and International Health at the Centre for Development Studies, University of Wales, Swansea. He specialises in the political-economic anthropology of fertility, and has undertaken fieldwork in the Caribbean, China, Cambodia, Kenya and Zambia. He has extensive experience of advisory and commissioned research with international agencies throughout Sub-Saharan Africa, Asia and Latin America. His main areas of advisory expertise are in the monitoring and evaluation of reproductive and sexual health programmes, and in social and institutional analysis in the health and population sectors. He has published widely in anthropology and development journals, and his Caribbean ethnography *Behind the Planter's Back: Lower Class Responses to Marginality in Bequia Island, St Vincent* is published by Macmillan.

Andrew Russell is Lecturer at the Department of Anthropology, University of Durham, and works on the Human Sciences, Health and Human Sciences and Medicine degrees at its Stockton campus (UDSC). His doctoral research was conducted in East Nepal and he has subsequently done fieldwork in North-East India. He is currently involved in a number of health-related projects in the North-East of England. He is editor (with Iain Edgar) of *The Anthropology of Welfare* (1998) and (with Elisa J. Sobo and Mary S. Thompson) of *Contraception Across Cultures: Technologies, Choices, Constraints* (2000).

Ines Smyth is Policy Advisor for East Asia at Oxfam, UK. A social anthropologist, she has taught and carried out research in various academic institutions, including the Institute of Social Studies in The Hague and the London School of Economics. Her areas of interest are gender theory, industrialisation in developing countries and reproductive rights and health.

Soraya Tremayne is the Co-ordinating Director of the Fertility and Reproduction Studies Group, University of Oxford and a Research Associate at the Institute of Social and Cultural Anthropology, University of Oxford. She was Vice-President of the Royal Anthropological Institute. Her current research interests are in the sexual and reproductive health and behaviour of young people in Iran.

Maya Unnithan-Kumar is Senior Lecturer in Social Anthropology at the University of Sussex. Her research in the early 1990s focused on kinship, gender and family relations in North-West India. This was published as a monograph, 'Identity, Gender and Poverty: New Perspectives on Caste and Tribe in Rajasthan' (1997). Her current interest is in the field of medical anthropology, especially the anthropology of reproduction and healthcare policy. She has published several articles on issues relating to reproductive healthcare and is currently editing a volume on 'Anthropology, Reproduction and Health Policy'.

Introduction

Soraya Tremayne

Human reproduction is a complex and intricate process which is determined by a combination of biological, environmental and social factors. Whilst evolutionary biologists may focus on the perpetuation of genes per se, the main interest of this volume is on the social dynamics of the reproductive process. By reproducing humans seek to ensure continuity and, to this end, they surround fertility and reproduction with complex social organisations, beliefs, norms and rituals. These take various forms in different cultures and manifest themselves in kinship, religion, law, economics and politics. Humans also create physical boundaries to preserve their social group from outside penetration and threats. They differentiate themselves from other social groups with whom they interact in terms of distinctive criteria such as language or religion, thus developing ethnic identities. Finally, to ensure stability and continuity, humans adopt appropriate strategies to respond to environmental and natural changes. Reproduction is therefore a dynamic process, which is not limited to two people reproducing biologically. It concerns the wider social group and interacts with economic, political, religious and legal institutions. As Robertson puts it, 'Reproduction is a relentless force in our lives, adding to and subtracting from the people around us, and obliging us to change our relationships with each other and with the wider world. It is a persistent strategic challenge, the outcome of which is as important for society as for the person in each household. Reproduction is simply too important to be left to the whims and fancies of individuals.' (1991:16). The dynamic nature of reproduction, and the fact that it concerns the community at large, requires that it be controlled and managed in order to preserve practices which are the result of 'numerous generations trying to make sense of the task of creating new life in a particular environment' (Robertson, 1991:17). To control and manage their reproduction, and to reach an ideal population size, people throughout history have adopted strategies to regulate their fertility, even though they may not always have been aware of the facts of procreation.

Background

Studies of the dynamics of human reproduction from an anthropological perspective are relatively recent. Although the significance of reproduction has always been recognised in anthropological discourse (Loizos and Heady, 1998), a focus on the dynamics of the social and cultural factors involved in reproduction has emerged as an important part of anthropological theory only in the past few decades. A brief look at the evolution of anthropological thought in the late nineteenth and early twentieth centuries shows that kinship, as the social expression of reproduction, has been viewed as the social institution which is 'the most transparently structured realm of human life' (Barnard 1994:785) and that it has been treated as the single most important aspect of society in anthropological theory. Beattie (1964:102) describes kinship as 'the idiom through which certain kinds of political, jural, economic, etc., relations are talked about and thought about' and portrays it as a 'contentless form which humans employ to create social relations'. In the history of anthropology it was through the study of kinship that the variety of human conceptual systems and the internal logic of diverse social structures came to be recognised. Barnard (1994:785) argues that 'kinship studies have promoted a quasi-fallacy that kinship is built on models that are more "real" than those of religion, of economics, of politics, or of law'; but, he goes on, 'kinship structures are not more "real" than those other notions, but they are more apparent cross-culturally than the structures studied by specialists in religion, economics and politics'. In Barnard's view, the apparent cross-cultural reality of kinship stems from an erroneous equation of 'kinship' with 'biology'. Despite the 'obsessive'[1] attention paid by early anthropological studies to questions of kinship, studies of reproduction remained narrowly rooted in the biological aspects of procreation and kinship in almost all societies

1. Coward (1983) cited in Franklin and Ragone (1998, Introduction).

was built on a supposedly biological foundation. Human reproduction was viewed as a 'natural' and biological phenomenon, and kinship studies paid more attention to cross-cultural differences than to the dynamics of reproduction. Anthropological studies also focused on paternity as the focal point of investigations of the social structure, and 'knowledge of physical paternity indexed the limitations curtailing analysis of "reproduction"'. (Franklin and Ragone, 1998:2) These factors, which resulted in the isolation of reproduction from its broader social context, have been one of the main reasons for its marginality in anthropological theory.[2]

The re-emergence of an anthropology of reproduction is the result of a number of marked shifts which have taken place throughout the world in the past few decades. As Sen, Germain and Chen (1994:3) put it, 'dramatic changes in the demographic characteristics of the world population are the hallmark of this century. At no earlier time in human history has the number, composition, and distribution of human population undergone such a rapid and profound transition.' Since the late 1960s and early 1970s policy makers have concentrated on finding solutions to the 'population problem' and 'population explosion' which became a central issue in development policy. Several factors have, from this time, shaped evolving attitudes and practices towards population, policy and reproduction. The most important, at the first stage, was a concept and practice of development which not only viewed population growth as an obstacle to economic growth, but linked the decline of fertility to an improvement in economic conditions. The argument put forward was that development is the best contraceptive, and that if people are educated their economic situation will improve and their fertility will automatically be reduced. Population policies subsequently underwent several changes (see below), and by the early 1990s, with the rise in awareness of the environment, public attention had focused on the connection of population numbers with both environmental issues and development (Sen, Germain and Chen: 1994:4). A second influential factor has been the advances in fertility and birth control techniques, with new pharmaceutical technologies offering choices to individuals, planners and policy makers. Thirdly, policy makers have sought to control population growth through the intervention of the state, justified in the name of the common

2. Ginsburg and Rapp (1991, 1994, 1995a) and Franklin and Ragone (1998, Introduction) have fully addressed the reason for the absence of reproduction in anthropological theory.

good, and wherever they have judged population growth undesirable, policies have been devised to control it. An increasing number of countries, especially those with high fertility levels, have thus adopted some form of population policy.[3]

The fourth factor, and one that has made a key contribution to recent shifts in the approach to reproduction, has been the rise of feminism, which addressed the reproductive experiences of women as a central element in the power structure of societies. In Ginsburg and Rapp's words (1991:312):

> Since the 1970s, the analysis of reproduction has been greatly enriched by the encounter between second-wave feminism and anthropology, in which women's reproductive experiences were analysed as a source of power as well as subordination. The fallout from this encounter was rich and impressive: some authors considered whether 'women's secrets' might be a power base, or even a site of resistance. Others used data from 'women's medicine' (like herbal birth control and prolonged nursing as a method of ovulation suppression) to show the effectiveness in scientific terms of such alternatives to medicalised systems. Western medical control of women's bodies, especially during pregnancy, became a focus of both popular and scholarly investigation.

The recent shift in the use of the term reproduction to 'reproductive health' and 'reproductive rights', and the medicalisation of reproduction in contemporary societies, have gone hand in hand with an increase in the intervention of states in the reproductive life of their citizens. In spite of this intervention and its pervasive nature, ethnographic research suggests that only those international policies which meet with people's reproductive ideals at the local level stand a chance of succeeding.

The dynamics of reproduction

The western development models of the early 1970s did not produce the expected results as it became clear that fertility in many parts of the world did not necessarily decline with better standards of living. The quest for solutions led to a considerable amount of research, including ethnographic research, which demonstrated the complexity of human reproduction. It became apparent that reproduction could not be viewed as a monolithic variable, and that it constantly interacts with social, economic and political institutions. As Ginsburg and Rapp put it, 'reproduction is a slippery

3. For a detailed description of different population policies, see Blake (1998).

concept' (1991:311), and any attempt to reduce it to a 'static classification which would make the task of defining it easy and convenient, would tell us as much about reproduction as a sketch of a wing tells us about how a bird flies'(Robertson, 1991:159).

Ethnographical literature provides abundant examples of the different ways societies, regardless of their size, regulate fertility and control it, thus increasing or decreasing their numbers. The ability to control and manage fertility therefore emerges as a crucial factor in the survival of communities. McLaren (1984:150) describes the need for this control as follows:

> Because the conceiving and bearing of children was so important previous generations elaborated a remarkable range of strategies to deal with each stage of the procreative process. It is difficult in fact not to think that we today have a much more impoverished sense of our own powers when contemplating parenthood. This is in part because in some ways we have developed a rigid, mechanical view of reproduction. Parents in the past perceived it as mutable – conditioned to diet, exercise, potions and charms. They believed that nature and culture interacted and that their fertility was accordingly their own social creation.

The individual reasons why people reproduce are too lengthy and controversial to discuss here. In Robertson's words (1991:60, 61):

> Whatever the reasons for producing children, various concerns and pressures force people to make choices to take control over rearing children, whatever our genetic and sexual urges may be. Throughout history and at every level of society from the individual and the family to the community and the state, people have had preferences about the number of children or their sex, about when they will have children and how much they wish to invest in them, and whether other people's children may be raised as their own. Our techniques for influencing these things have improved enormously in the last few decades, but it would be a grave mistake to imagine that 'family planning' is a modern innovation. Ethnography has shown the acute and active interest people have taken in the two counterpoised problems of the restriction and enhancement of fertility.

Nomadic and pre-agricultural populations generally have a low fertility rate and control their fertility through a number of measures, including late marriage, infanticide, contraception, abortion and child spacing. Agriculturist societies, on the other hand, have high fertility levels, as is also the case among the urban poor. The value of children and their role in society is therefore a central factor in reproductive decisions (Ginsburg and Rapp, 1991:326). Finally, as Robertson argues, 'perhaps the most serious mistake of all would be to assume that reproduction is inherently "irrational", devoid of any kind of calculation or strategizing, and therefore with no constructive role to play in the making of human history' (1991:25).

'Irrational' reproductive behaviour, both in a historical perspective and in contemporary societies, can only be understood in the light of the priorities people have over what might be considered 'logical' behaviour. Modern western development rhetoric, which serves as the basis for formulating international population policy, is often based on assumptions which, when put to the test, prove inaccurate. One of these is that societies lacking modern contraceptive technology cannot control reproduction and therefore have too many children they may not want. A second assumption is that when people become familiar with modern technological methods of contraception they will want to use them to reduce their fertility. The demographic theory which assumes that modernisation means a shift from natural to controlled fertility has been, and remains, at the core of the policies devised for reproductive health. However, Makhlouf's (1992) review of the data in the Arab region demonstrates the discrepancies that arise from such demographic models which relate high fertility levels of Muslim Arab countries to the lower status of women in Islam and lead to measures to improve the status of women.[4] As Makhlouf argues, neither the improvement in the economic conditions of women nor the efforts to raise their status have made a considerable difference in the fertility levels among the Muslim communities in the Arab World. Her analysis illustrates that when reproduction is treated as a single variable and is taken out of its social, cultural and historical context, crucial factors which are responsible for the reproductive behaviour of people, may be overlooked and be totally misunderstood and misinterpreted.

From reproduction to reproductive health

As awareness of the population explosion on a global scale has increased, the complexities of the issues involved in human reproduction have gradually become apparent to policy makers. In the decades that followed the first world population conference

4. For an illuminating example of the failure of such theories, see Makhlouf (1992).

in Bucharest in 1974, the critical role of women in population policies was acknowledged. Demographic research started to focus intensively on women and the links between fertility and women's status, associating high status with factors such as female education, female literacy and female labour participation which were, in turn, linked to low fertility, smaller families, later marriage and contraceptive use. The literature of this time indicates that women's development was bound up with demographic objectives, and was not concerned with the well-being of women as such. The next decade witnessed a shift from addressing women's health needs primarily through family planning and maternal and child healthcare programmes towards reproductive healthcare programmes. At the same time, mainstream development thinking began to focus on the alleviation of poverty amongst women. The approach was to address poverty rather than the subordination of women, with the expectation that greater economic independence would bring with it greater decision-making power. Women, in this scenario, would become less dependent on their children, and hence their views on the number of children they would like would change.

Further research has gradually revealed the complexity of the relationship between education, work, fertility and family planning, and it has become apparent, for example, that education does not affect fertility directly, but instead acts through many variables (Makhlouf, 1992). The simple approach of upgrading women's status, both economically and socially, was shown to be ineffective and incapable of dealing with the underlying factors which determine women's decision-making. The importance of understanding the principles that govern relations between the sexes, and the dynamics of power and gender relations is now recognised.

The 1994 International Conference on Population and Development (ICPD), convened in Cairo, took place amid general agreement that the focus of past programmes on demographic outcomes aimed at reducing population growth had not yielded the desired results, and that the notion of family planning and population control should be replaced by a broader concept of sexual and reproductive health and rights (Petchesky and Judd, 1998:9).

The resulting revision in population policies essentially suggested that reproductive health policies should take account of, and understand, the social contexts of sexual behaviour, and become part of a political agenda which is 'conversant with the economic and social realities being faced and which challenges conventional population and development policy' (Harcourt,

1999:8). As Hartmann (1993:xix) argues, 'rapid population growth is not the root cause of development problems in the Third World; rather it is a symptom of those problems'.

Agreement was reached that, in order to motivate people to have fewer children, it is not only necessary to improve their living standards, but also to give them the freedom of choice to decide on the number of children they want. In short, a consensus emerged at ICPD that population issues were not about demographic concerns, but about the rights of individuals and their freedom of choice regarding their sexual and reproductive life. These arguments implied that, in giving people the opportunity to choose the reproductive life they desire, health planners and policy makers should not be able to use reproductive health to meet demographic objectives. A second belief, namely that women who are in charge of their fertility will automatically choose to have fewer children, was also questioned. By referring to the 'rights of individuals' resolutions also explicitly referred to the rights of men as well, and articulated the importance of understanding the power relations and gender relations. As Moss (1994:9) puts it, 'Only an analysis that takes into account gender relations can shift the focus of "women and population programmes" from fertility reduction to reproductive choices'.

In short, the Cairo conference marked a paradigm shift in the formulation of international population policy, a dominant feature of which is 'the notion of individual attainment of sexual and reproductive health and rights as central to population policy, as opposed to achievement of demographic targets' (McKintosh and Finkle, 1995).

Agency and identity

Since the shift that took place at Cairo, and the consensus that emerged there, a considerable amount of both academic and applied research has been carried out, which have provided a take-off point for the scholars whose work is published in this book.

After Cairo, although the reproductive health of men was also considered as an important part of the Cairo agenda, and an increasing number of programmes concentrated on men, the majority of policies predominantly focused on addressing women as the main agents of change. But, in their eagerness to give women long overdue attention, decision-makers talked about 'women' as a universal category, and overlooked the importance of giving equal attention to the wider social and cultural context of reproduction. (Harcourt, 1997:8) As Harris and Smyth argue here, the notion of reproductive health may offer little support to the development and implementation of policies unless proper account is taken of the motives behind the strategies women adopt in relation to their reproductive health. These decisions, moreover, are not taken in isolation from the overall social network. Maya Unnithan-Kumar's inquiry into women's experiences of reproduction in Jaipur, India, shows that an understanding of women's agency in negotiating the various forces exerted on their lives must be paramount in any measures to improve their health and rights. The way women perceive and manage the physiological and social burden of reproduction and related healthcare at an individual level is the key to their survival. Unnithan highlights the ways women have to negotiate their reproductive health through the limited access they have to healthcare, and the choices open to them for making decisions. She argues that women's selection of who they should go to with their health problems (whether traditional healers, health services or private medical practitioners) depends on their interaction with specific members of their kin group and the extent of the power and control of the latter over them. Women have to navigate their way through an intricate web of social relationships and a social hierarchy which does not necessarily imply men, but often female in-laws. Emotions and desires are considered, in Unnithan's analysis, as the driving force behind these relations, the agency of women being central to the negotiations they conduct. The perception women have of themselves in relation to their reproductive functions is, moreover, a determining factor in the process of considering the options open to them. Unnithan points out that emotions are a much overlooked aspect of the motivations behind decision making and places them at the heart of the discourse of power, 'negotiating between one's own feelings and that of others'. Women's reproductive decisions, in her view, are not a response to the authority of the patriarchal system, nor that of the state, but are driven by individual interaction with various members of the kin group.

Kirstan Hawkins also takes up the issue of emotions in decisions regarding health, this time among migrant Aymaran women in El Alto, Bolivia. She examines the links between power and reproduction and uses Foucauldian analysis to explore, in Ginsburg and Rapp's words (1991:314), 'the dialectic between, on the one hand, the discursive strategies of the state, the market, and the international medical institutions, and, on the other hand, resistances to them' in order to show how power differences not only repress but also construct identities. Hawkins argues that most of the contacts women have with formal biomedical health result in emotionally negative consequences. These increase women's vulnerability to emotional disturbance and ill-health. Women's decisions as far as their reproductive health is concerned are formed by beliefs other than medical ones. The local constructions of health and illness are fluid, and different sources of knowledge represented in the different medical systems (modern medical and traditional) are drawn upon by women and are often used simultaneously, apparently without contradiction. Women's choices as far as their health and well-being are concerned shift according to context. Hawkins maintains that women's discourses on health and sexuality are embedded within the wider construction and negotiation of social identity and power relations. For example, they argue that through affiliation with the Methodist Church individuals are able to reconstruct and negotiate their identities according to their changing economic, political and social positions. Both Unnithan and Hawkins demonstrate the complexities involved in the shaping of reproductive decisions and strategies. Not unlike the Rajasthani women studied by Unnithan, who interact with other women in decisions concerning their reproductive health, the Aymara women of Bolivia interact with other women rather than men in the use of indigenous methods of fertility regulation which are controlled by women.

Human agency, identity and emotions are also a theme of the chapter by Andrea Cornwall who highlights the role played by children and their importance in the case of infertile women in Ado-Odo, South-Western Nigeria. The choices made by children to affiliate themselves to their mother or other members of the family as they grow older are extremely significant, especially for women who cannot bear their own children, and often allows them to actively craft relationships of intimacy through surrogate maternal practices; Cornwall also highlights the importance of emotions reflected in 'holding' a child which confirms the relationship of the woman with the child as a 'real' mother

Reproductive patterns do not change easily, and decisions to alter them are not taken lightly by communities, unless they are faced with some threat to their continuity. The complex context in which decision-making takes place when environmental changes encounter social and political ones is discussed by Kate Hampshire. She argues that the complex and varied ways in which different factors combine to determine fertility decisions can lead to results that are unexpectedly contrary to what might be called 'the predictable scenario'. For example, social and political coupled with environmental and climatic changes in the past few decades, have led to increasing economic pressures on the agropastoralist Fulani of Northern Burkina Faso. One of the consequences of these pressures has been male out-migration to towns with a resultant impact on fertility. In many parts of sub-Saharan Africa such migration has altered attitudes on a number of different levels and in many cases has led to the drop in fertility assumed to be a desirable consequence of modernisation. Hampshire argues that this is not so among the Fulani. Exploring the links between ethnic identity and the reproductive processes (which are also discussed here by Belaunde) she points to the multiple factors which affect fertility decisions among the Fulani: the importance of being fertile, the meaning of children, the preference for boys among agro-pastoralists, the low cost of bringing up children, the adoption system of children by childless relatives, the climatic changes leading to droughts and the increasing dependence of the kin group on each other. Hampshire also addresses another assumption about the impact of male out-migrations – namely that it increases female autonomy – showing that the drop in fertility in a society which values high fertility and blames women for childlessness creates a situation of increased vulnerability for many women.

As discussed earlier, it has been supposed that fertility and its regulation is generally associated with women, and is either decided by them, or affects their position within the society directly. Ethnographic evidence, however, shows that in some cultures men become directly involved in women's reproductive cycle and are responsible for the fertility of their wives. Elvira Belaunde argues that among the Airo-Pai of Amazonian Peru, the study of fertility is ultimately inseparable from the cultural construction and expression of emotions between the couple and towards children. She demonstrates that menstruation becomes an important factor in the social organisation of a population with low fertility, that menstrual taboos and rituals among Airo-Pai act as pro-natalist incentives, and that a wife's infertility is blamed on her husband's lack of care during her menstruation. Menstruation, one of the important markers of female fertility, has long been of interest to anthropologists. As Ginsburg and Rapp point out (1991:318), 'symbolic elaborations of menstruation have long received scholarly attention in anthropology, considered by some to be a central component in human social organisation'. A critical appraisal of both early and current work on menstruation points out that only recently that menstruation has been contextualised into larger cultural systems'. Belaunde also argues that a shift from a female-centred to a couple-centred approach is required in the analysis of fertility regulation. The Airo-Pai, unlike many forager-horticulturists who, under the pressure of external forces such as colonialism, became high fertility populations, still act according to a reproductive ideal of a few well-spaced children and rely for this upon a variety of traditional contraceptive techniques.

Reproductive decisions go beyond economic, political and environmental factors. Reproduction is fundamentally linked with identity, and the multiple values attached to reproduction come into force when people are confronted with undesirable situations which require negotiation of their rights. As Kligman (1998:5) argues, 'reproduction is fundamentally associated with identity: that of "the nation" as the "imagined community", that the state serves and protects, and over which it exercises authority, or that of the family and the lineage – in most instances, a patrilineage – in the protection and perpetuation of itself and its name'. She also argues (ibid.:5) that 'social reproduction and biological reproduction secure the continuity of peoples in social units – couples, families, ethnic groups, and nations all need to preserve their identity to protect and perpetuate themselves'.

The link between reproduction and identity is another recurrent theme in this volume. The example of East London sex workers studied by Sophie Day reveals an intriguing aspect of the way fertility per se, as a state which leads to reproducing, can be less important than proving to be fertile in order to gain recognition as a 'productive' member of the society. Day, in describing the constant search and anxiety for proof of fertility among East London sex workers, argues that 'fertility and infertility constitute a pair mutually implicating'. It is the fear of infertility that leads women to test out their fertility. The public image of sex workers as barren is a statement of their function and place in society which they seem to want to challenge. 'Proving' that they are fertile is often what they need in order to change the attitude of society towards them. While some of these women feel it is wrong to be a mother and a sex worker, they still want to become pregnant in order to challenge the assumption that they are both physically and existentially barren.

Establishing one's identity can take multiple forms, as several of the contributors to this volume point out. While Bolivian women resort to a change of religion (Hawkins and Price), the child prostitutes of Thailand (Montgomery) and the prostitutes of East London

(Day) choose motherhood and fertility as a bridge to achieve respectability and status. Cornwall provides a different perspective in her vivid description of the strategies employed by the infertile women of Ado-Odo of South-Western Nigeria, who are desperate to adopt a child to retain their status in the community. She draws a distinction between being fertile biologically, and other forms of motherhood. Mothering, in Cornwall's words, is a cluster of social practices in which virtually all women, irrespective of their fertility, engage at some point in their lives. Motherhood is more of a process and conveys the idea of not only having given birth to children, but having brought them up to adulthood. Cornwall uses the term 'mother' as a relational identity to describe dependency, care, guidance and relationships between women and the children of others. It is by becoming a mother that a woman can gain recognition by her husband's family. But Cornwall questions the portrayal by some anthropologists of infertile women as 'figures ostracised by others in the community, set apart from the flow of everyday social life and often stereotyped as "witches"'. She paints a quite different picture of infertility among Ado-Odo women, and demonstrates that the strategies they adopt, and the lives they create around themselves, are far from miserable and powerless. The status of infertile women is linked to the degree of success they have had in other spheres of life. From being ostracised as infertile, they might move on to become religious leaders, or successful businesswomen. The children that such women adopted in most cases proved more attentive than the 'real' children of fertile women.

Parenthood

The meaning of parenthood and the degree of involvement of men and women in the nurturance of their children varies greatly cross-culturally. Robertson (1991:6) argues that in western societies 'the family is understood as being determined by the fact of birth, rather than a matter of choice'. He mentions that 'the way we reproduce tends to make "family" a logical necessity, but the enormous variation in family and kinship patterns around the world is a reminder that these elementary relations of reproduction may be organised in many different ways'. Parenthood and childhood are two closely linked concepts which can be defined and understood within the rules of duties and obligations of the communities in which they are rooted. The more individualistic cultures of the west differ in their attitudes towards children and their 'ownership' from those of collective cultures. In the latter, parenthood is not limited to the biological parents, but is an integral part of the extended family where even today the wider kin network plays an active part. Ginsburg and Rapp (1991:328), in a literature review of the network of nurturance, mention that

> Ethnographic studies in New Guinea and Australia, in contrast to those in the West, provide notable cases in which nurturance and reproduction are broadly defined and a high value is placed on the role of men and women in 'growing up' the next generation. Such a work has focused on male fertility as a principle, paternal nurture as essential to the continuity of kin group, and reproduction as a cosmological principle.

They conclude that 'anthropological studies have given more attention to nurturance of children by non-biological parents than to fathering'.

Parenthood can include a broad range of variations such as fosterage and adoption. Cornwall and Belaunde provide two contrasting cases in attitudes and practices towards nurturance and reproduction. The Airo-Pai, Belaunde shows, place a high value on the role of both men and women in bringing up the next generation. Male attention and involvement in the process of fertility is viewed as essential to the continuity of kin group. In contrast, Cornwall distinguishes between fatherhood and being a father among the Ado-Odo. While in many cultures fatherhood automatically entails financial obligation towards the children, in Ado-Odo the impregnation of a woman is sufficient for a man to become a father and the 'owner of the child', regardless of whether he makes any contribution to the child's upkeep. This recognition by the father is important for both the mother and the child. The mother needs an officially recognised father to make claim on the child who would otherwise be stigmatised. Heather Montgomery's discussion of child prostitutes in Thailand also highlights the importance of motherhood and mothers. In Thai culture the mother is the linchpin that keeps families together; the moral basis for all kinship relationships and the economic and practical source of household survival. Child prostitutes may thus choose motherhood as a way out of prostitution, and as a solution which ultimately gives them recognition as worthwhile persons and acceptance by society. The low use of contraceptives by child prostitutes is linked to the importance of becoming a mother. Motherhood in this case is 'an ambiguous and shifting category'. Becoming a mother allows the young prostitutes to change status from child to adult, from dependent to carer and from having filial duties and obligations to having obligations owed to them. However Montgomery views this use of motherhood as continually open to reinterpretation and a flexible boundary between adulthood and childhood.

The value of children

The motives for wanting children are numerous. Children can be valued for their economic contribution, for looking after their parents in their old age, for providing the numbers needed to increase a social group's ethnic and national strength, for the pleasure and emotional affection they bring to their parents, and finally the desire among humans 'to get their genes into the future generation' (Betzig 1988:9). The value of children can change through time and cross-culturally. For example, traditionally children, especially boys, have had a higher value among agriculturists as labourers than among pastoral nomads. Infant and juvenile mortality has also been a cause of the desire for a large number of children. In non-industrialised societies parents support their children while they are young, and depend on them in old age. Robertson (1991:68) refers to this exchange as 'the transgenerational notion of "patrimony". The idea that we derive our assets from the parental generation and hold them in trust for the next generation.' In modern industrialised societies, where the state takes care of the elderly, and parents do not expect their children to support them financially, children have a different value. Robertson (1991:67) argues that in modern societies children have no immediate and direct economic value for their parents, and are 'sacralised' in the sense that they have been relieved from work and often from household chores. Indeed, in fully capitalised societies, children of certain social classes have become 'priceless' (Zelizer, 1985). In addition, with the increased participation of women in the workforce in modern societies, the value of a large number of children as a source of security for old age has diminished. As a result, defining the value of children has become a perplexing issue. The emotional aspects of having children, or the achievements of children as a confirmation of their own achievement in the upbringing of the next generation may themselves be valid reasons for reproduction to modern parents.[5]

However, the impact of modernity on traditional family structures does not necessarily destroy long-held values attached to children. Diana Martin's chapter in this volume provides an interesting example of the Hong Kong Chinese, who have retained their traditional values in one of the most affluent and

5. For detailed analysis of value of children, see Robertson (1991:51–71).

sophisticated societies in the world. For the Chinese, children, especially male children, are of great value to the family. But, Martin explains, their importance is not justified by economic and practical considerations alone. They are also valued from the point of view of ritual and religion although the preference for boys is explained by the fact that they are also future income earners. The central fact, however, is that children are indebted to parents for giving them life and therefore have duties towards them. The potential value of children is in what they will become, which is of greater importance than what they are intrinsically. Filial duties to parents and the hierarchical family system determine the place of the children. Martin argues that the Chinese family is parent-centred rather than child-centred, and the understanding is that children will eventually repay their parents and look after them. In this context, emotional bonds are an important aspect of a mother's relationship with her sons, as in future it is the son who will look after her. Such an ethos, which regards children as serving their parents, completely denies personhood to children who die early. Only people who reach adulthood and marry and reproduce are complete. Martin points out that the traditional values and attitudes towards child-bearing have been retained among the Chinese in Hong Kong in spite of the change in family structures and relations, and a decline in fertility levels.

Vulnerability

Vulnerability is an all enveloping concept increasingly used by policy makers to describe situations in which people are either actually or potentially exposed to harm, and are helpless to counteract it. Like many other terms used for the purpose of planning, vulnerability is a general expression which rarely distinguishes the specific contexts in which harm might be inflicted and how it is counteracted. Many local practices and responses to situations arising in the process of change become 'problems' when viewed through a global lens. Research is increasingly revealing that the definition of vulnerability is context specific, and that it is a combination of factors such as poverty, gender and sexuality in the society that determine vulnerability. Furthermore, the 'vulnerable' may themselves have different perceptions of the concept from those of policy makers. Interviews with street children around the world testify to the danger of applying the universal assumptions adopted by policy makers about vulnerability. One of these is that 'home is the safest place for a child'. But street children themselves often have an explanation of the logic behind their choice of living in the street rather than staying at home that challenges this notion. As Baker and Panter-Brick (2000) explain, in many cases life in the street is a deliberate and calculated choice and not due to desperation on the part of children. Many of these children express the view that life in the street is hard and exposes them to occasional abuse. But they prefer to live in the street because at least they are not exposed to the systematic abuse of home, where 'every night ... we get abused in different ways by various members of the family'.

Youth as a vulnerable group

Because youth is viewed as 'the demographic future of the world' (Population Council), one of the main items on the agenda of policy makers is the reproductive health and behaviour of young people. There are good reasons to worry about the young since the population of under twenties already forms the largest age group in the developing world, and their number is on the increase. Price argues that young people share many characteristics, especially in the developing world, which affect their behaviour globally. Factors such as urbanisation, globalisation, the influence of media, and the increase in consumerism combined with better access to education, an improvement in some aspects of health (especially a noticeable reduction in mortality in general, and maternal and infant mortality in particular), have created similar trends worldwide. The apparent similarity of these trends has been taken as a cue by policy makers to search for universal solutions. In an effort to respond to the needs of different groups, universal age categories such as children, young people, adolescents, youth and young adults, have been identified, without differentiating the specific social and cultural contexts which determine these categories. The discrepancies which exist between the international definitions of children, young people, teenagers, and other age categories, and local practices in the many societies which have retained their traditional practices and values as far as life trajectories are concerned, are creating constraints at several levels. What definitions of this kind do not take into account is the extent to which such concepts are social and cultural constructs grounded in their unique historical and economic settings (Harcourt, 1997:11). For example, while according to WHO anybody under eighteen is a child, in many developing countries married twelve-year-old girls are considered adults with the full responsibilities and status of an adult, while a seventeen-year-old boy at school is considered a child.

Jo Boyden's chapter provides a detailed analysis of the sociological, psychological and medical aspects of childhood, and maintains that one of the major effects of gaps in research is that scientific conceptualisations of childhood and youth often appear more consistent with popular stereotype than with sound human development theory. Price also points to the inadequacy of definitions of various approaches and methods of educating and training the young (and their educators) in various socio-economic settings.

Likewise, the concept of adolescence needs clarification in its specific context. Indeed it is a relatively new one in most cultures. According to Harcourt (1997:12), even in the west it has a history of only a hundred or so years and has been introduced to non-western cultures exposed to development through the process of modernity. Adolescence is generally defined as the transition from childhood to adulthood encompassing the 'development to sexual maturity, and to psychological and relative economic independence' (IPPF, 1994 cited by Price in this volume). Adolescence is therefore linked with the physiological state of reaching puberty. This is an ambivalent state which separates young people from children, but does not accord them the criteria of adulthood. Development and modernisation in transitional societies require that children spend several years between childhood and adulthood at school. This new stage of life, referred to as adolescence, is therefore a new age category in many developing countries, where the link between childhood and adulthood is marked by rituals of initiation and marriage, with no in-between stage. It is not therefore surprising that for young people in transitional societies this new stage of life has become a source of confusion as far as their status and behaviour are concerned. The conflict arising from the competing ideologies of traditional cultural practices and modern rationalities, leads to a certain type of behaviour by 'adolescents', which is often viewed by society as 'pathological', especially when it concerns their sexual behaviour.

While the 'pathological' behaviour of young people, and its undesirable consequences, have been the focus of attention of planners especially health planners, it seems that girls and young women have been the main target of the new world awareness of sexual and reproductive debates. As Tumbo Masabo (1994b:213), cited in Harcourt (1997:40), in a critique of the medicalisation of human procreation explains:

> Teenage girls are now on the international agenda and given priority as an issue. For years they have been viewed through the neutral lens of 'reproductive health' – an umbrella term not only signifying

> the absence of sexually transmitted diseases, HIV/AIDS, high-risk pregnancies, abortions, low birth weight, etc., but also implying additional goals such as 'safe motherhood' and reproductive well-being. In this manner, the regeneration of life was subsumed under a medical concept, health. What once occurred in the West was repeated in Africa; a moral order was replaced by a scientific bio-medical system; the priest and the shamans gave way to doctors.

Price argues that sexual activities, especially in poorer countries, start at very early ages, and that class, ethnicity, education, gender, residence, parenting and kinship patterns, and social networks are all variables which shape experiences and influence sexual behaviour. They point out that the imbalance of gender relations, cross-cut by conditions of poverty, places many girls and young women at a high risk of unsafe sexual activities. Another outcome of gender imbalance linked to poverty and cultural practices is early marriage in cultures which value high fertility.

One aspect of adolescent behaviour, which has become a highly controversial issue worldwide, is their sexual activity and early pregnancies among them. Teenage sexual activity, and the resulting, often unwanted pregnancies and abortion, is on the increase and has become a major cause of concern for parents, officials and often young people themselves. An estimated 5 million out of 40 to 60 million (WHO) unwanted abortions in the world are among teenage girls, many of whom are unmarried with no access to safe health services.

Teenage pregnancy is an ambiguous and loaded concept which requires some clarification. In the developing countries, high fertility among young women is greatly valued in many cultures, for example in Muslim countries and several sub-Saharan areas in Africa. In such cultures, becoming pregnant in one's teens, where it happens within the prescribed norms of the society, is viewed favourably. Bledsoe and Cohen (1993:7) mention that twelve and thirteen are not uncommon ages of marriage in some areas and cite Kulin (1988), who points out that 'teenage pregnancy of unmarried mothers in sub-Saharan Africa are the only ones deemed wrong'.

In the developed world teenage pregnancy is also a cause of both moral and health panics, but does not necessarily carry the same values and stigmas as in the developing world. Kulin (1988:727–35) argues that in many European countries adolescent pregnancy is perceived as a health risk, while, in the United States and Africa, by contrast, it is generally perceived as a moral problem: one of illicit sexual activity. As Andrew Russell in his contribution to this book argues, Teesside in the UK, which has the highest rate of teenage pregnancy in Europe, presents a different picture from the one Kulin draws of Europe. The reaction of the public to teenage pregnancy is not simply that of health concern. Becoming a mother as a teenager places a young woman in an 'increasingly distinct category' as the headline of the British tabloid newspaper cited by Russell, which describes teenage sexual activity as 'Our World Record of Shame', indicates. The value of motherhood and the value of children are the main issue here. 'Although girls have been having babies since time immemorial, too-early pregnancy or motherhood did not arise as a *social problem* until the last few decades' (Gordon 1997:260). As Harcourt (1997:11) mentions, it is assumed that women of reproductive age in most societies will get married and become mothers, but modernity has transformed this aspect of women's life. Now women have greater control of their own fertility, bear fewer children, and are less taken up with mothering. Statistics show that the actual rate of teenage pregnancies in the UK has not gone up in reality (Russell in this volume), but the shift in attitudes towards these has brought them into the forefront of public attention.

Russell also questions one of the public's arguments about teenage mothers in the UK, namely that they try to change status and become pregnant to benefit from the advantages the state offers to single mothers. He argues that the route to motherhood for a teenager is a fairly traumatic one, revealing various underlying social and cultural values which still prevail in favour of marriage and the family. The stigma of becoming a mother out of wedlock is confirmed throughout his case studies. Teenage pregnancy is associated with single parenthood while babies, in the public mind, are still associated with nuclear families. One study on cohabitation and single parent families (Kiernan. cited in Russell) states that 'younger mothers tend to form partnerships more quickly and in Britain solo mothers are a different group of women than the rest of Europe. In Britain they are teenagers and tend to be socially excluded, whereas in the rest of Europe they tend to be in their twenties'. Russell maintains that the 'panic' of the interventionist authorities, and their clear lack of understanding, and often negative attitudes towards the causes of teenage 'problematic' behaviour, is the main reason for the relative lack of success in dealing with it. The contribution of anthropology to policy is clearly demonstrated in Russell's chapter which points to the shortcomings of research that fails to take into account the local voices for whom programmes are devised. The increasing bureaucratisation of 'planning' for the sexual health and behaviour of teenagers is reflected in a recent radio interview, when a senior health official referred to 'improving services for people's "sexual career"'.[6]

Refugees as a vulnerable group

The chapter by Harris and Smyth raises the question of vulnerability in the different context of refugees and their reproductive health – a subject which encapsulates every kind of disruption in the life of an individual. The situation of refugees is a traumatic one of utter dependence on the outside world, mainly on the international community, which tends to treat them as homogeneous group, and which renders them totally powerless. The International Conference on Population and Development (ICPD) Plan of Action describes them as follows: 'This group has been singled out because of the conditions of poverty, uncertainty, stress and other forms of vulnerability.' Reports from the Red Cross and Red Crescent (1996) put the number of refugees in the world at over 37 million. Refugees represent a new type of population living in a political vacuum outside the 'normal' life of any country. While international aid is reasonably well organised to attend to their immediate needs when displacement occurs, working under emergency conditions means it often fails to pay attention to their long-term and specific needs. The state of being a refugee seems to invoke a single image. According to UN statistics, at least 75 per cent of refugees are women and girls living in camps with reproductive problems such as a rate of maternal mortality 200 times higher than in western nations (Poore 1995 cited in Harris and Smyth).[7] This is compounded by the fact that refugee women's ability to draw on the support of their kin group is usually dislocated by displacement. In addition, they are frequently subject to rape and violence. The result can be unwanted pregnancies, sexually transmitted diseases, HIV and AIDS. The difficulties faced by refugees, including their reproductive health problems, are often viewed as technical problems with technical solutions. Decisions are made on the basis of 'western' and 'technical' assumptions, and policies are devised as a result of superficial intelligence gathered through insensitive interviewing techniques. Once the refugees are settled, and their urgent and basic needs seen to, no further research is deemed necessary to provide information on the processes which affect their reproductive conditions.

6. The Today programme, BBC Radio 4, on Friday 15 December 2000, when a health official mentioned that 'in the UK we are trying to provide better services throughout people's sexual career'. Whether 'sexual career' can be defined and institutionalised, is a matter for debate.

Furthermore, as Harris and Smyth argue, the past two decades have concentrated on the needs of women at reproductive age, but have neglected the reproductive needs of the elderly, such as women who have reached menopause, men and children.

Conclusion

The case studies in this volume, drawn from different parts of the world, provide a strong proof of the dynamism of reproduction. They testify to the sensitivity, complexity and diversity of the strategies people adopt to manage their reproductive life in contemporary societies. They are by no means a comprehensive account of the motivations behind people's reproductive decisions and choices, or the strategies they choose to achieve their reproductive ideals. The examples presented reveal only the tip of the iceberg as far as the variety of methods used in managing reproduction is concerned. But in so doing they succeed in demonstrating the intricate processes which act as determinants of reproductive decisions cross-culturally.

Several interlinked themes emerge from the work presented here. Firstly, the management of reproductive life in each cultural context is unique to that community, and assumptions cannot therefore be made that those societies which share certain socio-economic and cultural and environmental characteristics (pastoralists, agriculturists, the urban poor) will necessarily follow the same pattern of fertility behaviour. It is clear that fertility decisions are often taken at a micro level by communities, and that people's reproductive decisions are shaped by their social world. The attempt to understand reproduction in isolation from its broader context is a barren exercise. Secondly, fertility decisions are based on deeply rooted values and ideals and are not easily influenced by outside factors, unless these correspond to those ideals. Thirdly, global trends, such as urbanisation, migration, consumerism, the media, famines, wars and displacement affect people throughout the world and tend to support state intervention in the life of its citizens, especially their reproductive life. The encounter of global processes with local realities provokes reactions and triggers consequences which are often unforeseen. These reactions are not always active responses of acceptance or resistance. They can be passive or indirect, often frustrating policies and plans if they do not suit people's ideals.

Modernity has brought about considerable improvements in the lives of people in the developing countries. Education and health have improved living conditions in many parts of the world. Better access to resources by more people has resulted in new and better life chances, and has created an awareness among many, especially the younger generation, of their rights and entitlements. Inevitably these processes have entailed some negative outcomes. Modernity often disrupts traditional systems of support such as kin and other networks among social groups where change is introduced. Case studies in this book show that change has had less of a negative effect on the reproductive life of those communities which still rely on their 'traditional' networks than those who can no longer benefit from such support. The disruption of traditional knowledge leads to incomplete guidance for reproductive life among young people, especially young women. Young people no longer have the opportunity of learning from their parents and grandparents, and the new channels of information such as school, media and the peer group can only provide partial information (Harcourt 1997:188).

Modernity also affects the relationship between the generations. Concepts of parenthood and childhood as important milestones in defining people's sense of self in society, are also shifting. The traditional power structures were reflected in family and household relationships and in concepts of motherhood, fatherhood and childhood, and varied culturally to reflect societies' economic and existential situation. They are being redefined in modern and modernising societies and take on many variations. The concept of parenthood is changing in many societies. The relations of reciprocity between parents and children is no longer sustainable, and the gradual loss of parental control over children is one of the most noticeable features of the societies which go through modernisation. The impact of the disruption is reflected mainly in the sexual behaviour of the young generation.

The tendency of international planning, which is often echoed at a state level, is to think of women at the reproductive age as the main arbiters of reproduction. This ignores the full reproductive cycle and 'life stages' affecting the reproductive decisions made by women. The role of the wider community, gender relations, intergenerational relations, and the role of men in making reproductive decisions have hitherto only partially been addressed. The fact that people are now living longer and reproducing later in life presents new challenges and directions.

Finally, the case studies show that despite the pervasive effect of policy intervention, people continue to make their own reproductive choices. Though the ethical aspects of state interventions in the reproductive life of citizens has been debated fully at an international level and there has been a recognition that freedom of choices for the individual is the best way forward, policy makers must show a genuine commitment to understanding the local forces which shape the dynamics of reproduction, or they are unlikely to achieve their goals.

Part One

AGENCY AND IDENTITY

CHAPTER 1

EMOTION, AGENCY AND ACCESS TO HEALTHCARE: WOMEN'S EXPERIENCES OF REPRODUCTION IN JAIPUR

Maya Unnithan-Kumar

Introduction

Set in the context of the cultural perceptions of bodily processes, demographic trends, kinship relationships and poverty, this chapter focuses on the motivations underlying rural Rajasthani women's selection of a range of reproductive health services. It shows women's reproductive agency to be especially reinforced by the emotions generated by social intimacy, anxieties about fertility and social performance, and women's desire to decrease the mental and physical burden of reproduction on their lives. As a result, reproductive healthcare is primarily sought from spiritual healers and private gynaecologists, by-passing the vast health delivery sector of the state.

Jaipur district in Rajasthan is characterised, like most other districts of the province, by poor demographic indicators, such as high fertility, high mortality – especially infant mortality – and high maternal morbidity. One in every fourteen children born in Rajasthan die in the first year of their life (Government of India, NFHS: Rajasthan, 1995). Most maternal deaths, which are close to the average Indian figure of 437 per 100,000 live births, are due to anaemia, haemorrhage, toxaemia and abortion complications (Government of India, NFHS, 1995). The area is marked by poverty with a low average income, marginal subsistence farming and low paid jobs in the service sector. Apart from economic hardship, there are great social constraints, especially on women, and in reproductive terms this translates into pressure for early and continuous childbearing.

The negligible resort, overall, to any form of control over conception makes the burden of fertility especially great for women. This burden is significantly increased by the high vulnerability to reproductive tract infections, the scarcity of water in the region, and the lack of access to appropriate nutrition and healthcare. Reproductive tract infections not only increase the physical vulnerability of women, but also render them vulnerable to social marginalisation and related anxieties. For example, cases of secondary sterility often result from infections in the fallopian tubes, ovaries, cervix or uterus, making women unable to meet the social expectations of childbearing placed upon them. Of central concern in this study is the manner in which Rajasthani women perceive and manage the physiological and social burden of reproduction[1] and related healthcare. The issue of healthcare delivery is approached in terms of women's perceptions as users and their access, in particular the constraints and motivations which underlie their selection of healers from the different health services on offer (in both the private and public sectors). I talk about women's agency in relation to their access to healthcare as the intentions, motivations and desires that result in certain kinds of health-related decisions and actions in which women are involved.

Though unrecognised by the public health sector, women's emotional attachments, desires and knowledge of reproduction are critical factors which influence their health-seeking behaviour. The question is not whether women decide, or not, to address their reproductive conditions but what makes them decide to take up certain options rather than others, when these decisions are taken, and who or what facilitates the process. As an anthropologist, I am interested in exploring gender and healthcare issues in terms of the emotional context of women's and men's lives. Emotions have not been considered in relation to healthcare issues outside the frame of psychology, as far as I

1. I follow Ginsburg and Rapp's working definition of human reproduction as meaning, 'the events throughout the human and especially the female life-cycle related to ideas and practices surrounding fertility, birth and childcare, including the ways in which these figure into understandings of social and cultural renewal' (1991: 311).

know. And yet I have found them to be crucial in understanding the differences in women's health-seeking behaviour *within* a particular cultural context. Healthcare policy in India is predominantly driven by demographic statistics, which is not surprising given the power of demographic and economic analyses in modernist discourses of development (for example Greenhalgh, 1995). As yet little is known in India about the cultural, let alone emotional and experiential aspects of women's lives which underlie the figures on fertility and reproduction, and which shape the ways in which women address the effects of repeated childbirth on their lives and relationships.

The chapter draws on my perceptions of the experiences of reproduction and healthcare of women who frequented a small, rural voluntary health centre in a village approximately 20 kilometres south-east of Jaipur city. The inhabitants of the area belonged to a mix of Hindu caste and Muslim communities. The health centre received patients from both groups, although the single largest group were Sunni Muslim women. For most of the Nagori Sunni Muslim women I met, menstruation commenced when they were from fifteen to eighteen years old and they had their first child when they were between seventeen and twenty. Women joined their husbands shortly after their menarche and most would be bearing children within the first year of their marriage.[2] Like other rural women in the area – Meena, Khateek, Raigar, Rajput and Brahman, for example – rural Muslim women were thus initiated into childbirth soon after their first menstrual period. The demographic information I collected from 107 rural Muslim and Hindu caste women in the area showed that nearly 60 per cent of Hindu caste and Muslim (Sunni Nagori) women had four or more children with a birth interval of one-and-a-half to two years between their children. Fifteen to 18 per cent of rural caste and Muslim women alike had one to three children where the birth interval was as large as five to nine years due to the problem of secondary sterility.[3]

There was a high incidence of foetal death or miscarriage (*bachhadani mein bachha kharab hona*; literally, the child going bad

2. On average, Sunni Nagori women in their thirties at the time of my fieldwork had been married when they were between two and thirteen years, following the Rajasthani custom of child marriages where the *gauna* (or consummation) for those who were married below nine to ten years, took place approximately three to four months to one year after menarche.

3. The women who have less than three children, and usually with large birth intervals between them, are a small but significant population. Yet, they remain invisible in the health statistics which are focused on curtailing rather than enabling women's efforts at childbearing.

in the child sac) among Muslim and rural caste Hindu women alike. Nineteen out of forty-eight Muslim women (40 per cent) and twenty-five of fifty-five rural caste women (36 per cent) reported one to three miscarriages of foetuses between two and six months. There was an even higher incidence of infant deaths with the majority occurring in the first year after birth.[4] These staggering figures, particularly on infant mortality, further reinforced what I heard from the women I met. I found maternal mortality occurring in isolated cases (four–five women among women known to the women I met), although information was not systematically available. There is an absence of state-wide or community-wide information on maternal mortality figures in the National Family Health Survey.[5] A high incidence of reproductive morbidity (mainly related to infections in the reproductive tract), however, was all too evident to see.

From my observations in rural Jaipur, which I shall shortly turn to, women's thinking, feeling and acting on fertility, reproduction and healthcare issues is a complex combination of their individual and community beliefs, their own knowledge and standing, the emotional universe of village and kin relationships, their individual physiology as well as their relation to poverty, especially indebtedness. I want to argue that over time the nature of the women's desires and actions in relation to reproductive health may shift as a result of a shift in any of these conditions, but also as a matter of course, over the reproductive cycle itself. Women's reproductive agency, then, may be less in their early reproductive years because of the dislocation of their relationship with friends and family at marriage. Women's kin are very important people who influence their desires and actions with regard to health as in other matters. Yet, not all kinspersons exert influence just because they are kin, neither do all kinspersons have equal control over the other, nor is their influence necessarily constant. The importance of certain kin above others in decisions related to health and reproduction follows, I find, the lines of emotion, an important dimension for understanding women's health-seeking actions.

4. Twenty-three of 48 Muslim women reported 43 infant deaths (25 girls, 18 boys). Twenty-five deaths (58 per cent) were among children under the age of five; 21 of these deaths (84 per cent) were infants under the age of one year. Seventy-seven per cent of infants among caste Hindu women died before they reached their first birthday. The general figure on infant mortality for Rajasthan is 73 deaths per 1,000 live births (Government of India, NFHS: Rajasthan, 1995: 136).
5. The NFHS survey blames large sampling errors for the absence of figures for individual states or population subgroups (Government of India, NFHS, 1995: 226).

Fertility, emotion and agency

I see women's reproductive agency[6] (their desires and motivations) as linked to emotions in two senses. Firstly, the stimulus to act in particular ways often stems from emotional involvement with those who surround us, and often the decision to carry out a particular action, or even the thought that a particular course of action is the most suitable, is based on a negotiation between one's own and other's feelings on the matter. For rural, lower class Rajasthani women I suggest that reproductive healthcare practices are influenced by what women and men in marriage regard as spousal affection and responsibility,[7] as well as what is considered to be socially appropriate gender behaviour. Secondly, in physiological terms, emotions are crucially linked to one's state of feeling and sense of well-being. Depression, often manifested in a lack of motivation, and accompanied by feelings of weakness and anxiety, is significantly connected to poverty and may be related to inadequate nutrition as well as the vulnerability and powerlessness associated with the lack of finances, assets and inability to commandeer people and resources. Poverty as a factor in the inability to access healthcare has to be further qualified in conjunction with the prevailing gender ideologies. This means that even if some women have access to better foods, ideas of appropriate behaviour may result in a denial of these foods by the women themselves. In both the physiological and social aspects, I see emotions as connected with issues of power, as Lutz and Abu-Lughod have so clearly stated (1990). In the early 1980s, Rosaldo (1984) was already arguing that the socially and culturally constructed nature of emotions should be considered, and criticising the conventional division between thought and emotion. She emphasised the necessity of conceptualising emotions as

6. In my use of the concept of agency I will draw on some of the many works on the subject (Bourdieu, 1977; Giddens, 1984; Scott, 1993, for example) and, in particular, the relatively recent focus on agency in current demographic and medical anthropological discourse. I use human agency to mean, following Giddens, a 'reflexive monitoring and rationalisation of a continuous flow of conduct' (1984) in which practice, as Bourdieu suggests, is constituted by the interaction between the *habitus* and the setting of people's activities, or in Bourdieu's words as the relation between the *habitus* (as a socially constituted system of cognitive and motivating structures) and the socially structured situation in which the agent's interests are defined along with the objective functions and subjective motivations of the practices (1977: 76). Here the cultural concepts (values assigned to different behaviours) and the political economy (forces creating the setting) become ingredients of action (Greenhalgh, 1995: 19).
7. K. Sivaramakrishnan first suggested this to me.

processes, not things, which cannot be understood apart from their cultural contexts.[8] According to Rosaldo, 'feeling is forever given shape through thought and that thought is laden with emotional meaning ... what differentiates thought from emotion is the engagement of the actor's self. Emotions are thought *felt* in flushes, pulses, movements of our livers, minds, hearts, stomach and skin. They are embodied thoughts – thoughts seeped with the apprehension that I am involved.' (1984:143). Therefore our responses to situations will depend on how we conceive the world and what such things as the body, affect and self are like.[9] Rosaldo is not suggesting that the self /individual dichotomy is non-existent, but that one must be open to the possibility that notions of 'I', that is the individual, need not always be separated in a dichotomous fashion from the self or 'me', the social person. This view, it seems to me, is important in thinking about women's desires and actions in the Indian context where socialisation patterns encourage the development of the 'me', or collective aspect of the persona. Emotion then provides us with the means of getting at the experience of embodied socialisation, as Lyon and Barbalet (1994, 48) suggest, in which women simultaneously experience their body as both belonging to them and as alienated from them (Petchesky and Judd, 1998, introduction; Unnithan-Kumar, 2001). In terms of rural women's health-seeking actions in Rajasthan, I would suggest that, while there are cultural restrictions on the possibilities in selecting satisfactory healthcare options, women do nevertheless have a range of health specialists to choose from. Which particular option a woman will choose depends on a number of factors, including her emotional state and relationships, which are specific to her situation alone. Such an argument would explain perhaps why education does not play as significant a role as imagined by health policy makers and planners.

The connection between emotions and agency in cultures where there is an emphasis on the collective is an issue of debate. Abu-Lughod (1986) has suggested that the longing expressed by Bedouin women in their love poetry actually underscores the collective importance of suffering rather than the 'real' expression of an individual's grief. However, as Reddy points out, one of the major difficulties in regarding emotions as culturally constructed

8. Scheper-Hughes, in her work on the political economy of emotions, also emphasises that emotions do not precede or stand outside culture (1992: 431). She shows, for example, how the inevitability of high infant mortality in the Brazilian shanty town she studied replaces the show of motherly grief by one of detachment bordering on indifference.
9. Lutz, 1988 and Wikan, 1990 are important studies in this vein.

(what he terms 'constructionism', 1999:259) is that all resistance also becomes a collective construct making individual non-conformity difficult to detect.

Early writing on women's agency drew inspiration from James Scott's work on the less visible forms of political action among peasant groups. Scott (1993) argues that much of the politics of subordinate groups falls into the category of 'everyday forms of resistance' which include such acts as foot-dragging, feigned ignorance, desertion, pilfering, slander, sabotage, threats, i.e., acts of non-compliance. Scott also suggests that although these may be individual acts, they cannot take place without some level of tacit compliance among other, similarly positioned, individuals. While intentions are built into Scott's definition of resistance, it also allows for the fact that many acts of resistance may not have the desired outcomes or may lead to unforeseen consequences.[10] In a similar vein, early women's studies literature aimed to show that women do not passively follow the cultural roles allocated to them, but are often engaged covertly in undermining patriarchal and cultural authority.[11] Women can, it was argued, be seen as initiating their own rather than following other's actions. This is notwithstanding the fact that a woman might initiate action without necessarily getting the outcome she desires, or might be active in decision making but unsuccessful in her attempts to influence others.[12] More recently, Raheja and Gold (1994) have argued that women's resistance and agency is more overt and distinct than has been previously imagined, occupying the realm of narrative, songs and stories. The distinction made by Raheja and Gold between imagining resistance (song) and living it (domestic work) may, however, be somewhat artificial.[13]

Although I see the work on resistance as very important, my own emphasis on women's agency is not so much in terms of resistance, namely the view that women, in making decisions about their bodies, are in effect challenging patriarchal control or seeking to influence or contest the authority of individuals or groups. Rather, I see agency more in terms of motivation, the desire to seek out healthcare, to which the contestation of

10. Here we find echoes of Bourdieu's work where the habitus is a series of moves which are objectively organised as strategies without being the product of a genuine strategic intention (1977: 73).
11. Some examples that spring to mind are Dube and Leacock's *Invisibility and Power*, Rama Mehta's, 'Inside the Haveli' (1976) and L. Holmstrom's, *The Inner Courtyard* (1990).
12. My thanks to Ursula Sharma for making me see this point clearly.
13. My thanks to K. Sivaramakrishnan for pointing this out.

authority may be a related, perhaps largely unintended, secondary outcome. This is because I find that patriarchy in Rajasthan actually favours the medical care of women for reproductive ailments. In his work on fertility and agency, Carter (1995) has also shown that even in pre-transition, high fertility and high mortality populations, at the micro-level there are often household strategies operative which effect a balance between household personnel and resources (such as ideas about appropriate periods for conception or breastfeeding).[14] It is imperative not only to move beyond the stereotypic ideas of patriarchy and culture wherein women are seen as the compliant victims of reproductive regimes, but also the idea that women's responses, as in controlling fertility, are necessarily those of resistance (a point also made by Kielman). The way forward lies in women's perceptions of their own actions as resistance or not.[15] The point is whether women themselves construe their actions as resistance. I see women's reproductive experiences, especially in non-contracepting populations, as forming a part of their *doxa* (taken for granted/ natural), the normalised part of their lives. By taking this approach we can begin to understand why, for example, infected vaginal discharge is regarded as 'normal' rather than problematic. I would argue that women in such populations have a different understanding of the relationship of reproduction to their lives than women in contracepting populations. The idea that there is a possibility of individual achievement after the reproductive stage (or, 'life after children') is less dominant than the idea that a woman's life is all about reproduction.

While both men and women in rural Rajasthan see women's lives as being all about reproduction, the bodily experience of the cultural regulation of fertility and reproduction for women, in contrast to men, makes for a gender differentiated conception of the world. Yet women's identities are seldom defined by their

14. Carter finds both the passive and active notions of agency dominating demographic discussion to be unsatisfactory because, while the former is based on the mindless adherence to cultural rules and thereby denies people agency, the latter, which involves conscious decision making, expects people to engage in complex fertility level calculations which are difficult to sustain in reality. For Carter, human action with regard to fertility lies more in micro-level actions which, as Giddens suggests, are reflexively monitored and rational, continuous flows of conduct.
15. For Kielman, then 'endowing particular bodily practices such as gestures, habits and symptoms with meanings of resistance or subversive action is problematic – unless women themselves envisage and express the possibility of options separate from orthodox frameworks of meanings around the body, bodily knowledge and bodily practices' (1998:136).

own perceptions of their reproductive experiences, reflecting their powerlessness to control the social processes of which they are a vital part. The idea that the dominant view of women is one over which women have little control, or as one which is removed from women's bodily experiences, is not new. As Emily Martin (1987) has so forcefully shown for the west, medical discourses predominantly construct women's bodies in negative terms, in terms of a purpose that has failed. These discourses may both stand apart from women's own experiences and yet influence the way they conceptualise them. It is not that women are unaware of the gender injustices of reproductive regimes but that, as Scheper-Hughes (1992) suggests, the reason they collude in describing themselves negatively (for example as 'worthless' or 'used-up') is because they participate in the same moral world as their oppressors (Lock and Kaufert, 1998). For Kielman, on the other hand, the ambivalence of women's agency also allows them the possibility of alternative action.[16] Moreover, inaction cannot always be interpreted as a lack of desire, but may simply reflect the inability to translate desire into action. I found that women in rural Jaipur had a tendency towards inaction (not difficult to understand given the effort, cost and their negative experiences) in seeking healthcare services. Yet, given a certain level of support, particularly from kin, they were also willing to seize the opportunity of exploring further possibilities of healthcare. Lock and Kaufert, in their recent edited volume (1998), make a similar argument in understanding women's relationship to technology.[17] What is clear though is that even common sense actions are based on some fundamental calculations.

I now turn to a description of the experiences of reproduction and healthcare of women in rural Rajasthan. Zahida was one of the Sunni Muslim women I got to know particularly well over the year and I recount her story here.

16. For Kielman wherein the practices which women carry out as individuals serve to undermine their own claims of conforming to the cultural norms, is the position from where women engage in creating sometimes opposing possibilities for meaning and conduct on the margins of the dominant discourses regulating their bodies, which allows them to both mediate between social orders and to invent new forms of knowledge (1998: 138).

17. According to Lock and Kaufert (1998: 2), 'women have always had to make the best use of what is available to them', and, 'if the apparent benefits outweigh the costs to them selves and if technology serves their own ends, then most women will avail themselves of what is offered'.

The ethnography

Zahida's Story

Zahida had her first period when she was thirteen and in her natal home; she was married at fourteen. One year later she had her first child. She was totally unaware of her pregnancy; her period stopped but she did not tell anyone, she did not know. Her whole body became swollen. When she was in her ninth month she became very sick. She could not walk, could not go to the bathroom, could not see, could not hear; but she had little help or sympathy from her husband or in-laws. Then her mother, father and father's sister paid her a visit. Her mother saw that her breast was leaking, told Zahida that she was pregnant and called a midwife. The midwife said Zahida might have a child at any moment, but she should not give birth in her married home as it would be dangerous for both mother and child. Her father said they would take her home. Her husband became angry, tore her father's *kurta* (shirt) and said, 'if she dies, she will die here, I will not let her go with you'. Later, her *jeth* (husband's elder brother) intervened and told his brother to bring her to the city where he would show her to the doctor. Her husband and husband's sister tied her with a rope, as she was too weak to sit up, put her on a bicycle and took her to the government women's hospital. The doctor admitted her and asked her husband and his younger sister who they were. They told him that they were Zahida's neighbours, that she had no kin, that her parents were no longer alive, and that her husband stayed outside Jaipur. According to Zahida, they lied because they were frightened. Besides her husband's sister – with whom she gets on well – had been told by her in-laws not to say anything, to let her brother do the talking.

Zahida was left alone in the hospital where she was treated for fifteen days until she had a son who weighed 1.5 pounds and 'was like a rat' (*chuha jaisa*). After she had given birth, Zahida stayed in the hospital for another fifteen days and the child was kept in a machine (incubator). She also received two bottles of blood from a rickshaw *walla* paid for by her husband's elder brother. She does not know what sums were involved but says that her brother-in-law did a great deal for her. She had visitors from her mother's house, but no one, except on one occasion her *jethani* (sister-in-law), went to see her from her affinal home, not even her husband, not even after the child was born. When, after a month, she was discharged, she travelled home by herself. No one came to collect her. Her husband was ill. There was nothing to eat at home when she returned. Her mother sent 20 kilograms of wheat, and her husband's younger sister (*nanad*) gave her some broken wheat porridge (*thooli*) which she roasted and boiled in water. She had no clarified butter (*ghee*) and no milk.

Zahida did not conceive again for another seven years. Her mother-in-law and father-in-law said she could not conceive and told their son to divorce her (*talaq de do*). Her husband kept her son, hit her and sent her back to her *piyar*, where she stayed for two months. A meeting of elders called to consider her situation decided that, because Zahida was a good woman, her husband must be forced to take her back. Zahida subsequently sought medical advice from a private infertility specialist. She became pregnant but the specialist said the foetus was not growing. When somebody in the village said it was because of *oonpar ki hawa* (literally 'wind from above', ill wind) she sought help from a man of the Meena caste who became possessed by Bhairu (*bhairu bhav*), had a *tabeez* (charm), arranged a *jhadan* (literally 'sweeping', exorcism), and told her to wear a *kada* (amulet) on her upper right arm. She continued to take the specialist doctor's medicine and advice whenever she had some money. She also saw a *bhangi* (lower caste Hindu man) and got a thread to wear around the neck (*gale ka dora*). When she was five months pregnant she had a lot of white vaginal discharge (*safed pani*) and went back to the doctor specialist who recommended a sonography and gave her medicines which made her better.

Zahida finally gave birth to a second child (a son), this time at home. Her third son was also born at home, as was her fourth after a gap of a year. The fifth child (also a boy) miscarried at five months after a cow hit Zahida and its horn ruptured her uterus. She bled for three days at home without treatment. When the bleeding did not stop, she sent her son to call her mother who took her to Sanganeri Gate (the government's women's hospital). Zahida was refused treatment at the hospital and, fearing that she would die, went to 'Neetu', a private gynaecologist who had treated other women from the village. Rs. 7,000/– was spent at the private hospital. The money was taken on credit and repaid at a rate of 700/– per month (totalling Rs. 8,400/–).

Two years later, Zahida's twins were born at Neetu's clinic. The bill came to Rs. 15,700/– of which Rs. 3,700 were arranged from the household resources (the TV and a goat were sold) and Rs. 12,000/– was taken on credit from a Brahman, to be repaid within fourteen months. Afterwards Zahida used the Copper-T. She finally had a girl and wanted no more children. The Copper-T gave her pain but she could not remove it for fear of becoming pregnant again. She wants to have an operation but does not know exactly when. She says her husband is useless because he does not work and somehow she has to feed the children. He is really bad when he beats her. But, she adds, he is a good man because he lets her go where she wants.

I think what emerges most forcefully from Zahida's story is that reproduction is a specific, complex experience of a combination of physiological, social, economic and psychological factors which form part of women's everyday lives, and that any one decision in this story can only be understood in relation to the whole context of Zahida's life – among other factors marital relations, poverty and support from specific kin. Zahida's initiation into childbirth was both early and difficult and she was unprepared and unknowing of what it would entail. Her story emphasises the importance of her parents as a source of knowledge, in initiating healthcare services, as well as in the comfort they provided in emotional, physical and financial terms. While it was her mother who explained Zahida's bodily changes to her, it is perhaps surprising that she had not transmitted this information to Zahida before. I was told that mothers and daughters do not discuss intimate matters such as menstruation or childbirth in any detail as it is embarrassing for them. I encountered a number of women who, like Zahida, escaped the attention of family and kin when they were in the early stages of their pregnancy because of the very minimal development of the foetus.

Apart from her parents, the role of certain in-laws, particularly her husband's elder brother and her husband's younger sister was central to Zahida's ability to use the health services she required. The intimacy she shares with them is in contrast to her relationship with her mother-in-law or her husband's elder brother's wife who quarrel with her about the rota of work they have to divide in the household. Besides, Zahida's husband Rafiq has never been able to hold a job for long, although he is the darling of his mother. He is known to drink and beat Zahida. Zahida would become depressed about his behaviour and told me she had left him a couple of times. Yet she said she wouldn't marry another man; she loved Rafiq and enjoyed having sex with him.

Zahida's lack of independent access to money on the one hand, and to food on the other, severely restricted her ability to recover completely from her childbirth experiences. She was unable to conceive after her first child and came under tremendous social pressure as a result. She felt depressed, fearful and anxious, not only about her inability to conceive but also about her status as a wife, which was called into question. She approached all the agents perceived to provide effective cures for infertility, whether spiritual healers or private gynaecologists. As a result of her efforts, she had four more children, albeit in difficult circumstances. At the time I met her, Zahida was in her thirties, and was using the Copper-T intra-uterine device. She wanted to carry on having sex with her husband but did not want to get pregnant. She had several sons as well as the daughter she desired and was even contemplating a tubectomy (locally referred to as the 'operation').

As I write, I have heard that Zahida is pregnant again. Given the number of children (including sons) that she has borne, there is little social pressure on her to continue to conceive. Zahida has also effectively used contraception. It is difficult to fathom why she has become pregnant again. The following sections allow us to understand her action as her resolution of the conflict between reducing her own physiological burden and following the various reasonings of those who matter to her.

The proximity of Nagori women to their the natal kin, following the specific marriage patterns among Muslims, allows them to draw on much wider kinship structures of support in healthcare matters than caste Hindu women who marry much further away from their natal kin. The Hindu expectation that the pregnant woman will return to her natal home for her first birth was not, I found, so much of an issue among the Nagori. One of the major implications of the Nagori pattern of marriage and settlement is, I suggest, the confidence based on the emotional and financial support provided by the natal family, which greatly facilitates women's ability to access healthcare assistance. Nagori women, in contrast to caste Hindu women, can draw on a greater pool of kinswomen to substitute for them in their housework, or accompany them to health specialists (which is vital in a cultural context where women do not travel unaccompanied). The support from kinswomen and men in the affinal village increases the longer the duration of residence and hence the more advanced women are in their reproductive cycle.

Intimacy, anxiety, desire and the access to health services

The emotions generated by social intimacy, anxieties about fertility and social performance, and the desire to decrease the burden of reproduction on one's life are, I suggest, some of the driving forces behind the healthcare options chosen by the poor, rural women I met in Jaipur district. Kinswomen and kin-midwives (midwives of one's own community) as well as spiritual healers are the dominant healthcare agents for Nagori Sunni and Hindu caste women.

This is primarily because these traditional healers function within the same cultural framework as the women who seek their advice. Both healers and patients have similar beliefs about bodily processes, the power of substances as well as in the social connectedness of a person's physical and mental states. At the same time, fully aware of the limitations of 'indigenous' practitioners, particularly in the areas of the termination of pregnancy, spacing of children and the complete termination of fertility, rural women consult known, expensive but efficient private women gynaecologists. Which healers within these categories are actually consulted depends on the influence of specific kinspersons, the healers themselves and the individual disposition (desires, capabilities) of the women concerned. Focusing on emotions in addition to kinship or gender enables us to understand the politics between kin and within the community on issues relating to women's reproductive health (see also Unnithan-Kumar, forthcoming).

Much of the discourse on maternal and child health in the Nagori and lower caste Rajasthani communities revolves around the perception of childbirth and related reproductive processes as 'natural'. It therefore becomes important to understand what are 'common sense' practices and emotions in reproductive terms. Moreover, as the rural Sunni Muslim and Hindu caste women and men alike talk about their ailments (*bimari*) in general terms for pain (*dard/dukhna*) it is important to consider both everyday complaints, which may not be reproduction related, as well as those for which reproductive specialists are consulted.[18] At the same time, despite the generalist language employed to describe ailments, I found there was an unstated understanding that certain complaints were reproduction related. For women in particular, reproductive ailments constituted a special category as they were considered important enough for an unquestioning allocation of household finances which were otherwise unavailable to women (including for non-reproduction related health problems).

Intimacy among kinswomen: menstruation and childbirth

In this section I show that the knowledge of childbirth and menstruation is diffused among a large group of kinswomen (including kin-midwives who are aunts, sisters-in-law and women of one's peer group). As a result, the decisions about who will give advice on menstruation or attend the birth of one's child are primarily a function of social intimacy rather than expert knowledge.

18. Kleinman (1980), makes a similar argument for a contextualisation of illness and disease in terms of everyday processes.

Most of the reproductive problems of rural women in this area of Jaipur district are related to menstruation (*mahawari/maheena ki pareshani*) and infected vaginal discharge (*safed pani*). Nagori, rural caste and lower class women attending the health centre mainly complained of either excessive bleeding (menorrhagia), irregular bleeding (polymenorrhoea), painful bleeding (dysmenorrhoea) or an absence of bleeding (aminorrhoea).[19] As in most patriarchal cultures, in rural Rajasthan there is shame attached to menstruation. All the women I met explained to me that menstruation (*maheena, mahawari* or 'MC', the abbreviation for 'menstrual cycle' which was part of the local vocabulary as a result of contact with healthworkers) was a flow of waste or dirt (*kachra/gandagi*). In practical terms this means that women must learn to covertly manage their menstrual periods. Zahida and Jetoon changed their menstrual cloth, at the most, three times a day in the summer. The first change was early in the morning when a group of kinswomen would perform their ablutions in the field while it was still dark. The second change was furtively made in the afternoon when there was no one in the fields because of the summer heat. The last change was made at night, after dark. Kamlesh, who has moved to a slum nearby, said she uses a single cloth for the whole day. Jetoon, Zahida and Kamlesh all said that the menstrual cloth had to be washed out of sight and hidden in cracks of stones or placed under other clothes to dry. Women felt equally constrained in passing urine or defecating. Kamlesh, Zahida and others said they restrict the amount of fluids the drink in order to control their urine for long stretches. Notions of shame and impurity thus combined in shaping women's menstrual practices and personal hygiene.

The secrecy attached to menstruation is regarded as essential by the women themselves because of the potential danger that menstruation has for women. Menstruating women become more vulnerable to *hawa* (wind; ill winds, referring to possession by dissatisfied spirits) and *nazar* (the evil eye; spells related to envy). This is often the reason why women do not venture far from the house when they are menstruating (or bleeding after childbirth), not even to the doctor if they experience pain or discomfort. The eyes are said to be vehicles through which spells are cast, and also to function as indicators of one's general condition. Dhanni, Kamlesh and Zahida all insisted there was a vital connection between menstruation and one's eyesight. An irregular or

19. The assistance of Dr A. K. Banerjee, director of the voluntary health centre, with the medical information presented here is gratefully acknowledged.

absent menstrual period signalled the weakening of the eyes with the blood in one's body turning to water. According to Kamlesh, the more blood there is in the body, the greater the menstrual flow. Kamlesh, only in her early thirties, said she spoke from personal experience. She said her menstrual cycle used to be for three days but now, as her body was weakened, she had only one-day periods. Kamlesh had given birth to twin girls nine years earlier, but had not conceived since. She explains her secondary infertility as a curse put upon her by father-in-law's father (discussed further in the section on spirit healers below).

In contrast to menstrual problems or those of infertility, infected vaginal discharge (leucorrhoea) was given less prominence by the women themselves and I suggest this is largely because the connection between an infection of the reproductive passages and a failure to reproduce is not so clearly made in indigenous terms. For example, conditions of pelvic inflammation, or the infection of the fallopian tubes, ovaries and uterus including the cervix were generally referred to by the local terms *ghav*, meaning wound, or *ganth*, meaning lump in the *nalli* or tubes and *bacchadani* or uterus. Although white vaginal discharge was a serious and widespread complaint, it was not considered significant enough by women to merit medical or an expert local healer's attention. It was also one of the physical states which caused shame (*sharam*) and was discussed only among women who were intimate with each other, some of whom would be familiar with the locally known herbal remedies. Prolapse of the uterus, bladder or rectum (*shareer nikalna*; literally 'body coming out') were also, like vaginal discharge, seen as conditions of shame, conditions which women had to manage on their own rather than seek treatment for. Unlike infected vaginal discharge, however, there were no herbal or other remedies generally sought or given for this condition (there were some exceptions).[20]

For guidance on matters relating to menstruation, sex, conception, birthing, nutrition and lactation, as well as for information on the best spiritual healers or private gynaecologists to consult, women turn to specific kinswomen from within a particular age group. Information on menstruation is usually obtained at the time of menarche and is most often provided by older sisters and sisters-

20. Mehmuda, an elderly Muslim woman from the neighbouring Pathan community, said her uterus gave way when she lifted a weight when she was three months pregnant with her third child (she has had five children since). She had used the rubber ring (*choodi*) advised by a private woman gynaecologist but discarded it because of discomfort. She had previously also applied the extract of the bodjadi bush but found it to be ineffective.

in-law (brothers' wives who have married into the natal home and village). For both Nagori and Hindu caste women, after marriage it is again the category of sisters-in-law (this time the husband's brothers' wives and husband's sisters) who form a peer group in which intimate matters such as sex, menstruation and vaginal discharge are likely to be discussed. It is this group of women and their experiences who, above all, influence individual women in their choice of specific healers or the type of medication taken. These are also the women who wash and bathe together and share household tasks. In late pregnancy, it is usually the sister-in-law who helps out with work tasks, and it is she who usually bears the responsibility of caring for the mother during and after childbirth. When Jetoon's child was born, for example, her sister-in-law disposed off the placenta (considered highly polluting and the work of lower status midwives; Rozario 1998, Patel 1994). According to Zahida, the newborn child is first put to the breast by the mother's sister-in-law, acknowledging the important relationship between the two women.[21]

Among the Nagori Sunnis, it is women from the generation above that of the expectant mother, in particular aunts or elder sisters-in-law, who are the most important 'midwives'(*dai*). Lower caste midwives may also be present at the delivery, in which case the kin-midwives revert to a supervisory role until the baby is delivered (Unnithan-Kumar, forthcoming). Most women were knowledgeable about birthing, but some were considered to have greater experience than others as well as a knack for delivering babies. Samina was one such midwife in Zahida's community. She was in her late thirties and had delivered around 200 babies in her three to six years as midwife. Whenever Zahida, Jetoon or Rashida had a pain in their 'tubes' they would ask Samina's advice. She would usually refer them to either the spiritual healers or the gynaecologists the women of the community generally frequented. Samina herself did not prescribe any medicine. For abortions, she said that although she knew a fairly simple technique, there was a danger in performing abortions and as such it was better to visit the private gynaecologists (or another Muslim midwife in the city whose medicines, however, were known to cause great heat, dizziness and danger to women). Outside the actual context of birth then, midwives were regarded as having limited knowledge and capabilities. Even their knowledge of childbirth was diffused among a number of similarly positioned (in terms of generation and expe-

21. Due to the limitations of space, I do not go into the indigenous categories of breastmilk here, or the generational differences in women's perspectives on breastfeeding (for this see Unnithan-Kumar, 1999 and forthcoming) but rather focus on the areas where healthcare is actively sought.

rience) women. It is therefore not surprising to find that midwives were not highly regarded in the community.[22]

'Routine' matters of childbirth were largely managed within the community of kinswomen, an arena where health related actions are not so much a question of contesting the authority of men as of negotiating and testing the loyalties of kinswomen. It is the community of women, especially kinwomen of one's peer group, who suggest which healers to turn to when complications related to reproduction are expected or arise.

Anxiety, individual desire and spiritual healers

Spiritual healers are the dominant category of healers consulted by women, as well as a number of men, in rural Rajasthan. They enjoy this status for a number of reasons. As mentioned previously, it is only spiritual healers who address the 'evil wind' or 'evil eye' aspect of any illness. Certain conditions, in particular menstrual complications, are seen to result from the 'strength/force and work of the wind' (*hawa ka jor/hawa ka kaam*), while infant mortality is also frequently perceived to be the work of spells cast by jealous or disaffected women. Other conditions for which such healers are consulted – by both men and women – are, for example, unexplained fevers, insect and snake bites, depression and tensions. Apart from the fact that spiritual healers are able to offer women concrete explanations and solace for the more traumatic experiences in their reproductive life span, the low cost of visiting such healers places little financial burden on them. At the same time, because spiritual healers of any caste or religion tend to be equally respected by both men and women in their local communities, husbands or fathers find it more difficult to prevent their wives or daughters and sisters from visiting these indigenous healers. Women are thus free to consult frequently with spiritual healers without being construed as deviant. It is, then, this category of healers to whom women turn to with their innermost anxieties, grievances as well their secret desires.

All the terms for spiritual healers such as *jhar phunk wala, bhopa* or *jisme bhav ata hai*, referred to the fact of the healer becoming possessed. Most of the healers who were consulted by the women I met were men of either lower Hindu castes (Bhangi, Raigar or Meena), or Muslims.[23] Returning to Zahida's story, we find that when she

22. This observation is in contrast to the current popular health planning perspective in India, which believes that a solution to the dismal maternal morbidity figures lies in the empowerment of community midwives (Unnithan-Kumar, forthcoming; Rozario, 1998; Jeffrey et al., 1987).

had trouble conceiving her second child, she went to see a man of the Meena caste who was known to become possessed by the spirit of *bhairu* (popularly regarded as an incarnation of the Hindu god Shiva). She was anxious to conceive as her mother-in-law had rebuked her for being sterile (*bandhdi*) and the daughter of a mother who only produced daughters. Zahida's visit to the Meena proved unsuccessful and in fact, when she returned Munni, her sister-in-law (husband's elder brother's wife), accused her of casting a spell over her family (Munni's husband developed pains in his stomach and both he and his brother, Zahida's husband, were unable to hold any work). So before Zahida could seek her own treatment she had to get her name cleared of bringing misfortune on her affinal family. To this end she sought out her sister-in-law (husband's sister), Miraim's father-in-law, who was known to become possessed by a holy man called Shukker Baba, as well as an exorcist in Bassi (approximately 20 kilometres away) and in Jaipur city (approximately 12 kilometres away). They all ascertained that Zahida was not a 'witch' (*dakan*), in other words that she had not intentionally sought to cause harm. She then accompanied Miraim to seek advice about her infertility from Pooran of the Bhangi caste who lived at the railway crossing where he worked part-time as a linesman.

Zahida explained her inability to conceive a second child and her consequent visit to Pooran as being caught by the 'wind' at the crossroads behind the mosque in her affinal village. She said the spirit that had 'caught' her was that of a lower caste (Raigar) woman who had died in suspicious circumstances. It was the spirit of this Raigar woman which caused her infertility. (Lower caste Raigar women are called to assist Nagori women in complicated deliveries, where, I believe, in case of death they can take the blame.) Pooran was able to identify this woman and had successfully caught her spirit by tying his red and orange threads measured to Zahida's length and knotted before it was fastened around her waist. Pooran was consulted by Hindu caste and Muslim women and this is perhaps because he was possessed at different times by lower caste Hindu saints, Guru Nanak of the Sikhs, and a Muslim *pir*. Apart from the sacred threads, Pooran used cloves and lemons in his prescriptions. The cost of these items was borne by the women, and while they were no fees for his services, Pooran usually received cigarettes and gifts in money or kind, depending on how much the women could afford or wanted to spend.

23. There are some contexts in which healers in Rajasthan happen to be women (see Mayaram, 1997, for example).

Spiritual healers like Pooran are important healthcare agents because they are able to provide women with relief from the anxiety caused by social aspersions, not only on their reproductive value, but also their altruistic intentions with regard to family matters in general. In addressing the grief of loss and vulnerability so frequently faced by rural Rajasthani women, spiritual healers both complement and substitute the care and support provided by kinswomen and men. Women who have lost children or are anxious make public their show of grief by crying when they recount their experiences to healers or other kinspersons. At the same time, they are matter of fact in their search for satisfactory answers or cures for their predicament. Zahida's example shows that, while certain affinal kinswomen (her mother-in-law and her sister-in-law, Munni) undermine one's position within the family, there are others (especially her sister-in-law, Miraim), who being emotionally closer provide social security and solidarity enabling them to influence the healthcare sought by their kinswomen. Zahida's resort to several healers shows that women also evaluate the services that spiritual healers provide them and are not completely bound by the influence of their kinswomen and men. Furthermore, Zahida, Kamlesh, Samina, Jetoon and others are not bound by their community loyalty to consult only traditional healers and often use a combination of spiritual and biomedical prescriptions. In general, however, any well-being that results from medication is attributed to the work of spiritual and other local healers.

Culturally acceptable desires and biomedical expertise

The frequency with which rural women sought out local and known, private health specialists was, on the face of it, surprising, especially given the large and increasing public sector outlay on healthcare provision in Rajasthan (as elsewhere in India). The healthcare system in Rajasthan, as in other parts of India, consists of (i) a large public healthcare delivery structure (especially in terms of number of personnel, employed) which aims to provide healthcare at minimum cost;[24] (ii) a big private healthcare sector

24. In Jaipur district, for the rural population, there are 17 Primary Health Centres and Family Planning Centres, 35 dispensaries and 3 hospitals. By contrast, there are 14 urban hospitals and 15 urban family planning centres. There are 15 mother and child welfare centres. Apart from allopathic services, there are 259 Ayurvedic Aushadhalay (dispensaries) and 3 Ayurvedic hospitals (District Gazetteer, 1987). Each Primary Health Centre has a number of sub-centres depending on the population, with each sub-centre in Sanganer catering for between 2,500 to 5,000 persons which could include anywhere from two to eleven villages over a radius of 1 to 8 kilometres (personal communication, Sushma ANM).

(in terms of numbers of hospitals, dispensaries, clinics as well as numbers of physicians, Bhat 1993),[25] and, (iii) a network of popular, localised, informal, private practitioners who rely on indigenous knowledge techniques. Few women took their problems to the public health worker (the auxiliary nurse midwife, or ANM) who was also never called to assist in the delivery of a child despite her training. In cases where a medical termination of pregnancy (MTP) was desired, Nagori women went straight to women gynaecologists, preferring private women doctors (encouraged by the doctors themselves), and bypassing the free medical services provided by public health centres and hospitals.

In the communities to which Zahida and Kamlesh belong, biomedical expertise is most regularly sought for what is popularly called *safai* (literally; cleaning) and regarded as a D&C (dilation and curatage) by gynaecologists. Although meant to take place after a spontaneous abortion, a number of women I spoke to used the process as a means to induce abortion after any sign of bleeding. There is also a handful of women who have had tubectomies, although sterilisation is something that is talked about and desired more than actually undergone. In comparison to the actual resort to a D&C and the rhetoric of desired resort to tubectomies, there is a low demand and lack of use of contraceptives. D&Cs, I observed, are in fact used rather than contraceptives to space children, although this is not overtly stated by the women themselves.

The D&Cs are performed by private gynaecologists who are recommended by kinswomen and usually all the women of a village go to the same one or two. Most of the women of Zahida's village consulted 'Neetu', a gynaecologist working in a successful private hospital in a residential colony approximately 6 kilometres away in urban Jaipur. Village women prefer these private doctors, despite the relatively high costs compared to the public services, mainly because of the efficiency of the services they offer. By consulting the same gynaecologists as other villagers, women seek to establish a kin-like relationship with the doctors, mainly because they feel they will get a sympathetic hearing (most urban doctors are perceived as not listening to the patients' complaints in detail). Also, if the patient is known to the doctor, it is believed that she can negotiate a delayed or staggered

25. This is not a surprising observation as Bhat (1993), in his review of the private healthcare sector in India, finds that whether in terms of hospitals, dispensaries, clinics or physicians, the private sector far outnumbers the government sector.

payment. Private women doctors usually charge fees from Rs.400/– for foetuses of 2–2.5 months to Rs.600/– to Rs.800/– for foetuses of 4–5 months. Including transportation and medicine, women require between Rs.500/– to Rs.1,500/– for a medical termination of pregnancy.[26]

Usually a woman's decision to undergo a D&C follows signs of bleeding during pregnancy and therefore requires minimal consultation with the husband. As mentioned previously, financial outlay is sanctioned in reproductive matters as opposed to other ailments which women may suffer (in particular older women) because of the centrality of reproduction and the value placed on having children. Sterilisation, on the other hand, despite the minimal costs involved, is, in practice, not a popular option because it requires much more negotiation, not only with a woman's husband but also his family members. In any case, it is not even considered as an option, and not collectively sanctioned unless a woman has produced a specific number and mix of children (usually three sons and two daughters). Producing the right numbers of male or female children may take the woman through her whole reproductive cycle. There is also the prevailing notion, based on the negative experiences of a number of specific women, that sterilisation leads to future reproductive complications. Samina, who has been the primary kin-midwife for Jetoon, Rashida and Zahida, underwent sterilisation after producing four children (she had two boys, two girls, one miscarriage and one infant death). When I met her three to four years had passed since her tubectomy, and she was complaining about pain in her tubes, cold sweats and a lack of appetite which she put down to complications from the operation. Several other women I met from the Meena and Oswal/Brahman castes who had undergone tubectomies blamed them for their prevailing ill health. Most of these women had their tubectomies done at public hospitals where there were no follow-up checks, or even information on the operation they had undergone. Unknown to the women I met, it is possible to reverse the process through a delicate operation offered free of charge by the state's health authorities. But even a reversal requires tactful negotiations with family members. Mamta, a woman of the Brahmin caste, had lost a son after a tubectomy and very much wanted to have her tubes reconnected. Her mother-in-law could not spare her from the work of their joint household, and combined with fears of a debilitating recovery Mamta was persuaded to give up her hopes of trying for another son.

26. In 1998 one pound sterling was worth approximately 70 rupees.

Among the Sunni women, I was surprised to find that the negative talk about sterilisation was seldom couched in terms of religious injunctions. In fact Jabunissa, Shakila and others laughed when I recounted that I had heard from a *maulvi* (priest) that Muslim women who underwent the 'operation' would be troubled in their coffins by the spirits of their unborn children. They retorted, 'Who is there to check on what happens in the coffin!' Nevertheless, it is acknowledged that sterilisations can only be undergone with the support of kinsmen, in particular the husband. A couple of Nagori men actively encouraged their wives to be operated, explaining that their attitude was a response to their wives' ill health or their poverty.

Women's talk and experiences of contraception are also largely negative. This is understandable given their physical weakness. The intra-uterine devices available, such as the Copper-T and even hormonal pills, as is well known, cause excessive bleeding in weak and anaemic women. The other option of using condoms (popularly known as 'Nirodh', a brand-name distributed free of charge by the public health workers), is difficult to put into practice given the cultural constraints on women. There is no doubt that this form of contraception aimed at spacing children involves most negotiation with a woman's husband. Shahnaz, in her twenties, was the only woman known to use condoms in the village. She was also among the eight women who had either completed class six or higher. Yet she was as ignorant of condoms as Samina. She and Samina asked me if Nirodhs were safe as they had heard they were unreliable, and could fill up and burst (*phatna*) inside the woman. I said I also used condoms and thought they were probably safe and also good because they prevent dirt and disease from spreading. They both wanted to know whether men and women stuck to each other during intercourse if they used condoms. The main factor behind Shahnaz's use of condoms, as she pointed out, was that her husband had 'progressive ideas'. He worked at a nearby factory run by an Englishwoman and had been influenced by the use of condoms among other middle class workers there. Shakila, also in her twenties, was as educated as Shahnaz. She too had had one child and did not want a second soon after. Shakila's husband, unlike Shahnaz's, was considered orthodox (a *namazi*; scholar of the Koran), and did not agree to using condoms. When she became pregnant during my stay, he refused her the option of a D&C (despite her aunt's guess that he might give in to Shakila on this matter). Indeed, he did not even let Shakila take any iron-enriched medicine during her pregnancy. So while education may be a factor in promoting healthcare behaviour, it needs to be seen in conjunction with patriarchy (in this case, the extent to which the husband is bound by tradition).

Given the active promotion of contraceptives by the auxiliary nurse midwives (ANMs), public health agents working at the village level, as well as by state health propaganda in the media, it is surprising that there was a significant gap in women's knowledge of the means to control their fertility. Zahida, who had her Copper-T inserted when she had her last D&C performed, said she was uncertain how it functioned. She agreed with Samina, according to whom the Copper-T stuck right up in the women's vagina and got full of 'meat', or it came right down to the mouth of the vagina and caused discomfort. Zahida said her husband complained of it during intercourse, so what Samina said must be true. In general, Samina, Zahida and others prefer to learn about contraceptive matters from their gynaecologists rather than the ANM. The ANM thus gets bypassed in matters concerning contraceptive advice, which is among her main tasks (her other duties are related to immunisation, the care of pregnant women and assistance with deliveries). As village women use kinswomen, kin-midwives and known midwives from the lower caste communities to assist in childbirth, ANMs are ignored again. Considering rural women's health-seeking behaviour in terms of their perceptions and desires goes some way in explaining why there is such a low uptake of the public health services on offer, such as those provided by the ANM.

Conclusions

There are several important observations that emerge from the issues relating to women's agency and healthcare discussed above. Firstly, it is clear from the examples of the processes underlying women's selection of healers, that they do not construe their actions as resisting the authority of men as much as that of certain women.

The analytic emphasis on emotions allowed us to understand the types of negotiation which women have with other kinspersons, in particular with affinal kinswomen who exerted the greatest influence over them in matters of health. Focusing on the desires and emotional attachments of Zahida, for example, showed us that not only is it sisters-in-law who as a kinship category are most influential, but also that there are specific individuals within this category who facilitate or debilitate the health-seeking initiatives of their kinswomen. Secondly, women's agency and ability to work towards their desires in healthcare matters is seen to shift over the reproductive cycle because of an increase in their emotional support and powers of negotiation within their husband's family over time. Thus women like Zahida, Samina, and Jetoon who are in their mid to late thirties, have greater abilities to negotiate with their kin about reproductive matters than younger women such as Shahnaz or Shakila.

Another significant point to emerge is the importance of relationships between spouses to women's reproductive agency. We find that Zahida's relationship with her husband, her love/sense of responsibility towards him, despite her portrayal of him as uncaring, influences her reproductive health-seeking behaviour (for example, her choice of contraceptive). While the education of women (Shahnaz, Shakila) allows them to be aware of and desire similar reproductive health outcomes, the ability to translate their desires into agency is dependent on the support and understanding of their spouse. This point is further reinforced by the predominant resort to spiritual healers who prescribe cures which aim to mitigate the social tensions and emotional conflicts attached to reproductive ailments. In relation to patriarchy as it is manifest in Rajasthan, we find it can facilitate women's reproductive healthcare as reflected in an almost unquestioning allocation of household income to meet the high expenditures incurred on married women's consultations with private gynaecologists. At the same time patriarchal practices interfere with reproductive healthcare, as in the case of Shakila who was denied the means of spacing her children.

Note

The paper is based on research on the healthcare provisions and access of women to reproductive health services in a rural area south-east of Jaipur city in 1998. The fieldwork was funded by the Wellcome Trust for Medical Research, UK. I should like to thank Ann Whitehead, Ursula Sharma, N. Sivaramakrishnan, Soraya Tremayne and members of the Oxford Fertility and Reproduction Group for their insightful comments. In India, the crucial support during fieldwork given by A. K. Bannerjee, G. J. and N. Unnithan, the staff of the Khejri Rural Health Centre, Zahidabano, K. Gogaram, V. Joshi, K. R. Vasanthan, M. Singh and S. Kumar is gratefully acknowledged.

CHAPTER 2

From International Policy to Local Reality: Women's Reproductive Health Strategies in El Alto, Bolivia

Kirstan Hawkins and Neil Price

Introduction

The Programme of Action (PoA) of the International Conference on Population and Development (ICPD) held in Cairo in 1994 appears to mark a major paradigm shift in the formulation of international population policy. The dominant feature of this shift has been described as '... a move from notions of population control to notions of reproductive health' (Basu, 1997:7). In the new policy discourse individual attainment of sexual and reproductive health and rights, rather than the achievement of demographic targets, is placed as central to population policy (Hempel, 1996; Petchesky and Judd, 1998). Central to the sexual and reproductive health and rights approach is the concept of the empowerment of women (Germain, 1997).

Despite the apparent international consensus reached on the objectives of the International Conference on Population and Development (ICPD), the universal validity of the concepts of sexual and reproductive health and rights and their application to diverse social realities and local contexts have come under question (Correa and Reichman, 1994; Harcourt, 1997; Petchesky and

Judd, 1998): '... until we know more about the local contexts and ways of thinking in which women in their everyday lives negotiate reproductive health and sexual matters, we cannot assume that reproductive health and sexual rights are a goal they seek and therefore one that has universal applicability' (ibid.:1). Analysis of the local and specific contexts of sexual and reproductive health is essential if the policy milestones set out at Cairo and at the Fourth International Women's Conference in Beijing in 1995 are to have any connection to the reality of the majority of the world's women (Harcourt, 1997:8).

While the PoA recognises the importance of social diversity and cultural context, the conceptualisation of reproductive health and rights contained therein is rooted in a biomedical paradigm and in the western liberal notion of the individual. Focusing on ethnographic case study material from Bolivia, this chapter considers the relationship between reproductive health policy discourse and how sexual and reproductive health is shaped and constituted within the social and cultural contexts and everyday practices of migrant Aymaran women.

Population policy and the shifting discourses on population and development

> Every social policy rests on some theory of how individuals, societies, governments and organisations operate.
>
> – Warwick, 1982:31

Much of the 'grand theory' concerning human fertility rests on the work of demography and the biological and medical sciences (Ginsburg and Rapp, 1995:161). Demographic theory and method have provided the knowledge base for the formulation of international population policy. Each of the United Nations intergovernmental population conferences has, it is said, epitomised the conventional wisdom or 'discourses' on population and development for that specific decade (see Smyth, 1994:2).

This chapter draws on Foucault's notion of discourse as specific socially and historically constructed 'bodies of knowledge' or 'technical fields' (McHoul and Grace, 1993). While scientific knowledge presents itself as a cumulative progression towards the truth, Foucault argues that 'official' and scientific discourses change radically over time. Thus, at any one historical moment there are competing discourses, which construct social and political realities differently (McHoul and Grace, 1993:19). For Foucault, fields of knowledge which represent themselves in different historical epochs as objective, continuous (i.e. linked by an evolutionary progression of ideas) and apolitical are socially, historically and politically constructed products and mechanisms for the operation of disciplinary power.

Foucault uses the term discipline in two senses. The first refers to academic disciplines or specialised technical fields such as medicine, psychiatry, sociology and demography; the second to operations of power practised through disciplinary institutions such as the hospital, school and prison to maintain social control supported by these specialised bodies of knowledge (McHoul and Grace, 1993:26). In other words, through the use of the term 'discipline', Foucault stresses the connection between techniques of power and the forms of knowledge that have developed alongside them (McHoul and Grace, 1993).

While demographic theories of fertility change have undergone a series of apparent revisions over the past three decades, all have been strongly influenced by modernisation theory, which assumes that societies undergo evolutionary and unilinear transformation from traditional to modern forms. Despite major theoretical developments in other areas of social science (such as postmodernism and social constructivism), demography has remained firmly rooted within the positivist paradigm, developing increasingly sophisticated mathematical methods to produce its specialised body of knowledge (Greenhalgh, 1996). While constructing itself as a social science within its institutional base in academic institutions, demography's funding base has largely been drawn from government departments which require policy-related products (Demeny, 1988; Greenhalgh, 1996; Hodgson, 1983; McNicoll, 1992). As such, demography has constructed and defended theoretical frameworks which are primarily considered to be of utilitarian value by its funders (Greenhalgh, 1996:32).

The neo-Malthusian position has dominated the formulation of international and national population policy in the post-Second World War era (Hartmann, 1987). Neo-Malthusianism combines classical fertility theory from demography (fertility transition as a result of processes of modernisation) with a rationalist economic theory of fertility behaviour. Fitting within the modernisation paradigm, neo-Malthusians argue that fertility behaviour is based on economistic calculations of the cost and benefits of having children, in which the unit of fertility decision-making is the individual or the reproductive couple. This is the dominant framework within which 'demand' has been understood and operationalised in mainstream family planning programming (see, for instance, Behrman and Knowles, 1998). Neo-Malthusianism has been operationalised through vertical programmes which assume that demographic targets of fertility reduction can be brought about through the implementation of well-planned and well-managed family planning services irrespective of social and economic context (Thomas, 1991).

At first sight, one of the most surprising outcomes of ICPD is the apparent consensus reached between the 'family planning establishment' (see Hartmann, 1987) and representatives of civil society groups (in particular feminist international women's health activist and women's health coalitions), who in preceding years had been the most vocal and persistent critics of the international family planning movement's neo-Malthusian antecedents. Nonetheless, a certain historical synergy can be traced between neo-Malthusianism and the radical feminist position on population issues, which underpins the new post-Cairo discourse. This synergy dates back to the early days of the birth control movement, at the start of which the western feminist perception of birth control as a source of women's emancipation intertwined (particularly in the work of Margaret Sanger) with a neo-Malthusian proposition that access to modern contraception would, through reduced fertility levels, lead to less poverty (Hodgson and Cotts Watkins, 1997).

The neo-Malthusian discourse on population and development came under sustained attack during the first World Population Conference in Bucharest in 1974, in which the overriding message of southern states was that equitable social and economic development was a prerequisite for fertility decline, not a consequence of it (Demeny, 1985; Hodgson and Cotts Watkins, 1997). However, by the time of the International Conference on Population held in Mexico City in 1984, there appears to have been a radical repositioning of international discourses on population and development. Many southern governments who had advocated that 'development is the best contraceptive' at Bucharest (such as India) had, by the time of Mexico City, formalised population policies implemented through national family planning programmes. Conversely, the US delegation reversed its previous policy position, advocating that population is not a priority for state intervention and financing (Finkle and Crane, 1985).

The US position at Mexico City was not so much a retreat from neo-Malthusianism as a statement of neo-liberal ideology which advocates a drastically reduced role for the state in social welfare and economic development and greater reliance on free markets, entrepreneurial initiatives and the aspirations of individuals to improve their quality of life (see Correa and Reichman, 1997; Demeny, 1985; Portes, 1997). The official US stance at Mexico City moved state policy in line with the ideology of the new right and the moral majority, and paved the way for the formation of new alliances between the population establishment and the women's health movement (Hodgson and Cotts Watkins, 1997). The US government's post-Mexico City stance on international family planning programming led to a re-packaging of the United States Agency for International Development's (USAID's) family planning activities under the heading of 'maternal and child health', which was later transformed into 'women's reproductive health' (Hodgson and Cotts Watkins, 1997).

In his *History of Sexuality*, Foucault identifies a synergy in the eighteenth century between the Malthusian discourse on population and emerging discourses on sexuality, in which sexuality refers to a 'historically constructed apparatus: a dispersed system of morals, techniques of power, discourses and procedures designed to mould sexual practices towards certain strategic and politic ends' (McHoul and Grace, 1993:77). In Foucault's analysis the modern society is typified by the replacement of the power of a sovereign authority with diverse and localised mechanisms for the 'administration of life' (McHoul and Grace, 1993). The emerging public discourse on sexuality linked control of the physical body as a biological organism with techniques for regulating the population, hence giving birth to the discipline of demography:

One of the great innovations in the techniques of power in the eighteenth century was the emergence of 'population' as an economic and political problem: population as wealth, population as manpower or labour capacity, population balanced between its own growth and the resources it commanded. Governments perceived that they were not dealing simply with subjects, or even with a 'people', but with a 'population', with its specific phenomena and its peculiar variables:

> ... birth and death rates, life expectancy, fertility, state of health, frequency of illnesses, patterns of diet and habitation ... At the heart of this economic and political problem of population was sex: it was necessary to analyse the birth rate, the age of marriage, the legitimate and illegitimate births, the precocity and frequency of sexual relations, the ways of making them fertile or sterile, the effects of unmarried life or of the prohibitions, the impact of contraceptive practices – of those notorious 'deadly secrets' which demographers on the eve of the Revolution knew were already familiar to the inhabitants of the countryside. (Foucault, 1990:25–6)

The ICPD definition of sexual and reproductive health and rights, which appears to offer a radical break from neo-Malthusian notions of population control through giving centrality to empowerment of the individual, is, however, far from unproblematic. Underlying the ICPD discourse is the continuation of a neo-Malthusian policy agenda. The transformation of family planning into reproductive health care '... is expected to translate reduced reproductive demands more effectively and humanely into lower fertility' (Thomas and Price, 1999:795). The elements of sexual and reproductive health are defined within the conceptual boundaries of a biomedical perspective which fits within the modernisation paradigm. Through the incorporation of radical feminist discourses on individual rights, the neo-liberal notion of the freedom and choice of the 'autonomous individual' is also placed at the centre of policy discourse. The fundamental belief in the 'ethical autonomy of the individual' has been a cornerstone of humanist western philosophy for the past two centuries (Armstrong, 1998:21). Within such a framework, '... these values can morally be peddled, imposed on, or used to judge, non-western cultures, and more significantly ... be used to interpret the past' (Armstrong, 1998:21).

Local knowledges as critical discourse

Anthropology has increasingly drawn attention to the theoretical limitations and conceptual weaknesses of demography. Far from being an individual 'rationalist' decision-making process, fertility-related behaviour has been shown to be embedded within a complexity of social relations and institutions at the local level, contextualised within wider social, political, economic and historical processes (Greenhalgh, 1990; Greenhalgh, 1995; McNicoll, 1980; Hammel, 1990; Lockwood, 1995; Ginsburg and Rapp 1995; Price, 1996; Price, 1998). Anthropological approaches to the study of fertility behaviour suggest a move away from meta-theories of demographic change to analyses which place the social and cultural dimensions of human agency and its structural constraints at the centre of fertility theory (Ginsburg and Rapp, 1995:161; see also Unnithan-Kumar, this volume).

Within the body of social science literature concerned with HIV/AIDS, increasing attention has been drawn to the limitations of standard demographic behavioural research which has focused on studying 'knowledge, attitudes and practices' using sample survey instruments. If social and behavioural research is to make an important contribution to HIV prevention, it must focus on the cultural systems in which behaviour becomes meaningful and the context in which sexual interactions occur (Parker, 1994:§309). Attention has turned to the analysis of '... sexual scripts that exist in different social settings, and that organise the possibilities of sexual interaction in a range of specific ways' (Parker, 1994:§310). This focus has in turn led to '... an increasing concern with the wider cultural scenarios, discursive practices, and systems of knowledge and power which, as Foucault argued, produce the meaning and experience of sexuality in diverse historical and cultural settings' (ibid.).

Central to Foucault's notion of discourse is the critique of official or dominant knowledges, and the investigation of forms of knowledge which are considered as subjugated or marginal. What is of interest are the methods, practices and techniques by which official discourses go about the process of normalisation and '... manoeuvring populations into "correct" and "functional" forms of thinking and acting', and in the process occluding forms of knowledge which are different from them (McHoul and Grace, 1993:17). Foucault's notion of discourse draws attention to subjugated or marginal knowledges that have been disqualified, taken less seriously, or deemed inadequate by official histories and discourses (McHoul and Grace, 1993:15). The critique of official and dominant discourses requires giving voice to these marginalised knowledges:

> It is through the re-emergence of these low ranking knowledges (such as that of the psychiatric patient, of the ill person ... parallel and marginal as they are to the knowledge of medicine ...) and which involve what I would call a popular knowledge ... though it is far from being a general common-sense knowledge, but is on the contrary a particular, local, regional knowledge, a differential knowledge incapable of unanimity and which owes its force only to the harshness with which it is opposed by everything surrounding it – that it is through the re-appearance of this knowledge, of these local popular knowledges, these disqualified knowledges, that criticism performs its work (Foucault, 1980:82).

The remainder of this chapter considers the relationship between reproductive health policy discourse and how sexual and reproductive health are shaped and constituted within the social and cultural contexts and everyday practices of migrant Aymaran women in the Bolivian urban centre of El Alto.

The entry of reproductive health into Bolivian official discourse

The past decade in Bolivia has seen significant changes in official policies concerning reproductive health. Prior to 1989 Bolivian policy was decidedly pro-natalist. The images of the film *Wawar Mallku*

(*Blood of the Condor*) which portrayed imperialist US agencies carrying out enforced sterilisations among rural Quechua women, and led to the subsequent expulsion of Peace Corps (and other foreign non-governmental organisations/NGOs) from Bolivia in the 1960s, remain strongly imprinted in popular memory. However, in 1989 the first national reproductive health programme was launched, and since 1991 modern family planning methods have been available through government health services (Rance, 1997). Despite the integration of family planning services in the health system, utilisation of modern contraceptive methods remains low.

In 1994, Bolivia launched its new reproductive health programme, Plan Vida, which has the reduction of maternal mortality as its central goal. Bolivia has one of the highest levels of maternal mortality in Latin America, with unsafe abortion being one of the major causes. The Bolivian delegation to ICPD stated that central to the reproductive health approach was '... respect for women's decisions concerning sexuality and fertility and democratisation of women's roles in the family and in society' (Rance, 1997:11). The official Bolivian country statement for Cairo was subsequently produced as the *Declaration of Principles on Population and Sustainable Development*, the first explicit national population policy (Rance, ibid.). In 1996 the National Safe Motherhood Committee was founded, and '... augured new advances in the prevention of maternal deaths' (Rance, 1997:12). However, the biomedical emphasis of the concept of 'safe motherhood' has been criticised for failing to consider the historically specific political and economic contexts of maternal mortality (Morsy, 1995:172). Rance (1997:12) suggests that 'safe motherhood', in Bolivia, now '... represents a conservative discourse when contrasted with the post-1994 emphasis on gender and sexual and reproductive health'. Morsy (1995:172) similarly argues that the emphasis on addressing maternal mortality in Egypt's reproductive health policy has the potential to further co-opt family planning programmes at the expense of addressing the structural basis for maternal ill health.

El Alto: the social and historical context of migration

The city of El Alto is a creation of the past two decades, and is being constructed and expanded on a daily basis. Situated on the *altiplano* directly above La Paz, El Alto is now one of the most rapidly growing cities in Latin America, with an increasingly diverse population, including Aymara speakers from the *altiplano*, Spanish speaking *mestizos* and Quechua speakers from the valleys.

The city began as makeshift accommodation constructed by impoverished *campesinos,* who were unable to extract a sustainable livelihood from their small and unproductive plots of land on the *altiplano,* and began to migrate to the urban market centres during the economic crisis of the 1980s.

Campesinos are the class of land-based Indian peasants, whose labour was (officially) controlled by the elite classes of Hispanic decent until the land reforms of 1952. The *campesinos* formed the heart of the Bolivian economy, labouring in the mines, on the *haciendas,* and on the land owned by the elite classes (Crandon-Malamud, 1991:18). Until the 1940s, the use of Indian dress and language was restricted in law, and education of the Indian masses prohibited (Crandon-Malamud, 1991:49). Until very recent years Indian women in *pollera* (traditional Indian dress) were refused entry to the restaurants and hotels of La Paz.

Mestizo is a term traditionally used to refer to 'mixed race' peoples of Hispanic and Indian decent. Historically, *mestizos* formed a broker class between the Indians and the landowners, overseeing the Aymara and Quechua labourers through the administrative powers vested in them by the elite landowners (Crandon-Malamud, 1991:241). With the 1952 land reforms, the administrative role of the *mestizo* disappeared. The class distinction between the *mestizo* and *campesino* is now more blurred than ever, the *mestizos* in El Alto struggling to survive along with their *campesino* neighbours in the declining economy of the *altiplano*. The term *mestizo* is now often applied to those of Aymara decent who have shed their ethnic identity in the quest to forge a new class position in the national economy (Crandon-Malamud, 1991).

Distinct from the land-based *campesino*s are the miners who form a large section of the migrant population of El Alto. Miners had the reputation of being the most revolutionary segment of the working class in Bolivia (Nash, 1979:2). In seventy years of exploitation, the miners transformed themselves from a peasant population with a 'localised world view' to a working class aware of and participating in a world market (Nash, 1979:2). In the mid-1980s, when most of the national mines closed and the remaining few were privatised, miners were relocated by the government to urban centres such as El Alto. While migrant *campesinos* were able to diversify their economic activities, and maintain their land and links with their rural communities, the miners not only lost their source of labour and income, but also their social identity as an organised working class. In El Alto many of the mining families are now the most impoverished, lacking access to the rural landholdings that their *campesino* neighbours maintain, their subsistence depending entirely upon selling their labour in the competitive cash economy of the city.

Health and healthcare

There are three main forms of health care resource available to the inhabitants of El Alto: biomedical services provided through government clinics; NGOs and private physicians; *medicinas caseras* or herbal cures sold in the market and administered in the home, and Aymara medicine available from indigenous healers or *yatiris*.

Family planning, maternal health care and STD treatment and diagnosis form part of the free package of services provided by the government, the primary source (along with the Catholic church) of reproductive health care services in the marginal outlying zones of El Alto. In recent years NGOs have established clinics in the market centre (the *ceja*), most of which function on a cost-recovery basis charging fees for family planning, maternal health care, child health services and diagnosis and treatment of sexually transmitted diseases.

Medicinas caseras are herbal cures administered in the home usually by the mother, in the form of *mates*.[1] They are the most commonly used health care resource among the poor in El Alto. The practice of *medicina caseras* is based on a humoral theory and hot/cold dualism, influenced by Galenic medical theory from the Spanish colonial era (Crandon-Malamud, 1991:24). It forms part of the 'everyday' knowledge of women and is central to women's role as healthcare providers in the household.

Aymara medicine falls into the domain of specialist traditional healers, the *yatiris*, diviners of coca leaves. A whole section of stalls in the central market place is dominated by *yatiris*. In El Alto the term *yatiri* is often used interchangeably with *kallawaya*. However, in the rural *altiplano* the *kallawaya* tradition is understood as a highly specialised and complex body of knowledge, practised by an elite group of indigenous healers whose knowledge passes from father to son. The Aymara version practised by the *yatiri* is a simplified folk version of the *kallawaya* (Crandon-Malamud, 1991:43).

The *yatiri* may be a man or a woman, who has usually received the gift of divination through surviving an auspicious event such as being struck by lightening. Through the divination of coca leaves the *yatiri* is able to bring luck and good fortune as well as cure illnesses of a supernatural causation. *Brujeria* (witchcraft)

1. *Mates* (pronounced matays) are herbal infusions or herbal teas.

and the casting of bad luck upon an envious or suspicious neighbour is rife in the neighbourhood, and the *yatiri* may also be classified as a *bruja* (witch), depending upon the social relations she has established with her neighbours and within the community. During fieldwork in El Alto,[2] three *yatiris* were interviewed on a regular basis. Two had survived being struck by lightening. The other, in a position of extreme social vulnerability and poverty (a single mother with three children, and partially disabled from polio) suddenly discovered her powers of divination. She is now able to earn a living on the strength of her recently found specialist knowledge.

Local constructions of health and illness are fluid, borrowing from different systems of thought. The apparently conflicting 'bodies of knowledge' represented in the different medical systems can be drawn upon simultaneously and without contradiction (Crandon-Malamud, 1991:24). 'Soul loss', for instance, is often treated initially in the home by the mother, using *medicinas caseras*, followed by consultation with a *yatiri*. Crandon-Malamud (1991:32) suggests that the three medical systems have '...value as a primary resource that facilitates negotiation of cultural identity and thus alters social relations and creates access to secondary resources'.

Losing souls and finding churches

The goal of reducing of maternal and infant mortality is central to Bolivian reproductive health policy. The experience of infant and child death forms an important part of women's discourses on sickness and health. By far the most common serious childhood illness category is 'soul loss' caused by fright (*susto*), most commonly following a fall or an attack by a dog (a daily hazard in the streets of El Alto). Fright sickness, particularly affecting babies and children, is a common feature of Andean ethnomedical systems, although its symptoms vary across different Andean contexts, from listlessness and lethargy, to diarrhoea and severe fever resulting in death (Greenaway, 1998).

Fright sickness is caused by the soul leaving the body. The Aymara identity is associated with the existence of three souls, the *animu*, the *ajayu* and the *alma* (Crandon-Malamud, 1991:133). In traditional Aymara categorisation the *animu* does not become solidly entrenched in the body until adolescence

2. The case study material presented in this chapter is based on fieldwork conducted by Kirstan Hawkins in 1998.

(ibid.). The *animu* is capricious, and in infants and young children can easily wander off and become lost. The *animu* may be coaxed back by the child's mother, who calls the soul at night enticing it by placing sweets and desirable items near the child's bed. The *ajayu* and *alma* are more entrenched in the body at birth (ibid.). Loss of the *ajayu*, which may be eaten or stolen by spirits that live within the earth and mountains, is severe and requires the skills and knowledge of a *yatiri* to cure it. The *alma* only leaves the body at death and cannot be retrieved.

A variety of opinions on the exact number of souls that constitute the Aymara and Mestizo being exist among members of the community in El Alto. Discourses surrounding soul loss and fright sickness shift according to context. Those who are members of the Methodist church, such as the midwife Dona Maria, claim the existence of only one soul, thereby dismissing the validity of the illness category soul loss.

Dona Maria, a Mestizo in social identity if not in ethnic origin, was born in La Paz and has lived a good deal of her life in El Alto. She is economically successful, running a thriving business making *pollera* (traditional skirts) with her daughters. She was initially a Catholic of Aymara parentage, but converted to the Methodist Church as a strategy to control her husband's alcoholism and violence against her and her young daughters. The Methodist Church, she explains, does not allow alcohol and preaches against violence. After she and her daughters started attending the Methodist Church, she persuaded her husband to go with them. He subsequently gave up alcohol and the violence stopped. Alcoholism and domestic violence, Dona Maria considers, is part of the Catholic way of life, the way of life of the traditional Aymara, the *campesinos*. Soul loss, she, explains is a superstition, a false belief which belongs to the traditional Aymara culture, and is maintained by those who follow the Catholic church. Dona Maria says she does not believe in *yatiris*, or soul loss. Her first baby, she explains, died of soul loss. He received a fright from a sudden loud noise in the night, developed a fever and died the next day. That was when she was a Catholic. Since she has been a Methodist and stopped believing in soul loss and *yatiris*, all her children have been well and have not suffered from fright sickness. Now she only has faith in God to cure her and her family.

Dona Rosa's story expresses a greater degree of ambivalence:

'I became a Methodist because my husband used to beat me. My first two babies died and a yatiri *told me the babies had died because the Methodist Church had brought me bad luck, the children had lost their* ajayu. *There are*

two souls. The animu *and* ajayu *are the same, they are the Aymara soul. The* alma *is the Christian soul that goes to heaven when you die. After my babies died, I went back to the Catholic Church and all the rest of my children survived. I was a Catholic until my children were grown. I became a Methodist a few years ago because my husband had other women and was getting drunk and beating me. Now he goes to church with me and is a good man.'*

Dona Nicanora is a *campesino*, a recent migrant to El Alto, who maintains a small plot of land on the *altiplano*. She is a Catholic, a *yatiri*, and a *partera* (traditional midwife):

Dona Nicanora became a yatiri *after lightning struck her when she was looking after her animals on her land in the altiplano. She moved to El Alto because she could not make a sustainable livelihood from her land and because her house was struck by lightning three times. Dona Nicanora and her husband built their adobe house on the periphery of the city. 'We are poor', she explains, 'there is no work'. She has five children and earns a little money as a* yatiri *and* partera. *Many things, she explains, can cause soul loss such as* susto *(fright) and* envidia *(envy). 'There are three souls, the* animu, *the* ajayu, *and the* alma. *They are the Father, the Son and the Holy Ghost.* Susto *in children is often caused by a fall or a dog barking. A neighbour shouting and saying bad things can also cause* susto. *Neighbours are envious and shout and say bad things, they say things in the street, about the* pollera *we are wearing, because we are poor. When people shout at you and say bad things it can make you feel weak because it makes your heart cry. The Methodists say bad things about the Catholics, they say we are drunk and poor, and that Catholics are evil because they believe in* yatiris. *The Catholic Church says that believing in* yatiris *is sinful because it is believing in false idols, that we must pray to God for our souls. Only the* yatiri *can cure soul loss.'*

Crandon-Malamud (1991) argues that membership of the Methodist church for the Aymara stands as a twentieth-century metaphor for social class and upward social mobility. Through affiliation to the Methodist church individuals are able to reconstruct and negotiate cultural identities according to their changing economic, political and social positions. Hence, membership of the Methodist church is congruent with Dona Maria's rising economic position and social standing as a successful businesswoman and sought-after midwife. Church membership varies according to the social and economic position and context of the individual, who may switch membership strategically over the course of a lifetime. Through her membership of the Methodist church, Dona Maria is reaffirming her *mestizo* class identity, denying the traditional Aymara belief system which she perceives to be represented through membership of the Catholic church. Her affiliation to the Methodist church is also a strategy for negotiation and control of gender relations and protection of the economic and social well-being of herself and her children. Dona Rosa has employed a similar strategy as regards negotiation and control of gender relations, but changed her church alliance to safeguard the health and the well-being of her children. For Dona Maria and Dona Rosa, shifting church affiliation has formed an essential part of their reproductive health strategy.

Feelings of vulnerability as a result of *miedo* (fear) and *envidia* (envy) form a major part of women's discourses on health and social relations. If a woman is economically successful, neighbours may become envious; and envy is another cause of *susto*. More seriously, an envious neighbour may use *brujeria* (witchcraft) to turn a person's good fortunes to bad. The individualism and competitiveness of the market centre make it a particularly dangerous place, rife with envy and the potential for *brujeria*. Feelings of social and economic vulnerability are expressed in the illness experiences encapsulated in soul loss, which embodies the cultural construction of the 'self'; the diagnosis of soul loss can be considered as '... an indicator of contradiction and ambivalence about identity that shift over the course of an individual's life span as social, economic, and political circumstances change' (Greenaway, 1998:996).

Fright sickness often befalls vulnerable or weak individuals. Vulnerability is understood not only in physical terms, but also in terms of social and cosmological positioning (Greenaway, 1998). Through the illness experience of soul loss, social and ethnic identity is reaffirmed. As a recent migrant in the competitive and individualistic urban environment of El Alto, Dona Nicanora finds herself in a position of extreme vulnerability, lacking access to primary resources and social capital. However, through her access to specialised bodies of knowledge as a *yatiri* and *partera*, which reaffirm her Aymara identity, she is able to access strategic power in the hostile context of El Alto.

Strategies of power, resistance and negotiation

The government health centres, improved and developed with the assistance of external development agencies, appear as clean, white (and usually empty) obelisks, amid the mud, dust and open sewage that typify the landscape of the peripheral zones of El Alto. The doctors, trained in quality of care and community health, are perplexed, concerned, and a little irritated that their health centres remain largely devoid of patients.

The only woman doctor in the area sees the major problem as women's oppression and lack of education. Women, she explains, lack knowledge and power. Her task is to draw women to the health centre so that she can educate them on ways to improve their health, and to offer them means of empowerment, for example through the use of family planning. Another inspired doctor spends his days organising health fairs, education sessions at mothers' clubs and broadcasting loudspeaker messages promoting the importance of child vaccination and antenatal care. As a strategy to reach targets in priority areas of health care identified by the government programme (maternal and child health and dental health) he has hit upon the novel idea of a 'raffle for health', the main prize being a cooker. The local perception of the raffle is that the doctor needs more patients to boost his income, or that he is trying to entice women into the health centre so that he can look at their bodies. The raffle results in vast increases in largely unnecessary dental work being performed over the course of the month.

Despite their differing strategies, both doctors ascribe to the 'health belief model' which underlies many of the health education approaches adopted by the government and NGO programmes. The health belief model is premised upon the notion that behaviour is determined by 'rational' calculations of outcomes, and 'rational behaviour' is that which is oriented towards objective scientific knowledge (Good, 1994). Thus, if people are educated and provided with accurate health information, they will change their behaviour accordingly. 'Investigate public beliefs about vaccinations or risky health behaviours using the Health Belief Model, ... [and] get people to believe the right thing and our public health problems will be solved' (Good, 1994:7).

Women's discourses concerning their health and well-being shift according to context. During the fieldwork, when women were asked directly about the health centre, the most common response was that they had not used it because they had not been ill. Nonetheless, in the context of discussions concerning children and childbirth, *sobre parto* along with *susto* were the illness categories most commonly referred to. Every woman has either experienced directly, or seen another woman suffering from *sobre parto,* which is described as severe fever and tremors, caused by coming into contact with a cold draught, washing in cold water or ingesting cold foods, following childbirth. Although many women who have given birth at home have experienced *sobre parto,* women who give birth in the hospital or clinic are more commonly perceived to be at high risk. Dona Maria, the *partera*, explains: 'Women often have *sobre parto* after they give birth in the clinic or hospital, where it is cold, where women are not looked after properly and are made to get out of bed and wash too early. None of the women I have helped have suffered from *sobre parto*. *Sobre parto* cannot be cured by doctors. The doctors do not believe in *sobre parto*, they say it does not exist, they say it is an infection and needs to be cured with antibiotics. But it cannot be cured that way, it can only be cured with special *mates*.'

While soul loss is the major cause of infant and child mortality, *sobre parto* is the major cause of maternal ill health and death. Neither can be cured with biomedicine. Both require specialised bodies of knowledge, accessed only through social relations and knowledge systems which, in the face of increasing poverty and lack of access to economic resources and power, reaffirm the separateness and autonomy of the Aymara cultural identity.

Most of women's experiences of interaction with formal biomedical health services are phrased in terms of negative emotional consequences. Use of biomedical services increases women's vulnerability to emotional disturbance and ill health. Reasons for the non-use of biomedical services are expressed in sentiments such as: 'tengo miedo' (I am afraid), 'the doctors shout at us, they look at us and criticise us', 'they say women are dirty because they do not wash, and do not wash after giving birth', 'I feel ashamed, when the doctor touches me'. The linkage of emotions to illness (see also Unnithan-Kumar, this volume), and the notion that individuals can bring on their own ill health through an inability to control emotions, has been noted in other studies of Andean ethnomedicine (Larme, 1998:1013). Larme argues that while men and women are both susceptible to ill health as a result of emotional vulnerability, men have emotional outlets, such as excessive drinking, violence and extramarital affairs, which are largely unavailable to women due to cultural views of proper female behaviour. Hence, the cultural construction of gender roles increases women's vulnerability to ill health as a result of emotions such as fear and shame. Women's discourses, used to describe the experience of interacting with biomedical services, are congruent with discourses used in relation to sickness categories such as soul loss and sobre parto which reaffirm women's social and cultural identity.

However, the health centre can also be an important primary resource (see Crandon-Malamud, 1991). Dona Maria, despite her dismissal of the efficacy of biomedical knowledge in treating serious maternal health problems, is proud of the fact that she has received some of her training as a *partera* from the health centre. In her work as a traditional *partera*, she is now also affiliated to the health centre, reporting numbers of births and infant deaths to the doctor on a monthly basis. Her affiliation with the health centre has not altered her knowledge base (as was hoped by the biomedical training programme). Indeed it has conferred on her an elevated social status, and she perceives that the powerful biomedical system has legitimated her practice and enabled her to expand her client base through contacts initially made through the health centre.

The negotiation of social relations and social identity is central to individual strategies such as church affiliation, use and non-use of biomedical services, and adherence to traditional medical systems. The choices made and strategies selected are affected by a wide variety of factors such as social standing, economic position, gender relations and personal history of migration. As the circumstances of each individual are different, and as circumstances change, different strategies and choices may be employed at different times and in different contexts (see Crandon-Malamud, 1991:150).

Conclusion: sexual and reproductive health in context

Women's discourses on reproductive health, sexuality and gender are embedded within the wider construction and negotiation of social identity and power relations in a society in rapid transition (see also Unnithan-Kumar, this volume). Far from being a question of access to, and utilisation of, sexual and reproductive health services, women's conceptualisation of 'empowerment' is embedded primarily in their relative economic autonomy. Indeed, within indigenous discourses, there exists an inverse relationship between women's empowerment and use of modern family planning methods. In discussing family planning at the health centre, women generally refer to lack of knowledge, fear of side effects and husband's disapproval as their main reasons for the non-use of modern methods. However, within women's discourses on sexuality and fertility control, women who are the least economically active, and therefore least empowered in the marital relationship, are seen to be most in need of modern family planning methods. Women who are not economically empowered lack the means to control and negotiate sexual relations with their husband and therefore to use abstinence as an effective fertility control method. The use of modern family planning methods intersects with women's constructions of power and control over their bodies, sexuality, esteem and empowerment.

Fertility regulation strategies form part of indigenous practices, in particular the use of herbal teas and massage to induce abortion, and the use of periodic abstinence (usually referred to as the rhythm method). Sexuality and reproduction are not openly talked about and it has been suggested that women learn reticence about sexual matters at an early age (Schuler et al., 1994:213). Use of indigenous methods is controlled by women, and information on methods of control is communicated through women's kinship and other social networks. Use of modern family planning methods, on the other hand, necessitates social interaction with biomedical health services and usually a physical examination by a male doctor, thereby crossing cultural boundaries of gender interactions.

Women's discourses on family planning shift according to their relative economic independence and their associated power both within the community and within the marital relationship. Dona Maria explains: 'Many women do not have esteem because they are timid and feel fear, they are afraid to work and have to stay in the house and depend on their husbands. This is dangerous because they cannot leave their husband and survive on their own if they have to. I have never used modern methods of family planning, my husband is a good man. He understands not to trouble me, he sleeps in a separate bed. The best method of family planning is the rhythm method. The best way to practise the rhythm method is to have sex once or twice a month. I have seen the IUCD and pills make women ill, and I try to explain to them how to use the rhythm method. Many women cannot use the rhythm method because their husbands are not good men. Many women are timid and cannot control their husbands.'

Dona Elena has recently had an IUCD (intra-uterine contraceptive device) fitted at a reproductive health clinic in the centre of El Alto.

Dona Elena is twenty-four and has six children. She was brought up in the *campo* (countryside) by her grandfather who beat her. She married her husband at sixteen to escape from her grandfather and they moved to El Alto. Her husband has occasional work constructing houses. Elena only works outside the house when her husband needs her to help him. He will not let her work alone because he is jealous. She does not want more children. Her mother has told her about the rhythm method but her husband does not understand. He agrees to use it and says he does not want more children, but when he gets drunk he hits her if she does not want sex. After the last baby, her husband agreed that she should use something to stop her getting pregnant, but she could not afford to go to the clinic. Eventually, her *comadre* (godmother) lent her money and she went to the clinic and had an IUCD fitted.

Dona Elena's decision to use a modern contraceptive method was a result of her increasing disempowerment due to poverty and lack of power to control sex within the marital relationship. Lacking her own economic independence, she had to draw upon social capital in the form of the *comadre* relationship to act upon the decision she and her husband jointly made for her to have an IUCD fitted.

The notion of control of sexuality as a source of empowerment has been noted in other social and historical contexts. Schneider and Schneider (1995a:190) suggest that use of coitus interruptus as a birth control practice in rural Sicily was imbued with a moral value of sacrificing pleasure for social betterment, supporting Foucault's argument that restraint can be empowering. Drawing on ethnographic material among the Yoruba of Nigeria, Pearce (1995:204) notes that the possibility provided by modern contraceptives to divorce sexuality from reproduction is not universally perceived as a source of women's empowerment. Among Yoruba women the practice of terminal abstinence to end childbearing is perceived as a well-earned rest: 'The Yoruba practice of abstinence, particularly terminal abstinence, conflicts with the western liberal view of female sexual rights and the biomedical perception of biological needs' (Pearce, 1995:203–4).

The Cairo discourses of empowerment and sexual and reproductive health and rights are largely premised upon a western neoliberal construction of the autonomous individual and embedded within a biomedical paradigm. Sexual and reproductive health and rights, however, cannot be understood as separate from other spheres of social and economic life. In the context of marginalised migrant populations in the city of El Alto, this chapter has shown that the concept of reproductive health only gains meaning when considered in the local and specific social and economic context of women's lives. Notions of sexual and reproductive health cannot be isolated from the wider historical and economic context in which health, sexuality and reproduction are embedded. The objectives of Cairo can only be achieved in the context of much broader development approaches, which enable poor and marginalised peoples to exercise citizenship rights to access resources which reach far beyond those of reproductive health services.

CHAPTER 3

Motherhood, Fertility and Ambivalence Among Young Prostitutes in Thailand

Heather Montgomery

Introduction

In many ways, child prostitution is a very well studied, and certainly much discussed, problem. Its legal implications have been extensively analysed, in particular how to deal with, and prosecute foreign men who abuse children abroad (World Congress Against the Sexual Exploitation of Children, 1996). Its role in the spread of AIDS has been of equal concern (Sittitrai and Brown, 1994). However, there are certain issues which have been almost entirely overlooked but which are vital for a fuller understanding of the lives of children who do become prostitutes. The most obvious surround matters of reproductive health and pregnancy, which have been almost entirely neglected except in the context of AIDS research. Yet grave threats though they are, and although they have been concentrated on to the exclusion of almost all else, AIDS and HIV are not the primary concern of young women and children who work as prostitutes. Young prostitutes are at great risk from all sexually transmitted diseases and from pregnancies occurring when they do not have the emotional or physical stamina to cope properly. It is therefore important to examine why contraceptive use is so low, why knowledge of sexually transmitted diseases is so patchy and, most importantly, how motherhood is perceived and experienced and how that affects the limited choices of children who become pregnant through prostitution.

The ethnography in this chapter is based on fifteen months fieldwork in a community in Thailand which survived through child prostitution. This community, called Baan Nua, consisted of around 100 people, of whom many either worked as prostitutes, or lived off their income. Baan Nua was situated on the edge of a tourist resort notorious for its large numbers of foreign 'sex tourists'. Within this market there was an underground demand for child prostitutes. Although not openly advertised, at the time of the research it was relatively easy for foreign men to find children for sexual purposes, and several of them had regular foreign clients.

Baan Nua was made up of migrants from the poorer north and north-east regions of Thailand who had settled on the site about fifteen years earlier. Many were originally farmers, but the land on which they built was very small and unsuitable for growing crops or raising livestock. As far as possible, therefore, they earned their living in the informal economy around the city, selling, begging, scavenging, and most importantly of all, through child prostitution. There were sixty-five children in this community (defined as those under eighteen) and over thirty of them had worked or were working as prostitutes. They included both boys and girls and ranged in age from eight to fourteen. For the purposes of this chapter, I will concentrate on a handful of girl prostitutes aged between twelve and sixteen who represent the problems involved when children give birth to children and who illustrate the difficulties and ambivalence many of the children feel about early pregnancy and motherhood.

The position of motherhood

The importance of motherhood in Thai society is a much studied phenomenon. The mother in Thailand is often portrayed as the linchpin who keeps families together, the moral basis for all kinship relationships, and the economic and practical source of household survival (Landon, 1939; Hanks, 1964; Potter, 1976; Potter, 1979; Keyes, 1984; Blanc-Szanton, 1985; Kirsch, 1985; Thitsa, 1990; Muecke, 1992; van Esterik, 1996). A mother has a pivotal role within the family as its moral centre, as the conduit of property through the matrilineal line and because of the customs of matrilocal residence (Hanks, 1964; Potter, 1979; Blanc-Szanton, 1985). However, in contrast to the western paradigm of parental self-sacrifice on behalf of children, emphasis in most rural communities in Thailand, including Baan Nua, is placed on reciprocity and the duties that a child has to his or her mother. To be born in itself incurs a debt of gratitude that a child can never repay. A parent once told me that 'even though Buddha showed his mother the way to enlightenment, he could not pay back the debt he owed her for giving birth to him'. This belief is expressed by the concept of *bun khun*, the debt of gratitude that children owe to their parents (and especially their mothers) for their existence (Mulder, 1979; Havanon and Chairut, 1985; Vichit-Vadakan, 1990). Tantiwiramanond and Pandey (1987) explain that '... according to the Thai Buddhist moral scale, parents are entitled to be "moral creditors" *(phu mii phra khun)* because of their presumably self-sacrificing labour of bearing and rearing children ...while children are moral debtors'. Similarly, van Esterik (1996:27) notes: 'In rural contexts, women express the idea that one raises a child in expectation of explicit returns. A daughter repays the debt to her mother by remaining in the parental household to care for her parents in old age, while a son ordains as a Buddhist monk to pay his mother back for her breast milk.' It is a child's duty, as soon as she or he is able, to support their parents and to repay the care they have been given. In a rural setting, this means working on the family farm, or more recently, in a factory in a nearby town, and sending money home (Ford and Saiprasert, 1993). In Baan Nua, it means prostitution.

For girls, motherhood is also the most profound marker of adulthood and the event that changes them into women. Even relatively recent studies of both rural and urban areas (Potter, 1979; Muecke, 1981; Rabibhadana, 1985; Mills, 1990; Muecke, 1992) have emphasised the continuing centrality of motherhood, while acknowledging that women are marrying later and having fewer children. Motherhood remains a defining event of women's lives and one that has a profound impact on their social status. Both Hanks (1964) and Yoddumnern-Attig et al. (1994) point out that it is the birth of a live child and not marriage that signifies adulthood. Keyes states that a 'basic status change occurs in these villages when a mother gives birth to a child; from that point on she will be known as "mother" by all' (1984:229). Motherhood becomes synonymous with adulthood because it means a change in status from someone who only has obligations to someone who can call on the obligations of others.

When talking about reproductive health, these briefly sketched cultural issues are important to remember. On the one hand, the girls in Baan Nua were in the worst possible position to have children. They were prostitutes with high levels of sexually transmitted diseases, their general health was bad, and many had drug and alcohol dependencies. Nevertheless, not all of them saw motherhood as something to avoid and although often accompanied by extreme ambivalence, many welcomed it. Motherhood brought with it the possibility of a new status and it meant a child who would be indebted to you and, in his or her turn, would be compelled to support you.

Prostitution and motherhood

Baan Nua survived more or less entirely on the income of children who worked as prostitutes and is was through this income that it continued to function as a community. All the children lived with their families and sold sexual services exclusively to the foreign tourists who visited the city. Unlike the stereotype of child prostitutes which is often presented in the media or by campaigners, these children had not been kidnapped, drugged or debt-bonded into brothels (Centre for the Protection of Children's Rights, 1991; O'Grady, 1992; O'Grady, 1994; Hiew, 1992; ECPAT, 1992; Hall, 1992; Ireland, 1993). Instead they lived in communities with their families, contributing their income to the family finances. While they suffered poverty and extreme deprivation, they were able to exercise a degree of physical freedom and autonomy forbidden to children living in brothels (Asia Partnership for Human Development, 1992; Asia Watch, 1993). Many children were the sole earners in their families, supporting parents and other siblings.

In order to understand why prostitution occurred and flourished, it is important to understand the dynamics of the community and the responsibility that children felt towards their parents. Issues of filial duty and reciprocity were central to the dynamics of life in the community as children felt duty bound to support their parents (Montgomery, 1996). Within Baan Nua there was no family land to farm and there were few jobs available to uneducated children from the slums around the city that would earn enough income to support a family. Activities such as scavenging on rubbish tips for scrap metal and begging or selling food in the street had often been tried and given up because they brought in too little money, were too dangerous or were more suitable for younger children. Prostitution was the only job which had adequate returns and many children turned to it as a way of fulfilling their perceived obligations (Montgomery, 1996). Although many outsiders have demanded that such children be removed from their families (Koompraphant, 1993:56), the children themselves lived in fear of being sent away from their parents.

Unsurprisingly therefore, motherhood was viewed ambivalently within the community, especially among the young teenage girls who were most vulnerable to becoming pregnant. Motherhood was alternatively feared and celebrated, and attitudes towards it were highly changeable. Despite the widespread availability of contraception in Thailand, and the considerable knowledge among these girls of the causes of pregnancy, birth control was almost never used. I will return to this point at the end of the chapter, but it is worth noting here that no active steps were taken to avoid pregnancy, even when the girls claimed not to want a child.

Teenage motherhood, like child prostitution, is problematic, not least because it blurs distinctions between adulthood and childhood. While early pregnancy is not uncommon in rural Thailand, it runs counter to western (and increasingly to indigenous middle class) views on the correct form of childhood. Childhood is viewed as an asexual time of innocence, play and seclusion (Ennew, 1986; Ennew and Milne, 1989; Holland, 1992). Sexuality and sexual experience are not considered to be part of a child's experience and juvenile pregnancy reflects an awkward gap between theory and reality. When teenagers become pregnant through prostitution, it becomes even more troublesome, especially when issues of abuse and exploitation are inescapable. In this case fertility and reproduction cannot be looked at in isolation from the wider context of these resource-poor settings (see both Unnithan-Kumar and Russell this volume). It is not remarkable, therefore, that motherhood in these circumstances is regarded with apprehension by the girls themselves and by outside agencies which aim to prevent prostitution. However, even in these conditions pregnancy and motherhood are not viewed entirely negatively and elicit a range of reactions. They may actually be welcomed as a positive change in both status and work patterns, or they can be ignored, denied or even ended through abortion or adoption. In the circumstances, the change in status noted by many previous authors is not always automatic, and the links between motherhood and adulthood are far from definitive. Motherhood among child prostitutes becomes ambiguous; it can be both an entry into, and a denial of, adulthood and the young mothers themselves respond to it in various, and often contradictory, ways.

It is worth mentioning the issue of fatherhood briefly. Although girls are the main focus of this chapter, it is important to note that boys also worked as prostitutes and undoubtedly fathered children.

However, because this was less obvious, it was almost impossible to obtain any information about it. It was possible to note that fatherhood did not bring the same status change as motherhood and men with children were not necessarily considered adults because they had fathered a child. It was hard to generalise about this because there were so few young men who had fathered children and then stayed around to look after them; but fatherhood did imply fewer of the burdens of reciprocity and filial duty. Children in Baan Nua did feel some sense of duty towards their fathers, but it was never as strong as their feelings towards their mothers (Mulder, 1979; Muecke, 1984). Many of the fathers were absent and this affected relationships with their children. But within Baan Nua men were usually peripheral. They could not work in the village and rarely held down jobs outside it, and they left all the important decisions about finance to their female relatives. Therefore, many young men drifted off to other villages or occasionally to find work in other areas of the country. The ties that bound women to Baan Nua – their children, their children's income, their lifestyle – were not so strong for men who were always marginal to the fundamental structure of Baan Nua which was based around women and their kin.

Lek

When I met Lek in 1993 she was around thirteen years old and pregnant with her first child. She had been working as a prostitute for many years and at that time was the only source of income for her family of five (her mother, father, brother, sister and nephew). Both she and her mother Saew claimed that she voluntarily became a prostitute. Saew said that she knew nothing about it until it was too late and had no idea how to stop it once she found out. Lek was insistent that the work she did helped to fulfil her obligations to her parents and immediately gave all the money that she earned to her mother who often gambled it away or simply lost it. Although Lek has up to twenty different clients a year – all westerners (*farang*s) – her most regular partner for many years had been a British man known as James whom she called a boyfriend rather than a client. While she knew she was carrying a child of mixed race (*luuk khrung*), she did not know which of her clients was the father.

Lek's feelings towards the child were highly ambivalent. On the one hand, she hoped that either James or one of her other clients would take responsibility for her and give her more money because of it. But on the other hand, she did not want the child, feeling that it would prevent her from earning money and would tie her down. She also felt that her nephew was already the favourite of the family and that another child would mean that she would be even more neglected by her mother. When James refused to give her any extra money or to pay for the expenses surrounding the birth, she tried to induce an abortion. There was no knowledge in the community about abortifacient drugs or money to pay for a surgical abortion and so Lek tried to induce an abortion by hitting herself repeatedly in the stomach and jumping off a wall. However, even these measures were ambivalent. Lek knew of nobody who had managed to induce an abortion in this way, and when her mother found out she forbade her to try again. Saew had very strong feelings about abortion and as a Buddhist believed it to be a form of murder. Lek did as her mother asked.

Lek continued to work for the full course of her pregnancy and continued also in her secondary work as a pimp for the other children in the village. She gave birth prematurely in March 1994 to a daughter who she wanted Saew to raise in the rural community in North-East Thailand from where she originally came; but her mother would not go. Lek thought about putting the child into an orphanage and allowing her to be adopted but eventually decided against it, returning to prostitution as a means of supporting the child. Six weeks after the birth, Lek was back at work, leaving the baby in the care of her mother. Her brother refused to give her financial help towards the birth so she turned to another western client who paid all her medical expenses and expected sex in return.

Lek's case illustrates many of the difficulties surrounding pregnancy and motherhood for young prostitutes. It shows quite clearly the exploitation and abuse perpetrated by western men who are not prepared to show any responsibility for the girls beyond paying for sex. It also depicts the conflicting dilemmas that the children face; between responsibility to their own children and to their parents, and the difficulties they have in obtaining any sort of help other than from the men who were guilty of the abuse in the first place. Apart from her mother forbidding an abortion, Lek's family gave her little help and support.

Others around Lek offered no different example. Lek's sister-in-law Tik had also had a child early. When she was fourteen, she lived briefly with Lek's brother Tam while working as a prostitute and gave birth to Tam's child. After they split up, their son was given to Saew to raise and Tam gave up work to live off Lek's income. I once asked Saew if she was worried about either Lek or Tik giving birth so young but she replied that she was not because she had married at twelve and given birth at thirteen and did not think it was an unusual or difficult thing.

The people of Baan Nua retained some of the traditional respect for motherhood and it was usual to address women with children as *maer* (mother). This denoted both status and respect, but among the younger generation it was inconsistent and based as much on social as biological factors. I never heard anyone refer to either Tik or Lek as *maer* even after giving birth. Both had children young, at fourteen, but there was no status change involved because they did not behave socially as mothers. In Tik's case this took the extreme form of pretending that she was considerably younger than her years and denying the fact of her maternity. She would claim that her son was in fact her nephew or her younger brother and whenever I asked her age she told me that she was fourteen whereas she was in fact about twenty. She insisted on going to school with the other children of the village and sitting with the other fourteen-year-old girls and acting as if she were still a child. Similarly, Lek did not deny her maternity but neglected her baby, forgetting to feed her and usually leaving her mother to look after her. For Lek, motherhood and adulthood were not the same and her neglect of her child suggested that she was not ready for the responsibilities that she saw as commensurate with adulthood. However, both Tik and Lek explicitly rejected adulthood by denying or neglecting their children and refusing to be responsible for them, which suggested that they were aware of the value placed on motherhood and of its role in marking the boundary between adulthood and childhood. Motherhood does not, therefore, automatically make a child an adult. To perform its transformative function it has to be recognised socially by the community and by the mother herself. In this instance, motherhood, like adulthood and childhood, had become an ambiguous and shifting category, continually open to reinterpretation (see Boyden, this volume).

Lek's ambivalence towards her daughter was clear. She did not want to give her up for adoption, and although she placed her in an orphanage, could not bring herself to leave her there permanently and reclaimed her after six weeks. Despite her inadequacies as a parent and the lack of help, she attempted to look after the child by working to provide an income for her upkeep. Although Lek was often deeply pessimistic and would not talk about the future, saying things like 'I don't dream any more', she was also quite adamant that she wanted a different life for her child away from prostitution. Unfortunately, however, she had little idea of how to make this happen and hoped that salvation would come in the form of one of her clients who would take her away from Baan Nua and provide for her. She clung to the notion that James was a boyfriend, not a client, and consistently and vehemently denied that he abused or took advantage of her in any way.

Lek's daughter also represented explicit returns. Lek had someone who had duties to her and was no longer someone who only had obligations. Although the majority of very young children (under seven) did not work as prostitutes in Baan Nua, they were still expected to bring in an income. Many of them begged from tourists or attempted to sell chewing gum and garlands of flowers to them. Several scavenged on the nearby rubbish dump and sold the scrap metal they found there to dealers. Although this brought in tiny amounts of money and had high risks, as soon as they were able, all children were expected to earn money. In as little as three years time Lek's daughter would be able to start contributing money to the household, and the community values of Baan Nua dictated that she would turn it over to her mother in a show of filial duty. A child, even an unwanted child, could be a source of moral and financial recompense.

A child also provided a source and focus of love which should not be underestimated, however obvious this point seems. There is always a tendency to assume that parents who allow their to children work as prostitutes must be abusive and exploitative and that if they loved their children, they would forbid such work. However, in Baan Nua deliberate abuse was uncommon and children were much loved by their parents who looked after them as far as they could, sent them to a rudimentary school run by a small local charity group, and shielded them from the authorities. But life was extremely difficult for everyone, and children had to contribute as best they could, even if this meant prostitution. There was no sense that parents deliberately inflicted harm on their children, and indeed in some cases this was explicitly denied. A mother of an eight-year-old boy prostitute once said, 'It's only for one hour, what harm can come to him in an hour?' Although this attitude might be viewed as wilful ignorance, children were far more than a potential source of income for their parents and were welcomed and enjoyed. This is not to romanticise their life or people's attitudes to their children; clearly children were being abused and exploited, but this was done more from ignorance or perceived necessity than malice.

Similarly, although none of the young women who had children expressed it in these terms, babies also gave uncomplicated love. The child prostitutes of Baan Nua suffered from inadequate parenting and exploitative sexual relationships and friendships could be hard to sustain when all the children were chasing the same clients. I would suggest therefore that a baby gave many of these children a kind of love they received nowhere else. Although parents did love their children and children reciprocated that love, it was clear that many mothers found it difficult to raise their children and often misused alcohol or drugs, especially glue. Several were coping with both young children and their own grandchildren and had little time for the older children. Lek in particular felt neglected and undervalued by her mother and was scared that another child in the family would further supplant her. Despite Lek's equivocal feelings about her daughter, the child provided Lek with a focus and a love she did not get elsewhere. This was not an issue the children ever talked about and it is important not to project feelings onto them, but it did seem that babies represented security, emotional, social and financial, for these young mothers.

Reproductive health

Despite the obvious health risks involved in prostitution, there is surprisingly little literature on the reproductive health of young prostitutes, except in relation to AIDS. It is very hard to discover how and if young prostitutes avoid pregnancy or sexually transmitted diseases. Campaigns by the media and non-governmental organisations stress the high risks of HIV infection among children released from brothels (O'Grady, 1994), but very little is known about other aspects of their reproductive health. What few reports there are suggest that fertility is controlled by pimps and brothel owners and that the children have very limited control over their own bodies (Centre for the Protection of Children's Rights, 1991; Asia Watch, 1993). A report by Asia Watch claimed that in brothels along the Thai/Burmese border, where many women and girls are held against their will, it is usual for children to be compelled or persuaded to take oral contraceptives (and to have abortions when necessary) by the owner to prevent any disruption to their working lives and the levels of income they earn (Asia Watch, 1993).

The children in Baan Nua, however, sold sex on a freelance basis and had no brothel or pimp to tell them to use contraception. Although pregnancy and sexually transmitted diseases were two of the most obvious physical dangers of child prostitution, the children took no steps to avoid them. Both the pill and condoms were readily available over the counter in pharmacies and even supermarkets in the city; but they were rarely used. Cost, of course, was a consideration, and many of the children did not have the extra money to pay for them; but there were other issues which made it harder for children than adults to protect themselves from sexually transmitted diseases. Condoms in particular were problematic as the children's clients usually refused to wear them and to negotiate their use would take a command of English and a level of confidence and power that they did not have. Although many of the children did struggle to gain some control over their clients, this usually took the form of negotiating higher payments for sex rather than protecting their own health.

It is claimed by O'Grady (1992) and Muntabhorn (1992) that there has been an increase in the numbers of child prostitutes because men are now demanding younger children who are believed to be free of sexually transmitted diseases, especially AIDS. In the absence of any detailed studies of the sexual preferences of the clients of child prostitutes, this can only be speculation. However, if true, it is a dangerous assumption since, far from being resistant to disease, children seem to be particularly prone. A child's body is not suited to penetration by an adult and the sexual act can inflict great damage in the form of tearing and bruising. The standards of health and hygiene in Baan Nua were generally poor, with no running water, poor food quality and non-existent medical care. As any disease to a child with poor health and a weakened immune system can be devastating, the danger of opportunistic infections among the children was high and the cuts and lesions they received from their clients made them particularly vulnerable to secondary infections.

More general aspects of reproductive health seem almost forgotten. The concern with AIDS has subsumed interest in all the other diseases from which these children suffer (Ennew et al., 1996a) and yet these other diseases, whether sexually transmitted or not, are of more immediate concern to the children themselves. Indeed, there is little point in getting tested for HIV. If they do test positive, the children have no access to medical help and they cannot insist on condom use. To inform a client of their status or to give up prostitution would mean losing their only source of income. It was therefore unsurprising that few of the children wanted to discuss AIDS or HIV even though their knowledge of transmission was relatively good.

I do not know what other diseases the children suffered from. Certainly most of them had open sores on their arms and faces and suffered from gastro-intestinal diseases. Many were addicted to glue sniffing and appeared to have breathing problems as a consequence. Over half appeared to be underweight or malnourished. I suspected that several suffered from tuberculosis and at least two had measles. It would also be reasonable to suppose that many suffered from sexually transmitted diseases. When one sixteen-year-old girl from the community was taken to the public hospital, she was found to be suffering from gonorrhoea, chlamydia and syphilis. Given that she shared clients with other children in Baan Nua, sexually transmitted diseases must have been endemic. Yet hospital visits were the exception rather than the rule. The people of Baan Nua did not like going to the hospital; they were afraid of being reported for letting their children work as prostitutes, for not sending them to government school, or for the illegal use of the land on which they were living. They also felt that the hospital staff patronised them and would test them for AIDS and other diseases without ever giving them the results. They relied therefore on pharmacies for medication (which in Thailand do not need prescriptions to dispense) and took antibiotics when they could afford them and were in serious pain, but rarely finished courses. More often they simply ignored the diseases until they went away or became asymptomatic.

Fertility rates were, therefore, not as high as might be expected. Certain sexually transmitted diseases such as chlamydia can lead to pelvic inflammation and infertility and the high levels of poor health and malnutrition meant that many girls did not menstruate and saw themselves as unlikely to become pregnant. Few precautions were taken against pregnancy since they were perceived as expensive and unnecessary. The rarity with which the children attended hospital meant that longer-term forms of contraception such as Depo-Provera or intra-uterine devices could not be given or even discussed, and in any case might not have been suitable given the poor health of the girls.

Underlying attitudes also made contraceptive use problematic. The expense and the hassle involved, and the perceived lack of need for contraception certainly influenced some of the children; but equally important was their belief in, and reliance on *karma*. *Karma* is a central tenet in Buddhist theology and (to over-simplify) refers to the responsibility of a person for the sum total of their actions in all their incarnations, past and present. Certain actions can make merit, such as filial duty and fulfilling family obligations, which in turn improve *karma*. Buddhists are always struggling to improve their *karma* in order to improve their position in their next life and to be reborn in a higher or more comfortable situation. Most of the children in Baan Nua claimed to be Buddhist, and although their understanding of the religion was very simplistic it provided a cultural and religious reference in their lives to which they referred continually.

However, the belief in *karma* often manifested itself in ways that may appear as extreme fatalism to outsiders. Contraception was not used as it was believed that if it was your *karma* to get pregnant or contract AIDS it could not be avoided. Writing about male sexual behaviour in northern Thailand, Graham Fordham makes a similar point (Fordham, 1995). Despite extremely high levels of AIDS awareness and the availability of cheap condoms, men did not use them. Condoms, they claimed, not only reduced their pleasure, but were unnecessary. If they were going to get AIDS, it was their fate and that could not be avoided. If they were not destined to become HIV positive, then it simply would not happen. In Baan Nua, this attitude was also prevalent. I asked several young prostitutes if they were worried about pregnancy. While they all replied that they did not want a baby in their circumstances, none believed that they had any control of it. If it was their fate to be pregnant, then it would happen.

Nuk

The case of Nuk illustrates the apparent fatalism that many children in Baan Nua felt about their lives and the difficulty many had in imagining any way of changing their circumstances. When I first met Nuk, she was fourteen and living with Paul, a regular buyer of sex in Baan Nua who later became Lek's client. Nuk had been with Paul for two years and had negotiated a deal with him whereby she agreed not to have sex with other men in return for a weekly sum of money. She lived with Paul in an apartment in the centre of the city, but he spoke only a little Thai while she spoke no English. As a result, she frequently became lonely and would return to Baan Nua where her family still lived. Nuk had a very serious addiction to glue and often, after a heavy bout of sniffing, she would collapse and become paralysed. Occasionally she was taken to the free public hospital, but they could do little for her and usually sent her home. She and Paul quarrelled constantly about her addiction and he threw her out regularly because she would not give up.

After one especially heavy session of glue sniffing, Nuk collapsed and was taken to hospital where she was diagnosed as being HIV positive and having TB. She had a great deal of difficulty breathing and had to be put on a drip, but as no one could afford to pay for long-term treatment, she discharged herself. She refused all treatment after that and her condition grew steadily worse. She died five months later, ostensibly of TB. She had spent her last few months telling everyone that she wanted to die and saw no point in fighting her fate by staying alive. She had lost her way of earning money and was now simply a burden on her family. In some ways she was right. Her HIV infection and ill health, as well as her lack of access to medical treatment and to the drugs that keep HIV from developing into AIDS, meant that she would probably have died sooner rather than later; but she never questioned the inevitability of her death or the path of her life.

Conclusion

Child prostitution is an extremely emotive and sensitive subject, and in the urgency to campaign and protest against exploitation, it is unsurprising that other issues such as pregnancy and reproductive health have been overlooked. Yet pregnancy, motherhood and sexual health are precisely the areas that need to be studied if the cycle of abuse is to be broken. There is still far too little data about the health of child prostitutes and the overwhelming concentration on HIV and their eventual deaths from AIDS-related illnesses means that more emphasis is placed on how children die than how they live. Yet communities such as Baan Nua show that although children may struggle they do have lives apart from prostitution and their communities do continue. Yet prostitution is so pervasive in such places that the perception is that selling sex is the only way to bring in money and sexually transmitted diseases and pregnancy are simply occupational hazards. It seems likely that many of the children born to young prostitutes will, in their turn, also become prostitutes, working to support their young mothers who worked to support theirs.

The anthropologist is not always the best person to make policy recommendations. Still, cases such as Baan Nua do show the importance of anthropological understanding. Campaigns against child prostitution and the spread of AIDS have reached Baan Nua and people are aware of them; but they needed more than information. Attitudes and belief in fate and *karma* mean that despite their knowledge, they took no action to protect themselves. It is vital to condemn child prostitution and campaign to end it; but it is easy to look at prostitution, fertility and reproductive health on a macro level and to overlook how these concepts are played out at a local level where they influence the way individuals see themselves as daughters, mothers and as members of their communities. For some of these girls, motherhood was a positive experience, bringing with it prestige and a change in status. Others struggled with it, yet were accorded little help. With so much money directed into AIDS research or to prosecuting their clients, the children themselves have been overlooked. Of course money should be spent on the former but by concentrating so exclusively own AIDS and prosecution, the causes of child prostitution are never fully tackled, only the symptoms.

CHAPTER 4

Biological Symptoms of Social Unease: the Stigma of Infertility in London Sex Workers

Sophie Day

Introduction

It is increasingly recognised that issues of fertility and birth control need to be understood in the broadest terms of sexual and reproductive health (Smyth and Harris; Hawkins and Price, this volume). In this chapter, I show that fertility and infertility constitute a pair, mutually implicating, for it is the fear of being unable to have children that leads women to test out their fertility. As many do not carry pregnancies to term, it is possible that these activities in themselves may promote the very situation that women seek to avoid, since repeated terminations constitute a risk to fertility.

While this process of testing fertility and then terminating subsequent pregnancies seems to be widespread, I describe a unique set of circumstances surrounding sex work in London. Popular stereotype casts sex workers as 'public' (or 'common') women, inevitably barren. In reaction to this pervasive stigma, sex workers attempt to demonstrate convincingly that they are not merely public women who go to work, but also private individuals. As such, many want children and, at times, some of the women I knew seemed virtually compelled to demonstrate that they could fall pregnant. I argue that a corresponding failure to conceive brings home the full burden of the job which is carried in an individual body, perhaps for life. In this way, sex workers who fail to conceive become individually accountable for, and suffer, the ills of the difficult and dangerous social relationships surrounding the sex industry.

This chapter derives from long-term anthropological research with sex workers in West London, and from collaborative research primarily with Helen Ward, a clinician who later trained as an epidemiologist.[1] We established a cohort of women and the research methodology combined structured interviews and conversations, clinical and laboratory examinations, fieldwork and other observational studies of working areas and sites such as magistrates' courts. Our research was also conducted on the basis of service provision, a kind of reciprocity, which was gradually expanded into what came to be known as the Praed Street Project, funded by the National Health Service from the end of 1991. This project continues to combine clinical care with drop-in facilities, outreach work and crisis counselling and advice.

Intimations of infertility

The sex workers I knew were anxious about their fertility, and I shall refer repeatedly to two histories of women whom I knew for three years (Caroline), and six years (Laura), in illustration.[2] I met both in 1986, soon after I had begun my research project. Caroline was a teenager, small, slight and very active. She talked constantly of having children. I learned of two past pregnancies and the absence of contraception (at work) other than condoms, 'because I couldn't prevent nature'. Caroline used nothing with her boyfriend. She disliked work because 'the threat of being infertile is not worth it' and 'I feel as though I'm nothing, nobody, alone. I want my own flat. I want to have a child'. Caroline did not explicitly say that her work was immoral, but she did explain that it was wrong to use technological birth control (she was a white Rastafarian), to have a termination, or to work in the industry as a mother. Laura was in her mid-twenties, tall, well-built, blonde and 'fed up'. I soon learned that she too wanted children, 'I desperately want them [children],[3] especially now. Now I'm with someone,

1. I should like to thank Helen Ward along with the many other individuals (in and out of the sex industry) and institutions with whom I have collaborated since this research began in 1986. The Jefferiss Research Trust, AVERT, the NHS Executive (North Thames) and the Wellcome Trust have supported this work.

2. Personal names are pseudonyms.

we have been trying for the last year and a half. Helen[4] said there was a doctor here I could see to test whether my tubes were blocked and things like that. I really have got to the stage where I am paranoid I won't have children. It's not a problem with him because he has a daughter in his last relationship ....'

Laura, in her mid-twenties, had wanted children ever since she could remember and had used no specific contraceptive device since she had stopped taking the pill in 1982. She always protected herself from possible infections and pregnancies at work. She told me during another interview, 'Obviously, I protect myself when I go out to work, pessaries and sheaths, but I don't use anything with him. When I go out to work, I have Durex [a condom brand], pessaries and sponges. I use Nuform too [another condom brand], which has a spermicide, so I protect myself as much as I possibly can ....' Laura and her partner tried to calculate optimum dates for conceiving over six months and Laura began to talk more and more about her feelings of inadequacy, 'The disappointment every month, and sometimes it's like I force myself not to come on. I know I've done it, I'll be really pleased and then a week or two later I'll come on. Each month I get more and more and more depressed. He wants a kid as badly; his daughter is six years old and he doesn't see that much of her any more. He really wants a son, like I said, Leo [his star sign], puffed up ego. I keep feeling he's looking down on me 'cos he's already had a kid, so he knows he's all right, he knows it's me that's the problem.' During our next few meetings, Laura would talk about not being able to conceive, about 'fooling herself' by not menstruating regularly, about the problem as hers rather than his.

Caroline and Laura attributed possible infertility to past infections that were a consequence of a 'private' promiscuity and had nothing to do with work; they wondered whether their tubes had been blocked or scarred. Very little about the women I knew is typical in the same way as these ideas about an inner, reproductive body.

Blocked tubes and the social aetiology of infertility

In the citation, Laura referred to blocked tubes and, on another occasion, she amplified this reference by talk of past infections.

3. [ ] indicate my own interpolations that are intended to clarify the sense of a direct quotation. ... indicate omissions in these extracts.
4. Helen Ward, my colleague, who was then the project doctor.

The most common explanation of perceived or feared infertility concerned these 'tubes' which might have been blocked, as shown by further examples. One woman had a child who lived with her parents and she told me after failing to conceive and subsequent to fertility investigations, 'I have no tubes'. Another reported investigations some two years previously, following a miscarriage. A laparoscopy had suggested, 'there was a scar from PID [pelvic inflammatory disease] – my tubes might be blocked'; investigations were to continue. A third complained that she did not know why she was not getting pregnant, perhaps it was her tubes; she had used no contraception other than condoms since she came off the pill long ago, and very much wanted a child with her new boyfriend. This reasoning is probably widespread in English society, for women's magazines and health care suggest that tubal damage may develop from sexually transmitted infections (STI) such as gonorrhoea or chlamydia. These are a major cause of sub-fertility and infertility (Aral and Cates, 1983; see also Hampshire, this volume).[5] Logic suggests that sex workers have more infections because of their relatively high numbers of partners.[6] However, such biological common sense about the transmission of infection can also be seen as a version of long-standing prejudice about the dirt and filth of prostitution (explored further below). This biological explanation was almost always intertwined with a sociological one, which attributed infection to specific social relationships, namely past boyfriends. Note the text of Laura's amplification, 'Funnily enough, I've been cleaner in my working life than before ...[Before starting sex work and soon after she met her current boyfriend], I had gonorrhoea, trichomonas and chlamydia and it had spread to the tubes. That's why I want to have my tubes checked out. Sometimes, they say that can make you sterile ....' Laura explained how she had started a new life after finishing college and, 'for six months, I led

5. While it was usually the tubes that were blamed, a number of other possible causes were mentioned, ranging from iatrogenic forms of contraception to malfunctions elsewhere in the reproductive system. For example, one woman explained that she had been trying to get pregnant ever since 1985 (five years previously) when her cervix had been cauterised because of a green discharge that no one could treat.
6. Our London data can be used both to support and critique this 'logic'. On the one hand, sex workers are assiduous in their condom use and rarely pick up infections at work (Ward et al., 1999). On the other hand, screening and medical histories suggest a relatively high lifetime prevalence of some infections such as gonorrhoea (e.g. Ward et al., 1993; 1999). As noted below, these infections are indirectly and not directly associated with work, for most are attributed to boyfriends rather than clients.

what I believed to be a promiscuous life. That's when I got diseases for the first time ever. And, after the six months, I started going with my present boyfriend and the diseases all stopped.'

Like Laura, many women attempt to redress apparent or perceived infertility by carefully working out their dates and avoiding contraception at work which might cause difficulties in conceiving at home. Working with sex then causes practical problems in falling pregnant and having a child.

Practical concerns

Although not particularly emphasised by Laura or Caroline, sex workers are beset by difficulties when they want to conceive. Devices such as oral contraception that will definitely prevent conception at work also affect conception at home. Yet, barriers such as condoms are not altogether reliable and women reported some kind of condom failure once a month at work, on average (Ward et al., 1993). Some women take time off so as to make sure that they conceive with the right person. Val had always assumed that she would stop working before attempting to have a child. Later, as her husband continued to earn nothing as a musician, she modified her plans:

> 'I'm fertile, I had three terminations before the age of twenty-five, but I haven't been pregnant since then. He has got one girl pregnant. I won't work because of the anxiety. It would be the time a Durex split or something. Anyway, he wouldn't like it. He doesn't want to father another man's child...I'm thirty-five. I want to have more than one...

> 'If I don't get pregnant in June [she was expecting to get pregnant in one month], I shall work the next month and then try again. I'll have one month on and one off...

> 'I've been so much more careful. I don't go down on them any more [fellatio]. I use Allergy condoms [a non-allergenic brand] even for oral. I still hate the taste but they're better [than other condoms such as those with spermicides] ...Lots of girls do oral [sex] without [condoms], but I tell them it's not worth the risk, especially if you're trying to get pregnant ... Nowadays, it's basically straight sex. Since wanting to get pregnant, I won't let them kiss me or round my face either.[7] I'm finding work difficult to do at

7. This is a literal transcription of a taped interview which suggests that Val tried to keep clients as far away as possible.

the moment. I don't work a lot. But, probably, I will work for a while, until June.'

Val did not become pregnant in the short term and I lost touch with her when the particular research project finished at the end of that year.

Brenda too intended to conceive after she had stopped working, in six months time. She thought she would start again when the child was about a year old. However, she had previously experienced problems in getting pregnant for, as her boyfriend kept explaining, she was too assiduous in cleaning up after sex: 'I always wash inside, even with my boyfriend. With clients, it is because Durex has something that takes off your nail varnish; with my boyfriend, it's because I hate the smell. I use dilute Dettol [to wash] after sex with clients, or soap and water.' Despite all her precautions, Brenda was worried that she might be pregnant when she told me about cleaning up. A contraceptive sponge had 'moved around' and a condom had broken. Brenda had taken five of her contraceptive pills at once and was relieved to receive a negative result from her pregnancy test. As far as I could gather, she did not take these pills regularly as a form of contraception.

Despite all possible precautions, doubts accompany pregnancy. When Jane decided to keep her pregnancy and have a second child, she said, 'if it is the wrong colour, I'm not taking it out of hospital'. She was white, had one black child and expected another but worried about a single condom failure with a white client. Successful conception is greeted by careful calculations of dates relating to previous periods, possible condom failures and sex outside work in order to establish paternity beyond reasonable doubt. But, it is unlikely that doubts are ever dispelled pre-birth.

Of the women participating in our survey between 1989 and 1991, 39/272 (14 per cent) said they had been referred medically for fertility investigations; eight of these women had never been pregnant. Clare and Karen were two of the thirty-nine women who had been investigated for infertility, and two of the eight who had never been pregnant; they provide longer examples illustrating these concerns about, and practical problems in redressing, possible infertility

Clare

Clare talked of having children when I first met her, like Laura and Caroline. In 1987, she announced that her tubes were blocked and complained about the unhelpful attitudes of doctors who would not investigate, 'A year ago, my tubes had become blocked. I'd come here [to the clinic] for a third check knowing something was wrong but they told me it was alright. I was abroad and went to see a private doctor who put me on antibiotics. My tubes had scarred over by the time I came back.'

When Clare made these comments, she was attending our project clinic with an infection which she attributed to her boyfriend – she had just left him: 'I was three months without any infection whatsoever. It's alright when you're single.' After some months with this man, she had acquired gonorrhoea and was attending the clinic for a third time because she was still bleeding. 'How can you get gonorrhoea otherwise? I know something is happening because I always use Durex ... I don't know who else is involved. I don't know if he has other partners. It's just not worth the worry. I'm sore and itchy and something else is involved.'

Clare commented that lots of girls had problems from condoms and she wondered if she had an allergy, 'It's very important to me 'cos you get your tubes blown and then you can't have a child.' She mentioned various investigations to see if she were infertile. When I next met her, she told me that she had never been pregnant. She had continued to bleed since our last meeting but recently wondered whether she might be aborting as she 'found skin in the blood'. She had another D&C (dilatation and curettage) and blamed her old boyfriend both for her lack of money – she wanted a deposit on a house – and for her blocked tubes: 'If it wasn't for him and my infections, I'd be out of it now and I wouldn't have this worry about pregnancy.'

She had had gonorrhoea twice and PID four times: 'I used to get things all the time and then, even though I wasn't working, I used to get things. A few years ago, every now and then, I didn't used to use a Durex, maybe once a month. Every week I'd be up here with something wrong. I used to take the blame for it. I thought it was work or just bad luck. But, I've had nothing these past six months [having split up with her boyfriend].' She had been taken off the pill since this could have exacerbated her bleeding and used only a cap to protect her cervix – 'I have problems with my cervix.'

In 1988, Clare announced that she now had two blocked tubes and would not conceive in five years, even with IVF [*in vitro* fertilisation]. Both she and her new friend now wanted children very much and planned to move to the Caribbean or open a business. It seemed that her sister was saving up for assisted reproduction and, later, I learned that this sister had IVF three times without success. I was told another sister had had a hysterectomy.

Some months later, Clare told a different story. She said that her boyfriend was 'over the moon' about her 'infertility' as he knew that she could not afford IVF. After two years' investigations, Clare had an operation to have her tubes unblocked. She split up with her (new) boyfriend and explained that her problem had been caused by a chlamydial infection which had blocked her tubes. Clare was worried about conceiving if she used condoms but, if she did not use condoms, she might acquire another infection.

It took great determination for Clare to pursue these investigations: in addition to the operation, she reported at least two D&Cs and two laparoscopies during the period she used the project, as well as countless consultations. She nearly stopped using the specialist hospital as she had been treated extremely badly. Soon after I met her, she explained, 'a doctor sent everybody else out of the room and asked if I was working. He then completely lost his temper and said he didn't expect prostitutes to come in demanding D&Cs.' She only returned when she found that she would not have to see that doctor again, and after we had discussed the confidentiality of her clinical notes at length.

Karen

Karen wanted to get pregnant while she had a relationship with her 'pimp';[8] in fact, she said she wanted to have a 'few kids'. She used only condoms and, if she had a period, a sponge; she had stopped taking oral contraception at the age of sixteen. She reported four previous episodes of gonorrhoea as well as PID and a long history of other infections. After trying to get pregnant for three years, Karen was referred for investigations. In April 1989, she had laser treatment for cervical abnormalities and had her tubes checked. She was referred for further investigations the following year and, eventually, was told that she was 'normal'.

Karen was convinced that her boyfriend would not want her to work if she were pregnant, or if they married. She spoke of a cousin who had just had a child, the two had come to London together to work as prostitutes[9] and this cousin had now 'stopped hustling altogether ...When she got pregnant, she just stopped and went home to her parents'.

Karen, like Laura, knew that her boyfriend was fertile as he had a child, but it was difficult to enrol his support in the rigid routines of hospital attendance, times of the month and so forth. As she said, 'Maybe if we bonked a lot something would happen,

8. The term is used in a general sense of a boyfriend or husband (sometimes a girlfriend) who is working his partner, that is, living off her earnings from prostitution and making a business out of her business.
9. I use prostitute as a synonym for sex worker.

but he hasn't got a strong sex drive'. She had to attend the hospital alone as her partner could not get himself there; although 'my bloke says he'd go through with assisted reproduction ... you know what ... men are like'.

Clare had been similarly awed by the practicalities before her operation: her investigations had waited a six-month period 'when we're to really try [and conceive], with thermometers, hours a day and so on'. Clare did not live with her boyfriend and could not imagine how they would follow these procedures.

Karen told her general practitioner that they had sex three times a week and she was promised that something would be put in motion if she were not pregnant by Christmas. When I saw her in the mid-1990s, she had separated from her boyfriend, stopped sex work and retrained. She still considered that she might be infertile herself but had no immediate plans to make a family.

These two examples show that women have to negotiate a thoroughgoing division between work and home when they test their fertility. In effect, the evident continuities between different sexual relationships have to be denied by creating a bodily boundary impermeable to sperm in particular but also to other fluids, to secretions, mucus, and to contraceptive fluids or cleansing agents as well. In addition, women have to sustain purely personal relationships with their partners and make themselves into a 'normal' 'heterosexual' couple for the purpose of dealing with the state, in the form of doctors and medical treatments which may relieve symptoms of anxiety and infertility. I address issues concerning the problem of partners further below, but first I note briefly a radical solution to the problem of constructing a complete division between different types of sex when testing your fertility.

Reproduction without sex

I remember first noting the novel idea of reproduction without sex, mirroring the earlier innovations of sex without reproduction, in the late 1980s when a woman came into the clinic very concerned about HIV infection. She had begun to use a condom with her boyfriend, and used to say that she did not much like sex anyway, claiming to treat all men the same as though all were clients, 'they all have to pay'. However, this woman wanted a child and decided that she would 'inject herself' when the time came. She pointed to her womb indicating a technical solution that would bypass the need for intercourse and involve a different bodily praxis – insemination via her abdomen rather than vagina.

Kay, similarly, said that she used condoms with everyone but remained anxious that she might have blocked tubes and worried about the cause of a previous miscarriage. She did not actively plan a pregnancy but nonetheless began to avoid contraception sporadically with her boyfriend: 'I want to know if I can get pregnant before I start anything serious.' Kay then split up with her boyfriend and became increasingly disillusioned with men in general. After a while, she came up with a radical solution which bypassed men and sex altogether, 'if I ever have a baby, I want it through my navel'. As I looked quizzical, she elaborated, 'I shall have IVF through a laparoscope'.

The difficulties of working with and building personal relationships around sex were so acute for some women that they developed novel and costly resolutions of this kind in order to become pregnant: sexuality as a whole was reserved for work but procreation was rescued, independently of sex, for the home. To my knowledge, neither of these women actually became pregnant through medical interventions but, for both, 'assisted' reproduction resolved the conceptual problem of inadequate barriers between work and the home.[10]

Ideas about the division between these two domains, about what properly occurs at work and what remains private and personal at home, lie at the heart of the prejudice shown towards sex work in the UK and elsewhere.

Stigma

London sex workers constantly come up against stereotypes which suggest that working with sex makes you sterile. Although these ideas seem specific, they illuminate the situation for those of us who work outside the sex industry, for they concern a widespread set of distinctions between our public and private lives. General media images, childhood memories, academic and official reports, and most people in the UK, assume that sex should not be sold; it belongs to the private person. To sell sex, it seems, is to give your inner self or private person away to the lesser domain of the market. This confounds the separation between economy (or the marketplace) and society (or the family) and makes it difficult for many to recognise prostitution as a form of work.

10. Equally, some women avoided personal relationships altogether, giving up 'sex' while they worked in favour of 'celibacy'.

Anthropological accounts of the person in the UK and elsewhere have attended to a kinship morality and, more recently, non-kinship identities such as those based on gender or class which contrast with behaviour at work.[11] In the economy, we act as though our person were a thing which can be bought and sold like any other commodity. We thus appear alienable and substitutable, operating as though we were autonomous and discrete 'individuals'. At home, by contrast, we are involved in relationships of sentiment, love and kinship. The private person is constituted relationally and, in some discussions, appears as an inner core (see, for example, Carrier, 1992). We appear as though we were inalienable and consequently more real or whole; this private person, who is constituted through a distinctive social or religious morality, is accorded the higher value. No one, it seems, would agree to the extraction of their labour power if this process did not simultaneously create a distinctive personal life for the subject, because work contains the promise of home.[12] This fiction is as central to an understanding of sex workers as of any other occupational group in the UK today and implies that what can be glossed in shorthand as 'work' and the 'home' are mutually referring.

It has long been argued that an imagined separation between economy and society constitutes the central fiction of capitalism,[13] and the interpenetration of public and private is increasingly recognised in popular culture as well as academic commentaries where workers of all kinds are seen to make their identities at work (Rose, 1992) or even to obliterate distinctions between work and leisure altogether. However, the extent of change in late modernity is easy to exaggerate and the distinctions between different domains of life remain important to many, including sex workers. By and large, sex workers do not simply reject prevailing fictions and they rarely dispute popular distinctions between different realms of life. To the contrary, they are extremely concerned to differentiate work from the rest of their lives and, specifically, to refute popular notions of sexual activity as a purely private property of the person. London sex workers constantly reiterate that

11. Schneider's *American Kinship* is perhaps the classic account (1969), addressed in a number of more recent texts on kinship in relation to other 'identities', for example, Yanagisako and Delaney (eds) (1995).
12. In illustration, see the excellent accounts of English and American capitalist culture by Willis (1977) or Martin (1987).
13. In practice, economic calculations clearly permeate private affairs. The value placed on private life is itself attributed to wider economic forces: 'The value that we place on personal identities and relations (indeed, the very notion that these are distinctive) is in an important way a consequence of the growth of impersonal economic relations' (Carrier, 1992:553). Similarly, a great many parts of the inner core of a person are sold on the market together with sex.

some of their activities constitute a legitimate form of work and they insist that these are separate from their private affairs. They tend to replicate a sense of division between the private and the public but they assert that 'sex' can fall on both sides of the division (see Day, 1994 for details). Perhaps the most important distinction between a private and public body is between the inner and outer parts. Outside are the visible body parts to which clients are given access and also the 'mask', 'pretence' or 'act' performed (see also Oldenburg, 1990); the inside is associated with pleasure and intimacy, and houses reproductive organs such as the 'tubes' described above. This inner body is marked by the cervix.

In London, sex workers find it difficult to construct this separate domain of work, for popular attitudes, together with legal restrictions and policing make women constantly liable to loss of earnings, arrest and violence. However, they generally find it even more difficult to sustain a distinctive personal life. Laws make it virtually impossible for sex workers to live legally with other adults, and especially with boyfriends or husbands who can be prosecuted readily for living off immoral earnings in the event of any shared moneys (Day, 1996). Prostitutes seem to constitute an exception in English society: for women who sell sex, there can be no division between work and the home; prostitutes are purely 'public' women whether they are operating in the marketplace or not. Dominant ideologies about prostitution are radical, for it is not just the status of work that is called into question but the status of life outside work too and the person as a whole.

Given the confusion greeting the existence of sex in the market, it is not surprising to find that attitudes about proper economic behaviour are twinned with ideas about proper sexual activity: this is why prostitutes are also considered to be 'barren'. These views have a long history – note Karras on medieval England: 'Medieval physicians believed that prostitutes were sterile because their wombs became clogged with dirt, because the great quantities of semen they received made their wombs slippery, or because they commonly got no pleasure from sex and therefore did not emit seed.' (Karras, 1996:82) Modern myths differ little, although the aetiology described above tends towards a biological rather than a religious morality tale.[14] As Laqueur has so percep-

14. Contemporary stereotypes often come in pairs and are likely to stress the image of sex workers who breed like rabbits (so as to obtain housing, and requiring intervention from social workers who will put their children under state protection), as well as putting forward the opposing image of one who suffers involuntary infertility. The former view can be related to a wider 'culture of poverty' which tends to presume 'lower-class promiscuity' (e.g. Schneider and Schneider, 1995b:181).

tively shown, this notion of infertility concerns the non-productive nature of prostitution, at least in the later nineteenth century, 'Prostitution is sterile because the mode of exchange it represents is sterile. Nothing is produced because, like usury, it is pure exchange' (Laqueur, 1990:231). Further, 'A deep cultural unease about money and the market economy is couched in the metaphors of reproductive biology ...the claim that sex for money, coition with prostitutes, bears no fruit' (1990:232).

Laqueur drew particularly on Simmel in showing how prostitution, like usury, came to exemplify a general unease with the impersonal nature of a rapidly expanding market economy. Simmel equated prostitution and 'pure exchange' in his 1907 article: 'Only transactions for money have that character of a purely momentary relationship which leaves no traces, as is the case with prostitution' (Simmel, 1971:121). In modern Europe, money is impersonal and thus suited to impersonal sex: 'Only money is an appropriate equivalent to the momentary peaking and equally momentary satisfaction of the desire served by prostitutes, for money establishes no ties, it is always at hand, and it is always welcomed' (ibid). In even stronger terms, Simmel claimed, '...the nature of money resembles the nature of prostitution. The indifference with which it lends itself to any use, the infidelity with which it leaves everyone, its lack of ties to anyone, its complete objectification that excludes any attachment and makes it suitable as a pure means – all this suggests a portentous analogy between it and prostitution' (ibid.:122). You cannot (properly) buy the personal and intimate aspects of a person; when you do, 'it leads to a terrible suppression of personal dignity' (ibid.:126). In this way, prostitution provides a metaphor for the money economy, which is dehumanising and alienating.

I follow Laqueur in arguing that metaphors from reproductive biology serve to describe proper and improper forms of economic exchange today, as in the past, and I demonstrate that in/fertility provides not just a central discourse but a key set of practices among London sex workers. The 'barren' prostitute is not only one of the most powerful symbols of the evils of a modern exchange economy, long evident in western writing, but also a core label that many sex workers spend much of their time seeking to overturn. In these circumstances, many sex workers worry about their fertility and some fall pregnant, even repeatedly, as I show below. I suggest that the examples I have given of blocked tubes, damaging infections and boyfriends who might have been pimps, all serve to express doubts about the legitimacy of sex work. The conversations and stories I have cited, which often spanned several years, suggest that many women considered that they might not, after all, be able to lay claim to two bodies and two lives. Perhaps, they – the prostitutes – will fulfil stereotype through misfortune, sin, ill health or occupational hazard and become barren because of their work.

There is interplay between biological and social aetiology in this logic. Ideas about relationships involve a biological common sense about the transmission of infection, as noted above: effective monogamy (that is, a single partner with whom sex is not protected) could not transmit infection, multiple partnerships could. Comments about the source of a particular infection during the research period were generally confirmed by independent clinical and epidemiological investigations into risk (Ward et al., 1993, 1999). However, the apparently authoritative nature of biomedical language cannot be sustained on closer examination. While infections are a major cause of infertility, sex workers do not always know if they have had an STI, nor whether it was treated soon enough or well enough. Accordingly, infertility can be attributed to infections that developed during past relationships without any direct evidence. Moreover, other aetiologies cited by sex workers are less plausible in biomedical terms: women explained how their wombs had become misshapen during years of work, and of the harm caused by sperm. For example, 'someone told me ... that sperm blocks your tubes [and, therefore, you should have clients wear condoms]. That's why you can't get pregnant.' These comments immediately bring to mind the distinctive stigma associated with sex work, in contrast to the apparently factual and transparent comments about biology. This stigma serves to underscore a normative separation of work from home, where sex properly occurs only in private.

Thus, biomedical idioms can be unpacked to reveal more than 'simple' common sense. Perhaps most significant is the way that some 'facts' are more visible than others. For example, women downplayed explanations that might suggest hormonal or anatomical reasons for their infertility in favour of 'work-related' causes, namely, infections. Moreover, these infections were linked with the valued domain of the home and the 'real' person. The discourse served to express in particular the difficulties of establishing significant relationships – it was hard to be sure whether private partners were working or not when they set up relationships with prostitutes.

The huge and particular burden of infertility helps to explain why sex workers want to get pregnant. To borrow a phrase from Foucault (1976) it seems that a pregnancy serves much the same purpose as the projected autopsy is said to have done for nineteenth-century Parisian physicians. It constitutes a diagnosis; prostitution has not robbed a woman of her real, inner self for she can have children and a future. I do not mean to imply that women worry on a daily basis about the status of their personal relationships, which are obviously different from work. Yet, this inner self becomes more visible in pregnancy: an interior body, guarded by a cervix, acquires a distinctive reality that creates a definitive rupture with other (non-procreative) sexual experiences. Quite literally, the inner body acquires weight and substance. At the same time, counter-stereotypes which suggest that prostitution is a perfectly dignified form of work become more convincing, more credible and more persuasive because public and private are mutually constitutive. In these circumstances, the outline of a growing pregnant body can establish a sense of personal productivity: you will take something from the present, unpalatable business of sex work into the future.

The spectre of infertility reveals acute difficulties and, if you remain 'barren', you may not have negotiated popular stereotypes successfully, nor everyday relationships with friends, customers and state functionaries. A dotted outline of this still infertile body implies a lack of personal productivity in all future relationships and work practices. Moreover, stopping sex work will not simply 'cure' infertility in the same way that it will resolve the problems of nightly fines or client duplicity. The importance attached to conception and pregnancy among many sex workers in London is strongly associated with the very permanence of the stigma of infertility, in striking and ironic contrast to sex work itself, which is commonly considered a temporary or ephemeral occupation. Moreover, this stigma is embodied in the individual prostitute who, in accordance with common stereotype, becomes accountable for the hazards of commercial sex in a way that contrasts with the relational character attributed to most problems of the trade such as the fines levied by police, the dishonesty of clients, or the exploitation of managers. To be unable to produce a baby shows that you have and will have nothing.

Pregnancy

The desire to conceive complicates the image of the barren prostitute drawn by Simmel amongst others. Pregnancy (re-)establishes the reality of a separate, inner body and over 70 per cent (200/277) of the women interviewed between 1989 and 1991 had been pregnant. However, a great many pregnancies were not carried to term: half of those who responded (134/267) reported a total of 225 terminations (range, 1–6).[15] Without suggesting that women readily or lightly undergo terminations, it seems as though they reconstruct a desire for future rather than actual motherhood. In conclusion, I return to my opening account of Caroline and Laura. Both women fell pregnant twice while I knew them but Caroline then had two terminations. With her first pregnancy in 1987, she was adamant that she would keep the child. As her parents would not help, she decided to stay with her grandmother and duly went home to another part of the country. On her return to London six months later, she explained that her parents had put so much pressure on her, threatening to cut her off, that she agreed to have an abortion, which had proved extremely upsetting. As she settled back into her London work, she found a new boyfriend and became pregnant some time later; once again, she wanted the baby, but this time her boyfriend was vehemently opposed:

> 'Yeah. And, he said, right from the beginning, I knew it was. And he said a definite no. So, I knew the only way I could have it was to leave him, you know, and have it on my own. And I just don't want the responsibility yet. I mean, I've got money in the bank but money in the bank don't last for ever, does it?...
>
> 'I mean it might sound hard to understand but what I do want eventually is a baby, house and kids. But, like, he proposed to me the other day and I just said, "No." God, not for the rest of my life. This for the rest of my life. Probably getting a job and having to get up early in the morning and coming home at tea-time and cooking his tea and what-not. It's not me. It's not my life ....'[16]

Caroline returned to the sex industry, agreed to another termination and was persuaded to take oral contraceptives despite her misgivings.[17] Eventually, in 1989, she stopped sex work and began to train as a teacher, living in the suburbs with her boyfriend.

15. Compare with figures from a national sample in Johnson et al., 1994
16. Unfortunately, my data are partial in that they derive largely from the women involved. However, partners were not even necessarily consulted in these attempts to conceive, keep or terminate a pregnancy and, as this chapter focuses on the significance of infertility to sex workers, I hope that the lack of data from the men involved do not pose too serious a limitation.
17. It may be recalled that Caroline was a Rastafarian and considered contraception immoral.

Caroline's history illustrates why women may want to put motherhood off for the future. Once pregnant, a woman may be anxious about paternity and consider her life too unsettled for parenthood. Few can afford to stop work. Most, however, remain preoccupied with their ability to conceive and are likely, therefore, to fall pregnant again. In the histories of these younger women, pregnancies suggest a concern to demonstrate, repeatedly, one's fertility more than any desire to actually give birth. This, I suggest provides a possible interpretation of the high rates of termination in our study.

When I last saw Laura in 1992, she was living in London with her two children and teaching in a nursery. As Laura progressed with her first pregnancy, she worked less and less as a prostitute herself and gradually raised enough to stop work altogether, to pay for her college training and, later, her childcare as well as daily expenses. She had been able to raise money through a small number of regular clients who she saw repeatedly, and through putting clients in contact with other sex workers. For Laura, as for many other women, children came to stand for a radically different future, far away from the messy world of sex work. However, Laura was exceptional in making sex work productive through a series of very difficult transformations which turned money into property, prostitution into teaching and sexual relationships into children (she no longer lived with their father). In contrast to Laura, other women appeared to become stuck. Most intended to work in the sex industry for a strictly limited period but found it difficult to earn enough money and acquire a legitimate identity through which to finance businesses or mortgages. They found it equally, if not more difficult, to make their private lives rewarding as boyfriends, such as those initially associated with Laura and Caroline, consumed inordinate sums. This made it hard to ensure that work and the home were sufficiently distinct. Of course, it should be reiterated that Laura and Caroline were separated by a decade in age, and motherhood or children seemed to become more important than proof of fertility over time.[18] In addition, it should be noted that the very desire for children is part of this context, part of sex work. For example, I knew Karen and Caroline after they stopped working as prostitutes. Both also

18. I cannot substantiate this claim fully but I can provide further examples. Another woman in her early thirties and very much in love wanted a sterilisation reversed. Likewise, a third woman wanted a daughter after many pregnancies and terminations, subsequent to her very first experience of intercourse which had led to a child. Overall, just over a third (35 per cent, 95/272) surveyed had children.

stopped wanting children with the urgency and desperation that they had shown previously.

Prescriptive fertility

The situation I have described is by no means unique.[19] To provide just one other example, Morokvasič wrote of the proof that pregnancy provided to both men and women of the former Yugoslavia; women knew they were fecund and men that they were virile. A huge proportion of pregnancies were terminated: three quarters of the women known to be sexually active had had one or more abortions and Morokvasič estimates that roughly two-thirds of all pregnancies in her study group of 258 migrant women (with access to contraception) were terminated. Whilst abortion provided a form of birth control from some perspectives, it could be described as a form of procreation as well, rather as I have argued in this chapter: 'Though abortion is the opposite of procreation, it is symbolically the same – physical proof that a woman is fecund' (Morokvasič, 1981:138). Despite arguing for the specificity of this ethnographic case in London, the Yugoslav and other examples show that many men and women are concerned to test their fertility without necessarily intending to bear children and without in fact becoming parents. About one-third of all births are said to have been from unintended or unplanned pregnancies in countries such as the UK or US.[20]

I have described implications of possible infertility in sex workers for our understanding of gender and sexuality more broadly in the UK by exploring a conceptual division between public and private. However, I have argued that the situation for sex workers is specific: they are stigmatised as 'public women' who have to bear the consequences – infertility – in their own bodies. It is not surprising therefore to find that their anxieties about fertility are particularly acute and take a specific form, relating to the work they do. In conclusion, I suggest further implications at a practical level. More sensitive interventions are needed in the field of sexual health where attempts to 'cure' infertility in sex workers or to 'curb' their fertility may be misdirected. Neither infertility nor

19. As well as the excellent Yugoslav ethnography about this process of testing your fertility which I discuss, see material on the quest for conception in very different circumstances, as in the book of this title on Egypt by Inhorn (1994).
20. For example, Westoff reported 30 per cent of births in the US were unplanned in the early 1980s and this despite a high contraceptive prevalence of 60 per cent (cited in Robinson and Robinson, 1997).

fertility can be addressed alone since they are intrinsically related: fear of one state leads women to demonstrate the opposite. Moreover, infertility in the individual cannot be cured without attending to the wider stigmatisation that constructs sex workers in a barren image. The same is true of an (unwanted) fertility that derives from a society and culture in which sex workers find themselves compelled to demonstrate their womanly essence.

Part Two

FERTILITY AND PARENTHOOD

CHAPTER 5

THE IMPACT OF MALE MIGRATION ON FERTILITY DECISIONS AND OUTCOMES IN NORTHERN BURKINA FASO

Kate Hampshire

Introduction

The Fulani of Northern Burkina Faso are a population in a state of flux. The combination of major social and political changes since independence (1960), in which the last vestiges of the slavery system were abandoned, and climatic changes, particularly two major droughts in the last twenty-five years, has brought increasing economic pressures on Fulani agro-pastoralists in this area. No longer able to eke out a satisfactory existence from agro-pastoralism alone, economic diversification has become a necessity for many. In particular, since the mid-1970s substantial numbers of Fulani men have begun travelling to cities during the long dry season to look for work in order to supplement and sustain agro-pastoral subsistence systems. This phenomenon is not unique to Northern Burkina Faso. Several other studies have shown that, in recent years, short-term seasonal movements of young men to cities are becoming an increasingly important part of the rural economy of the West African Sahel (e.g. Maliki et al., 1984; Findley, 1989; 1994; Cleveland, 1991; Painter, 1992; David, 1995; de Bruijn and Van Dijk, 1995; Davies, 1996; Cordell et al., 1996;

Guilmoto, 1998; Hampshire and Randall, 1999). The aim of this chapter is to explore the ways in which the increasing contact young men have with large urban centres might be altering attitudes, behaviour and outcomes regarding childbearing.

A review of other studies examining the impact of temporary male out-migration on fertility in sub-Saharan Africa suggests change may occur on a number of different levels. Firstly, such migration may result in changing attitudes towards the value of children, or a shift in processes of decision-making regarding fertility. Where male out-migration results in increased autonomy and economic opportunities for women combined with the commoditisation of labour, traditional supports to high fertility may be undermined (Timaeus and Graham, 1989, Monimart, 1989; Gould, 1994). Increasing knowledge and social acceptability of birth control as a result of contact with urban areas means any such desires to limit fertility can be easily translated into practice (Timaeus and Graham, 1989). On the other hand, the demand for children might increase with the added uncertainty that sons might leave permanently (Cleveland, 1991), and contact with 'modern' ideas might also undermine traditional practices such as post-partum abstinence and extended breastfeeding which increase birth intervals and thus restrict overall fertility.

Temporary male out-migration has also been shown to affect marriage patterns which, where most childbearing is within marriage, can substantially alter fertility outcomes. Men may delay marriage to facilitate migration (Timaeus and Graham, 1989; Monimart, 1989) and Timaeus and Graham have shown that migrants' marriages are at greater risk of early termination as traditional sanctions on marital breakdown are eroded. In other situations, migrants may marry earlier by using earnings to overcome bridewealth barriers (Cleveland, 1991). Finally, migration can have fertility-reducing impacts that are unsought and may be undesired, through reducing coital frequency between spouses (Massey and Mullman, 1981; Timaeus and Graham, 1989), or by increasing the incidence of sexually transmitted diseases causing sterility or subfecundity (David and Voas, 1981).

The Fulani of Northern Burkina Faso are a population relatively new to rural-urban migration. Gould (1994) distinguishes between 'dynamic regions', where out-migration tends to reduce support for high fertility, and 'lagging regions', where the traditional supports remain and may even be strengthened. Under this classification, Northern Burkina Faso would certainly constitute a 'lagging region': remittance levels are low and commoditisation of the labour market is extremely limited. However, it is certainly not a static region, and the new migration regime has been accompanied by important social and economic changes. This chapter combines demographic and anthropological approaches to begin to unravel the processes through which these changes affect reproductive decision-making and outcomes.

The Fulani of Northern Burkina Faso and temporary male out-migration

The data presented here come from a study carried out among the Fulani of Northern Burkina Faso (the provinces of Oudalan and Séno). This is a semi-arid area with highly seasonal rainfall, almost all falling in the short rainy season from July to September (Barral, 1977; Claude et al., 1991). The main economic activities are extensive pastoralism and rain-fed agriculture during the rainy season. The Fulani, who constitute about a quarter of the population (INSD, 1994), are thought of, by themselves and others, as nomadic or semi-nomadic pastoralists, and being a pastoralist is central to *pulaaku* (Fulani identity). In common with other Sahelian pastoralists, they are associated with large-scale transhumance, moving long distances with herds of cattle in search of pasture and water (e.g. Barral, 1977; Gallais, 1975, 1984; Bernus, 1988; 1991; Milleville, 1991).

However, since the major droughts of the early 1970s and 1980s, when herd numbers were drastically reduced, many Fulani in Burkina Faso and elsewhere have become increasingly dependent on alternative forms of subsistence, particularly agriculture. Major transhumance movements have become relatively rare; instead many Fulani are engaging increasingly in temporary migration to cities. With fewer animals to tend to, the dry season has become a slack season for many, and a good window of opportunity to travel to cities to seek alternative sources of livelihood to supplement an agro-pastoral mode of subsistence. Today, large numbers of young Fulani men leave each year in the dry season, mostly to work in Abidjan in the Côte d'Ivoire (numbers of women leaving are negligible). In a survey carried out in 1995, 15.8 per cent of men aged 18–64 had worked in cities during the twelve months preceding the survey, and 36.6 per cent of men in this age group had done such work at some point in their lives.

However, involvement in this temporary migration is not uniform across all Fulani. Multiple logistic regression analysis shows that variables associated with propensity to migrate include age, economic activity, household size and composition and, most importantly, ethnic sub-group (Hampshire and Randall, 1999). There are four major ethnic sub-groups of Fulani in this region. The FulBe DjelgoBe, who live mostly in the north of the area, are the most pastorally-oriented group. Although today few FulBe DjelgoBe survive exclusively from their herds, they are still strongly associated with pastoralism and are the most pastorally mobile, living in tents which can be dismantled and moved easily on transhumance. Among the DjelgoBe, transhumance typically involves whole households. The FulBe Liptaako are a much more sedentary group of agro-pastoralists, living mostly in stable villages in the southern part of the area alongside the RiimaaiBe Liptaako, who are a largely cultivating group and the erstwhile slaves of the FulBe Liptaako. The JawamBe are a much smaller group of Liptaako Fulani who also had slaves. Henceforth, the JawamBe and the FulBe Liptaako will be considered together. Finally, the FulBe GaoBe are also agro-pastoralists and occupy an intermediate position between the FulBe DjelgoBe and the FulBe Liptaako, both geographically and in terms of their subsistence strategies.

It can be seen from Table 5.1 that there is a very strong association between ethnic sub-group and the propensity of young men to migrate to cities. In a series of detailed interviews with men about the decision to migrate, answers were almost always framed in terms of ethnic identity. In particular, it is extremely rare for FulBe DjelgoBe men to engage in seasonal economic

Table 5.1. *Seasonal Economic Migration Characteristics by Ethnic Subgroup: Men Aged 18–64*

Ethnic Subgroup	Total Number of Men	% Migrating 1994–95	% Lifetime Migration	Mean Duration of 1994–95 Migration (Mths)
FulBe DjelgoBe	303	2.0%	3.6%	8.7 (N=6)
FulBe GaoBe	665	19.1%	36.3%	4.9 (N=124)
FulBe Liptaako	504	11.1%	33.9%	8.3 (N=53)
Riim. Liptaako	343	17.2%	59.2%	6.8 (N=58)
ALL	1815	13.7%	34.5%	6.2 (N=241)
Statistical Tests		$Chi^2 = 58.1$	$Chi^2 = 221$	ANOVA: F ratio = 13.1
		$p<.000005$	$p<.000005$	$p<.00005$

Notes

1. Seasonal economic migration is defined here as migration out of the Sahel Region of Burkina Faso, for a period of between 1 and 24 months, with the intention of earning money. For the rationale behind this see Hampshire and Randall (1999).
2. ANOVA excludes FulBe DjelgoBe because of the very small number of DjelgoBe migrants.

migration ('We are FulBe DjelgoBe – of course we don't go to Abidjan!') compared with the three other groups. Among these three there is some variation both in propensity to migrate and annual duration of the migration. FulBe GaoBe men migrate frequently, but the duration of migration is shorter than for the Liptaako groups, particularly FulBe Liptaako men, who migrate for almost two-thirds of a year on average.

This variation in temporary male out-migration within a single broad ethnic category in a fairly small geographical area provides a good arena to explore the processes through which such movements may have impacts on fertility strategies and outcomes.

Methodological issues and data quality

In order to understand processes of fertility decisions and their outcomes, a combination of demographic and anthropological methodologies was adopted in this study. There were two main phases of fieldwork. After a pilot visit to the field in August and September 1994, a quantitative single round demographic survey (SRDS) was carried out in April–June 1995 on a sample of 8,834 individuals in forty villages. This was followed by an intensive multiple round study (MRS) on a sub-sample of the SRDS population: 1,224 individuals in six of the original forty villages. Each village was visited for one week bimonthly over the year December 1995 to December 1996 (six visits).

Baseline fertility data were obtained from the SRDS. Full birth histories were not collected in this survey, so fertility rates for the population as a whole, and by ethnic sub-group, were estimated indirectly using the P/F method (UN, 1983).[1] Detailed birth histories collected subsequently in the MRS allowed cross-checking of the SRDS data and revealed more information about the timing and spacing of births.

In order to understand the physical mechanisms through which different fertility rates are achieved in this population, a proximate determinants approach was taken (Bongaarts, 1978; 1982; Bongaarts and Potter, 1983). The assumption made is that no differences in natural fecundity are experienced by the various sub-groups (due, for example, to differences in energy balances: see Ellison, 1995). Differences in fertility are attributed, at the proximate level, to various conditions and practices which reduce fertility from its

1. Details of the demographic techniques and methodologies used are not given in this paper, which focuses more on the issues involved. For further details refer to Hampshire and Randall (2000).

theoretical maximum of 15.3 (Bongaarts, 1982). The major proximate determinants identified by Bongaarts and others are: marriage patterns (which limit the number of women *at risk* of conception); use of voluntary birth control (contraception and induced abortion); sexual abstinence (particularly post-partum abstinence); the duration of post-partum infecundity (at a population level closely related to length of breastfeeding) and the incidence of primary and secondary sterility. Quantitative data allowing estimation of the magnitude of each of these were collected in the SRDS and MRS using various demographic techniques.

Overall, given the nature of the population surveyed and the demographic techniques used, the quality of the demographic data is surprisingly good. Careful supervision of enumerators and simple cross-checks performed on the data as they were being obtained allowed most potential problems to be identified and resolved. Sex ratios of reported offspring indicated a slight under-reporting of girls by one of the groups, the FulBe Liptaako. Corrections have been made for this in fertility estimates given in this chapter.[2]

During the MRS, qualitative methods were used to explore the meanings and importance attached to reproduction, childbirth, marriage, childlessness etc. in order to clarify the links between the proximate determinants of fertility and the underlying causes of these. In each study site, a series of informal and semi-structured interviews was conducted with individual women and men and with small groups. Discussions were wide-ranging and, as confidence built up over the course of the year, in many cases profound. Participant observation was also important. Observation of, among other things, the processes through which marriage, divorce and widowhood take place, the events surrounding childbirth, techniques of childcare, and the changes in domestic organisation which occur as a result of male absence brought a greater understanding of the processes through which social change can affect reproductive decisions and outcomes.

Fertility levels and differentials

Women begin their childbearing earlier than men (Figure 5.1): a pattern largely explained by the marriage regime (see below). Total fertility is estimated at 6.6: broadly similar to Burkina Faso

2. Where the mean sex ratio of children ever born exceeded 1.10, extra girls were added to reduce the ratio to this figure: (Hampshire and Randall 2000).

as a whole and other comparable Sahelian populations. Mean completed parity[3] is slightly higher than the total fertility estimates, which might indicate a recent minor decline in fertility, but might equally be an artefact of the relatively small (for demographers!) sample sizes.

Analysis of fertility by ethnic sub-group reveal substantial differences (Table 5.2). In particular, the FulBe DjelgoBe have much higher fertility than any of the other groups (higher parity is found at all age groups). It is unusual to find mobile pastoralist populations, like the FulBe DjelgoBe, with higher fertility than more sedentary cultivating populations living in the same area (Henin, 1968; 1969; Swift, 1977; Randall, 1984; Campbell and Wood, 1988; Bentley et al., 1993; Roth, 1993).

Ethnic identity as Fulani strongly influences some reproductive practices (see Belaunde, this volume). For example, female circumcision is practised partly in order to reinforce boundaries between Fulani and 'other' groups, perceived to be of lower status. However, although ethnic sub-group identity within the Fulani category is expressed through certain social practices such as migration, the same is not true for reproductive behaviour and fer-

Figure 5.1. *Age Specific Parity of Fulani Men and Women (SRDS Data)*

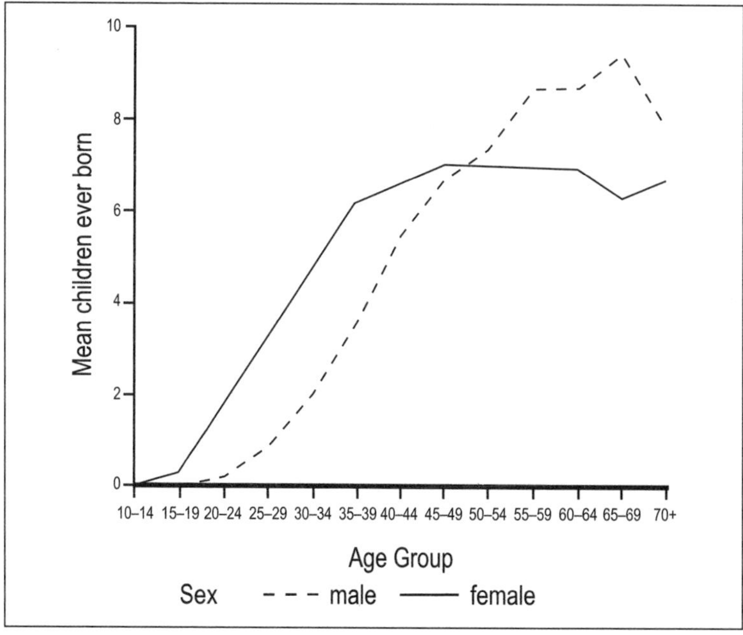

3. Parity refers to the average number of children ever borne (including those who subsequently died).

Table 5.2. *Indirect Estimates of Total Fertility by Ethnic Subgroup (SRDS Data)*

Ethnic subgroup	Total fertility: women aged 15–49		Completed parity: women 40–54	
	Total Fertility	N	Mean	N
FulBe DjelgoBe	9.2	302	8.0	66
FulBe GaoBe	6.3	570	6.5	145
FulBe Liptaako	6.4 (6.0)	395	6.9 (6.6)	99
RiimaaiBe Liptaako	7.1 (7.0)	299	7.1 (7.0)	65
ALL	6.6	1566	6.9	444

Notes

1. Total fertility estimates were made using the P/F method: for details, refer to Hampshire and Randall (2000).
2. All estimates are corrected for missing girls. Uncorrected figures, where different to one decimal place, are shown in brackets.

tility preferences. We must look elsewhere for reasons behind the observed fertility differentials. A strong possibility is that the lower fertility of the other groups is a recent phenomenon associated with their involvement with temporary male migration to cities. The remainder of this chapter is devoted to exploring the mechanisms and processes underlying these observed fertility differentials, with the specific aim of elucidating possible effects of seasonal labour migration on reproductive decisions and outcomes.

Changes in the processes and rationale of reproductive decision-making

It has been widely suggested that contact with urban areas and 'modern ideas' as a result of temporary migration to cities might produce changes in the processes and rationale of reproductive decision-making through some combination of the following: changes in the economic rationale of childbearing; an increase in the power, status and autonomy of women; and the increasing awareness and social acceptability of birth control and/or the undermining of certain traditional practices such as post-partum abstinence.

The impact of these changes on fertility is not straightforward: depending on the situation, fertility might decrease (e.g. Timaeus and Graham, 1989) or be raised (e.g. Cleveland, 1991). However, it is reasonable to expect that migrating groups might have higher levels of awareness of modern methods of birth control and might, under the right circumstances, be more disposed to use them.

As yet, however, contact with cities has apparently done little to alter fertility preferences or to shift the locus of decision-making within the domestic sphere. The great desire for large families and lots of children is ubiquitously expressed by this Fulani population, with no obvious differences between ethnic groups. Standard questions on desired family sizes are met by responses which range from the just about feasible (nine or ten) to the impossible (twenty-five or more) or simply 'as many as possible'.

This is not surprising, for there is still a very strong economic rationale for maximising the number of offspring. The commoditisation of rural labour markets in this area is extremely limited, and labour rather than land is the limiting factor of agro-pastoral production (particularly agriculture). Having lots of children is, therefore, necessary for economic security and well-being; without children it is very difficult for a Fulani man to become a full social being and form an independent household (cf. Stenning, 1958). This is compounded by the very rigid gender divisions of labour in Fulani society, which exclude women from participating directly in agro-pastoral production. Children are also important as a source of networks and social status. Alliances with other households formed through the marriage of children are a source of social status in their own right, and can become crucial to the survival of livelihoods in times of crisis – not uncommon in the Sahel (Iliffe, 1987; Adams, 1993). As well as building new alliances, the marriage of children to close kin can help reinforce and consolidate existing kin networks through which day to day cooperation can occur.

There are no perceived disadvantages in having lots of children. Children are never seen as a drain on resources. The availability of food is believed to be purely a product of the God-given fortune of the child, and nothing to do with the level of resources available within households or the number of mouths to feed: *'BiDDo fuu rimdatakena e tindem'* – every child is born with its own luck (literally 'forehead'). Moreover, there is a constant unmet demand for adoption or fostering by relatives who do not have enough children of their own, which can act as a safety valve, allowing children to be offloaded, either temporarily or permanently, if it becomes necessary.

Migration has done little to undermine this rationale for large family sizes and may, if anything, have strengthened it in ways similar to those proposed by Cleveland (1991). Where there is uncertainty about whether or not sons will stay around, it becomes even more important to have lots of children. And while large households and good extra-household networks are important to optimise agro-pastoral production and survive the occasional crisis, they are absolutely crucial to successful seasonal labour migration. Migrants without large families and good networks risk critically undermining domestic production during periods of absence, as I have shown elsewhere (Hampshire and Randall, 1999); men from large households and those with good kin/alliance networks are much better able to pursue optimal migration strategies than those without.

Children are also essential to the social and economic security of Fulani women. Women move to their husbands' homes on marriage, where their status is almost entirely dependent on reproductive success. Until a woman has borne at least one child (and usually a son), her position in her marital home is extremely vulnerable. Extended childlessness almost always results either in divorce, or, particularly if the husband and wife are close kin, in the husband taking an additional wife. In such circumstances the new wife displaces the childless one in terms of affection and status. One man in his sixties, who had been through several wives, said, 'you cannot love your wife if she gives you no children', a view echoed by many. Other men told of pressure from their families to divorce childless wives and/or to marry again. So, despite the risks to health and life inherent in childbearing (an estimated one in eighteen women die in childbirth[4]), the desire for children is expressed as strongly by women as it is by men.

It has been suggested (e.g. Okoth-Ogendo, 1989; Monimart, 1989; David, 1995; Timaeus and Graham, 1989; Gould, 1994), that temporary male out-migration can lead to shifts in gender divisions of labour and/or power. When de facto female heads of household are left behind, the rights of women to own productive wealth and be economic decision-makers may be expected to increase, which may in turn increase the opportunity cost to women of childbearing and provide opportunities for economic and social status through routes other than childbearing alone.

In Northern Burkina Faso, however, there is very little evidence of these sorts of changes occurring. The majority of Fulani households,[5] particularly among the GaoBe and Liptaako groups, are of an extended structure, made up of several closely related

4. Estimate based on SRDS data on proportions of sisters dying from maternal causes (Graham et al., 1988).

5. It is recognised that the term 'household' is not straightforward, particularly where units of consumption, production, reproduction and socialisation do not necessarily coincide (Roberts, 1991). Here, a local definition is used: the *baade* or *wuro*, equivalent to the largest unit at which regular economic cooperation (herding, cultivating, cooking, eating etc.) takes place.

men (father and sons, brothers, occasionally brothers' sons) and their wives. Thus most households can tolerate some male absence without needing to shift male duties and responsibilities to women. Of the 116 households included in the MRS sample, only eight were left temporarily without men as a result of seasonal migration to cities in 1996, and even here there was little sign of either a change of workload or empowerment for the women involved. Four of the eight units were immediately incorporated into other households – usually the husband's kin. In these new, temporary households, the women only performed tasks which normally fell within the female domain; the male, agro-pastoral work was carried out by men. Far from becoming empowered, the women in their husbands' brothers' households occupied an even lower status position than they did in their own marital homes. Two of the other temporarily manless households remained formally and spatially separate, but cooperated heavily with kin close by. In these cases the husbands' kin took over the productive agro-pastoral labour and economic decisions. The other two households were de facto female-headed households in the first place. Both were effectively run by competent widows in their fifties whose sons, although officially household heads, actually had less control over the management of the households than their mothers. The few cases like these of post-reproductive aged women gaining control of productive resources obviously have little effect on reproductive decision-making.

It is hardly surprising, therefore, that none of the Fulani interviewed had ever used any form of contraception for the purpose of birth control. A few men had used condoms with prostitutes, largely as a result of an AIDS awareness programme, but not as a means of birth control. A large number of Fulani interviewed (particularly women, but many men also) claimed to be completely unaware of the existence of contraceptive methods. While migrants were more likely than non-migrants to have heard of contraception, none thought they were ever likely to use it.

The only possible source of unmet demand for contraception might be among young, unmarried women. However, there are very strong social sanctions against pre-marital fertility. During the period of fieldwork, there was only one case of a never-married woman giving birth. The woman was about twenty-five but unmarried because she suffered from mental retardation. Immediately after the birth she and her family were forced out of the village permanently. Several other members of the village talked about the shame the event had brought on them. Birth rates among never-married women are, therefore, negligible, so it is unlikely that access to birth control would alter their fertility rates substantially.

Induced abortion is, for similar reasons, confined exclusively to young, unmarried women and even then it is extremely rare. Potions for inducing abortion are greatly feared, as it is believed they are so strong that if one woman were to drink some, it might cause all the pregnant women in the village to miscarry. It is clear that a voluntary reduction in fertility, mediated through birth control, is not responsible for the lower fertility observed among the migrating groups of Fulani.

'Modernisation', through contact with urban areas, may undermine certain traditional practices which limit fertility. In several West African societies, prolonged post-partum abstinence is an important constraint on fertility (e.g. Page and Lesthaeghe, 1981). Cleveland (1991) identified the relaxation of the traditional extended post-partum abstinence in Ghana as a result of temporary male migration to cities as a cause of increased fertility in the sending areas. Likewise, any reduction in traditionally extended periods of breastfeeding, due to contact with 'modern' ideas would result in reducing birth intervals and increasing fertility. However, as yet there is no evidence of these sorts of changes in Northern Burkina Faso. Breastfeeding among the Fulani is extended (median length twenty-three months), which has a substantial impact on post-partum infecundity (a population mean of sixteen months using Bongaarts' [1982] model), and thus on fertility. However, no differences are observed between ethnic sub-groups, and there is no evidence whatsoever that extended breastfeeding is being in any way undermined by male contact with urban areas, although it is, of course, possible that this might happen in the future. And while post-partum abstinence is observed, it is too short (usually just the forty days prescribed by Islamic law) to influence fertility, given the practice of extended breastfeeding.

Changes to social institutions: marriage

In societies where fertility outside marriage is very low, the amount of her fecund life that a woman spends in a married state is an important determinant of her fertility: this is the case among the Fulani who have strong sanctions against fertility outside marriage, particularly pre-marital fertility. Changing marriage patterns have been identified by several researchers as an important mechanism through which temporary male out-migration can have an impact on fertility. Timaeus and Graham (1989) found that migrants delayed marriage and were more likely to experience marital dissolution than non-migrants, thus limiting their fertility. Cleveland (1991), on the other hand, found that migrants were able to marry earlier than non-migrants as they were able to overcome bridewealth barriers.

Marriage among the Fulani of Burkina Faso is universal (Figure 5.2), and the economic migration of men has done little to change that. By the age of twenty nearly all women are married. Men always marry too, although rather later on average.

While there are no differences between the ethnic sub-groups in the universality of marriage, there are differences in age at first marriage (Table 5.3). FulBe DjelgoBe men marry significantly earlier on average than any of the other ethnic sub-groups involved in temporary male out-migration. Interviews with migrants suggest that, as found by Timaeus and Graham (1989), some men are delaying marriage for reasons connected with their seasonal migrations to cities.

But, as indicated earlier, there has been no change in the social need for women to marry and begin childbearing as soon as pos-

Figure 5.2. *Proportions Never-Married of Fulani Men and Women by Age Group (SRDS Data)*

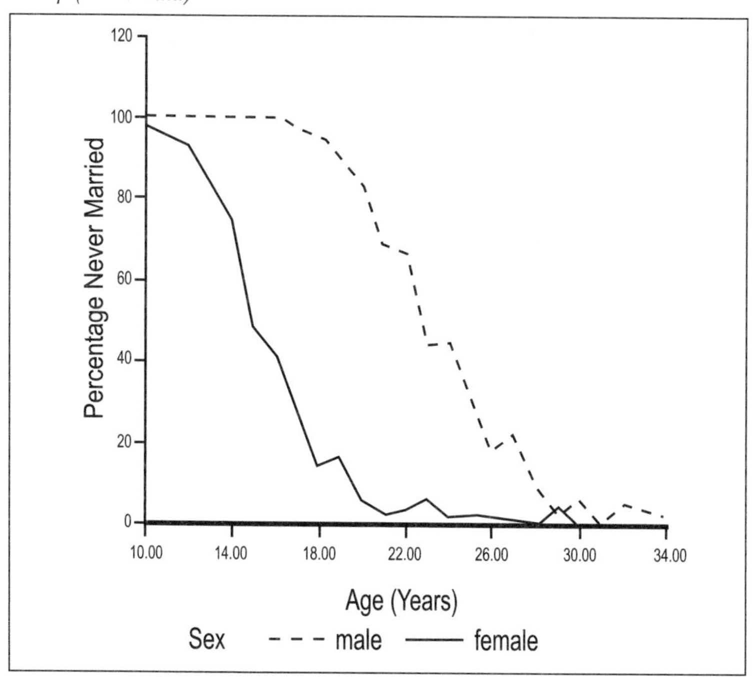

sible. The existence of mild polygyny among the Fulani (7.6 per cent of currently married men and 13.5 per cent of currently married women were in polygynous unions in the 1995 SRDS, mostly involving two wives) decouples any simple relationship between age of marriage for men and that for women, since all the women can be married without all the men needing to be married. Differences in age at marriage among women are very much smaller (Table 5.3) and, if anything, FulBe DjelgoBe women marry slightly later than the other groups (the opposite of the male trend), but the differences are too small to have any significant effect on fertility. The differences in age at marriage mean that FulBe DjelgoBe spouses are, on average, closer together in age. It is possible that this has a positive effect on coital frequency, and thus on fertility, but the data here do not allow such a hypothesis to be tested.

A similar point applies for marriage stability. Marriage among all Fulani groups is relatively unstable, and divorce is accepted as a common part of life. However, analysis of length of marriage by ethnic sub-group and migration status suggests that temporary male out-migration increases the probability of early divorce, supporting the findings of Timaeus and Graham (1989). Interviews with migrants and their wives suggest that long periods of male absence may weaken marriages. It is also possible that male migrants become freer from kin obligations to remain married to close relatives.

However, again, the pressure on women to be married, combined with the flexibility offered by polygyny, means that most women remarry very quickly following the termination of one marriage. Subsequent marriages are less formal than the first and can be arranged rapidly. Median length of the first inter-marital gap (i.e. the time between the end of the first marriage and the start of the second) for women is 1.8 years, with no significant

Table 5.3. *Age at First Marriage of Fulani Men and Women (SRDS Data)*

Ethnic Subgroup	Men		Women	
	Mean age at marriage	N	Mean age at marriage	N
FulBe DjelgoBe	21.2	471	17.1	461
FulBe GaoBe	25.2	953	16.4	867
FulBe Liptaako	25.1	734	15.8	597
RiimaaiBe Liptaako	23.9	518	16.4	461
ALL	24.5	3139	16.3	2795

Note: Indirect estimates of singulate age of first marriage are given (Hajnal, 1953).

differences between sub-groups. (Subsequent gaps may be slightly longer but rarely exceed two or three years.) This is very short in terms of the reproductive lifespan of a woman, so the impact on fertility is small.

So, while there is little doubt that temporary male out-migration is affecting marriage patterns, through men delaying first marriage and through increasing marital instability and mobility, the continuing pressure for women to be married throughout their reproductive years, facilitated by a mildly polygynous marriage system, means that these differences do not translate into very large differences in the proportion of women's reproductive lives spent in the married state, and thus on fertility.

Unsought and unwanted changes in fertility outcomes: spousal separation and sterility

Finally, temporary male migration to cities may have direct effects on fertility that are neither sought nor desired. One consequence of this migration is spousal separation, found to be an important mechanism for depressing the fertility of seasonal labour migrants in both Mexico (Massey and Mullman, 1981) and southern Africa (Timaeus and Graham, 1989).

Over half of married women of reproductive age in the MRS (117/211) were separated from their husbands over the year 1996 for at least one week in any two-month period. The most important single cause of spousal separation was temporary male migration (fifty-seven cases; others included: transhumance, visits, illness and childbirth, which is excluded from calculations because it has no impact on fertility). Given that migration is highly correlated with ethnic sub-group, it is hardly surprising that the mean annual duration of spousal separation for the FulBe DjelgoBe (0.7 months) is significantly less than for the other groups (2.4 months). Interviews with migrants, combined with various regression analyses indicate that men are not timing their migrations to coincide with their wives' infecund periods, so differences in lengths of spousal separation are likely to translate into fertility differences. In practice, however, the proportionate reduction in fertility due to spousal separation between the ethnic sub-groups is small, and the differences between sub-groups are too small to explain much of the observed fertility differentials.

Another possible unwanted consequence of temporary male migration to cities is an increase in sterility rates. A large number of African populations are seriously affected by high sterility: it has been estimated that total fertility in countries such as Cameroon or Gabon might be increased by two or three live births per woman if sterility rates were reduced (Larsen and Menken, 1989, 1991; Larsen 1989, 1994).

A number of sexually transmitted diseases (STDs) are known to lead to reduced fecundity and, ultimately, secondary sterility, particularly gonorrhoea and chlamydia (e.g. Retel-Laurentin, 1979; McFalls and McFalls, 1984; Brunham and Embree, 1992). David and Voas (1981) explain differential fertility among Fulani populations in Cameroon in terms of the higher prevalence of STDs among seasonal migrants. Other research (Bakouan et al., 1991; Painter, 1992; Anarfi, 1993; Garenne et al., 1995) has found migrants to engage in high risk sexual contacts and thus to be more exposed to various STDs than non-migrants. In particular, recent data from Abidjan (Garenne et al., 1995) show a rapid increase in the deaths of young adult Burkinabè men, an increase whose timing ties in with the AIDS epidemic. It seems safe to assume that young migrants are also disproportionately exposed to other STDs.

Sterility is a major source of concern for the Burkinabè Fulani, but problems of sterility are always blamed on women and no explicit connection is made between sexual promiscuity, STDs and sterility. Extra-marital affairs are tolerated among the Fulani as long as they are conducted with discretion. It is widely accepted that seasonal trips to cities offer the best opportunity for extra-marital sex for men. An extensive series of interviews with migrants (in groups and individually) revealed that they virtually all have frequent, unprotected contacts with prostitutes while away (while such accounts are prone to exaggeration in either direction, I believe this general finding to be accurate.) Although many men had heard of condoms, very few claimed ever to use them. Male migration also provides Fulani women with plenty of opportunity for extra-marital sexual contacts. One young woman said: 'While the men are away, they go with other women. Why should we keep our legs closed?' Infidelity of wives is tacitly accepted and tolerated by migrants. Given this information, the hypothesis that STDs, acquired by migrants and passed on to others, are leading to high rates of secondary sterility and subfecundity is certainly plausible.

There is substantial variation in age specific sterility by ethnic sub-group (Figure 5.3). FulBe DjelgoBe have much lower sterility at all age groups than the other FulBe populations, and the levels of DjelgoBe sterility, particularly among the younger age groups of women, differ little from Burundi levels, found to be the lowest of all African populations (Larsen, 1994). RiimaaiBe Liptaako

Figure 5.3. *Age Specific Sterility of Fulani Women (SRDS Data)*

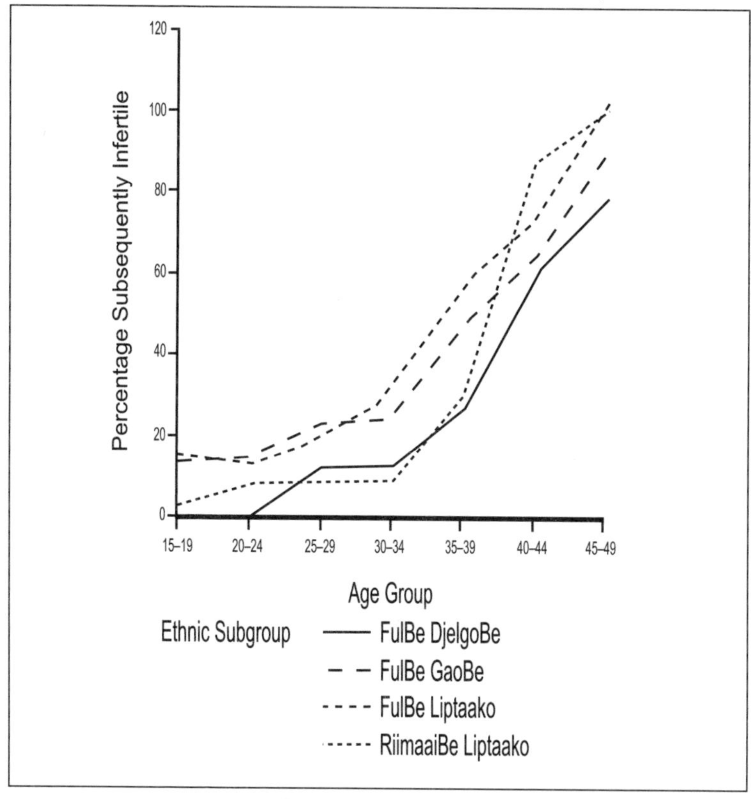

also have low levels of sterility among younger women, although there is a very sharp rise among women over thirty-five compared with the other groups. Sterility is highest overall among the FulBe GaoBe and the FulBe Liptaako.

Unlike spousal separation, differential sterility is large enough to have quite a big impact on the fertility of the sub-groups concerned. Given what is known about the sexual behaviour of migrants and the prevalence of STDs among prostitutes in destination areas (particularly Abidjan), the supposition that the high level of sterility among migrating groups is due to STDs contracted is, although circumstantial without clinical data, not unreasonable.

Summary of the proximate determinants of fertility

It is possible to quantify and summarise all the proximate determinants of fertility discussed (see Table 5.4; for details of the methods used, derived from Bongaarts [1978, 1982], see Hampshire and Randall [2000]). Each separate proximate determinant (C value) represents the *proportion reduction in fertility due to that particular constraint.* For example, the C_m value for the FulBe DjelgoBe is 0.92, so in the absence of constraints imposed by the marriage system, the total fertility of the DjelgoBe would be increased from 9.2 to (9.2/0.92) = 10. Theoretically, c values can be multiplied together to show the combined effect of all the different proximate determinants: these are shown in the column 'product'.

Of the proximate determinants, it is C_i, post-partum infecundity, that has the greatest overall impact on Fulani fertility, but there is little variation between ethnic sub-groups. Marriage exerts a relatively minor impact, and there is little variation between the sub-groups due to polygyny. It is sterility which shows the greatest variation between sub-groups, and in the right direction to explain the observed fertility differences. While the evidence surrounding the causes of sterility remains circumstantial, it is highly likely that it is closely connected with temporary male labour migrants picking up sexually transmitted diseases through unprotected sexual contacts while away. Spousal separation also shows variation in the right direction to explain the fertility differences, but the size of the effect, and of the differences between groups, is too small to explain much of the fertility differentials.

Conclusions

The evidence presented in this chapter suggests that temporary male migration to cities *is* having an impact on the fertility of send-

Table 5.4. *Summary of Proximate Determinants of Fertility by Ethnic Subgroup*

Ethnic Subgroup	C_m	C_i	C_s	C_{st}	C_c	C_a	Product
FulBe DjelgoBe	0.92	0.57	0.98	0.94	1	1	0.48
FulBe GaoBe	0.88	0.58	0.95	0.82	1	1	0.40
FulBe Liptaako	0.94	0.58	0.91	0.77	1	1	0.38
RiimaaiBe Liptaako	0.90	0.57	0.94	0.86	1	1	0.41
ALL	0.90	0.57	0.95	0.84	1	1	0.41

Key: Proximate determinants represent the proportion reduction in fertility due to:

C_m: the marriage system: a proportion of reproductive aged women being unmarried at any one time;

C_i: post-partum infecundity, largely a product of length of breastfeeding;

C_s: spousal separation;

C_{st}: sterility;

C_c: use of contraception;

C_a: induced abortion.

ing groups. However, this is not the result of the sorts of social changes expected: modernisation, changes in power structures and the autonomy of women, changes in social institutions such as marriage etc. There *are* important social changes which have come about as a result of migration, such as shifts in marriage patterns and changes in systems of domestic organisation to accommodate temporarily lone women, but these have not yet led to a re-negotiation of reproductive decision-making. There is still, for both men and women, a strong rationale for high fertility, and the sorts of changes which might alter this have not yet occurred.

Instead, fertility among migrant populations is declining primarily through the unwanted mechanism of increasing sterility. This has several important implications for migrant populations. Firstly, there are obvious health implications of the apparently increasing prevalence of sexually transmitted diseases, particularly if, as seems likely, other STDs are acting as a marker for the transmission of HIV. It is too early to say yet whether HIV will become the catastrophe in West Africa that it has in parts of East Africa, but the data available from Abidjan (Painter, 1992; Garenne et al., 1995) suggest that it might already be posing a threat to some migrant communities.

Secondly, there may be serious economic consequences. Since the major droughts of the 1970s and 1980s, dry season labour migration has become an important way in which people have been able to maintain and increase the security of rural livelihoods. But the success of this migration is dependent on large families: both large households and good extended kin networks. In the absence of these, migration becomes much less successful and often not possible. If sterility rates continue to rise, future generations of migrants, as well as current ones, may be compromised.

Thirdly, there may be detrimental social consequences of increasing sterility in a society where having children is a pre-requisite to becoming a full social being. Where the status and security of women depend largely on their ability to produce children, the gender implications might be serious. Already it is clear that male out-migration has not (at least yet) had the positive impact it has elsewhere on the position and autonomy of women. If anything, women whose husbands migrate become economically disempowered in their new, temporary households. For the moment, the widespread institution of fostering and adoption buffers the problem of childlessness for many women, but if sterility becomes more widespread, it may be increasingly difficult to find children to adopt. Far from the predicted scenario, where male out-migration increases female autonomy and leads to fertility reduction through choice, the reverse may be happening: male out-migration leading directly to undesired fertility reduction through increasing sterility, which, in a society where women are blamed and rejected for childlessness, creates a situation of increased vulnerability for many women.

Of course, the balance of these effects may shift with time. The Fulani have only been migrating to cities in significant numbers for the last twenty-five years and the numbers involved have only increased sharply in recent years. It may be that attitudes take longer to change, especially among those groups, such as women, who are not exposed directly to the urban areas and different ways of life. Certainly it is too early to be overly pessimistic. However, in common with other papers in this volume (Montgomery, Hawkins and Price, Smyth and Harris) it is clear that changes in fertility and reproductive behaviour cannot be understood in isolation from the social and economic context. In particular, it is worth taking note that one should be careful before assuming that a drop in fertility as a result of apparent 'modernisation' is either chosen or desirable.

Note

This research forms part of a collaborative research project, funded by the EU DG XII STD3 Programme (ref 921028), under the direction of Professor Katherine Homewood, involving University College London in collaboration with ISG (University of Amsterdam, IDR (Université de Ouagadougou), IRBET (Ouagadougou) and the Université de Cotonou. Parts of the fieldwork were also funded by the Boise Fund (Oxford University), the Nuffield Small Grants for Social Sciences and the UCL graduate school. I am very grateful to Dr Sara Randall who supervised the research and who read and commented on earlier drafts of this chapter. I also thank Faty Dicko, Bila and Guida for their help in data collection.

CHAPTER 6

Menstruation, Birth Observances and the Couple's Love Amongst the Airo-Pai of Amazonian Peru

Luisa Elvira Belaunde

Fertility regulation amongst contemporary forager-horticulturalist societies is not confined to indigenous methods of pregnancy control isolated from other aspects of people's reproductive lives. A wider conceptualisation of fertility also includes a variety of observances associated, among other things, with menstruation, delivery and post-partum periods. In order to gain a fuller picture of indigenous attitudes to fertility, it is necessary to cover a variety of practices linked to different stages of the reproductive cycle and to draw out their cultural significance. A methodological shift from a female to a couple-centred approach is also required. There is a need to integrate both male and female perspectives into the analysis and assess the implications of different fertility practices for the development of long-lasting sexual and emotional relationships. Ultimately, the study of fertility is inseparable from the cultural construction and expression of emotions between a couple and towards children.

Menstrual and birth observances were once common in forager-horticulturalist populations the world over. Ethno-historical studies show that during the colonial and post-colonial periods western officers and missionaries fiercely opposed local fertility practices. At a later stage, government and economic policies indirectly contributed to their further erosion and disappearance. As a consequence, many traditionally low fertility populations now have high fertility levels (cf. Caldwell and Caldwell, 1987; Berlin, 1995; Bongaarts, 1981; Hern, 1994; Jolly, 1998). In Amazonia a few cultural groups, such as the 400-strong Airo-Pai of North-Eastern Peru, still act according to a reproductive ideal of a few well-spaced children and rely upon a variety of traditional contraceptive techniques to achieve it (Belaunde, 1997). Notwithstanding the importance of indigenous contraception, it is but one aspect of a much wider complex of fertility regulation held by both men and women.

Airo-Pai notions of sexual companionship and parenthood rest upon the long-term involvement of men in their partners' reproductive lives. Well before a woman becomes pregnant, her partner is held responsible for her well-being while she is menstruating. During pregnancy and around the delivery, his daily behaviour has a direct impact upon her and upon the child's health, an Amazonian practice known as couvade (Rivière, 1974; Rival, 1998). Finally, as long as a child is breastfeeding, the father must not jeopardise its growth by making his wife pregnant. There is a continuity of responsibility between menstrual seclusion, couvade and contraception, three ritualised practices by which men actively contribute to the cultural construction of women's bodily processes.

Young people learn to take responsibility for their fertility gradually. As they mature, they often stumble upon conflicts which may either strengthen or destroy their relationships. Fertility practices are therefore key to the long-lasting success of marital partnerships, shared parenthood and the experience of culturally specific emotions (cf. Lutz and Abu-Lughod, 1990; Scordas, 1994; Gow, 1991). In particular, the expressions used by men and women to talk about their feelings during key moments of their reproductive lives are revealing of the strong emotional significance invested in fertility practices. Both the couple's affective tie, and their feelings towards their children, are constituted and manifested by these practices. In agreement with other contributors to this volume (see Hampshire, Hawkins, Russell and Unnithan-Kumar), I argue that the culturally specific meaning and desire for children is a prominent aspect of fertility decisions and experiences.

Fieldwork for this chapter was carried out in 1988–89 in the Airo-Pai community of Huajoya with a population of seventy people. Qualitative research methodology included participant observation, (I lived in peoples' houses, sharing their food and family life), interviews and the recording of narratives and songs. Far from being a pristine forest people, the Airo-Pai have been in contact with westerners since the sixteenth century and have survived a history of political intervention, epidemics of infectious diseases and economic marginalisation (Vickers, 1989:35; Cipolletti, 1988:11; Casanova, 1998:26). Four centuries ago, their ancestors formed part of the highly populated Encabellado nation of Western-Tukanoan speaking peoples. Today, only a few hundred of them remain in the frontier area between Peru, Ecuador and Colombia. Nevertheless, they have a distinct language and cultural identity. In Peru, there are seven communities which are closely linked by kinship and residential movements. They are surrounded by Quichua groups and Spanish-speaking colonists. The bulk of their livelihood is derived from traditional subsistence activities, but most men periodically seek paid employment in local businesses, coca farms and logging centres. Among the aspects of the Quichua and colonists' lifestyles which the Airo-Pai dislike the most are perceived reproductive failures such as the absence of menstrual seclusion for women, large families with many children and short birth spacings, and the maltreatment of young children. These features figure large in some of the arguments advanced by both men and women to discourage intermarriage and to contrast themselves as a distinct cultural group. Reproductive practices thus stand at the core of self-perceived ethnic identity (cf. Hampshire and Hawkins in this volume).

The experience of seclusion

One of the most important aspects of Airo-Pai life was brought home to me soon after my arrival to Huajoya when I had my menstrual period. When I began to menstruate I carried on as usual. One day, as I was taking a bath in the river, several older women came towards me in the water, giggling and talking amongst themselves. 'Are you making *sitsio* (dirt)?' asked one of them. I was not sure what she meant, but the glint in her eye made me guess. 'You must not walk around like that,' she said, 'the men will fall ill. Next time you must let us know.' They were evidently amused at the thought that I should observe their custom, but they were determined to see me doing it. They left me to finish my bath and in the following weeks did not raise the subject again.

A few days later, I noticed that one of the women was secluded in a corner of her home. The floor around her was covered with banana leaves. She was sitting in an old hammock and wearing old clothes. 'I am sad and silent,' she said to me in a high-pitched, plaintive, and yet slightly jocular voice. 'I cannot cook any more. My husband cooks now. I just sit here peacefully, watching what others do.' I observed that her husband was preparing the food. He served it to the rest of the family, but, instead of handing his wife's food to her directly, he poured it into a banana leaf and gave it to a child who took it to her. It all seemed very strange to me because the woman was sitting only a few feet away from her husband. They were talking to each other as usual, but he avoided getting too close to her, or touching anything she had touched. She remained secluded for five days, spending most of the time sitting alone or talking to friends who came in for a visit. On the fifth day, she asked her daughter to warm some water in an old pot and take it to an isolated place down river. The girl took some clean clothes and also collected a big bunch of leaves from the inga tree (*inga edulis*) which grew along the river shore. Her mother left the house through the back door, avoiding the main paths used by men. She sat by the river with her legs stretched in front of her rubbing her body and hair energetically with wet inga leaves. Then she poured warm water over herself, stood up, took a short bath in the river and put on clean clothes. On the way home, she picked a handful of leaves from hueoco (unidentified) bushes and chewed them. A few minutes later her teeth and lips were covered with the black juice of the leaves. Ornamented with this natural black lipstick, she looked rather different from the person who was lying in a corner of the house minutes ago. 'I am rejoicing now,' she said to me, 'I have thrown away the dirt.' She resumed her domestic tasks and released her husband, who returned to his own work.

I was secretly hoping the women had forgotten about my periods, but they soon showed that they were keeping a good record on me. One night after dinner, when people were setting their mosquito nets to sleep, Eugenia, the lady with whom I was lodging, called me to her doorstep. She pointed to the moon in the sky and said 'you will soon be making dirt'. She was using the moon as a calendar, and like everybody else in the community she knew perfectly well when my next period was due.

I confess that I did not enjoy the experience of menstrual confinement and found it hard to sit on banana leaves for five days. One of my most striking memories, however, is people's concern for my mood and appetite. During the day, I was often left alone at home. 'Sit still here waiting for us, watching the house,' Eugenia would tell me before she took off for her garden. When she returned two or three hours later, she would smile at me and ask, 'Are you feeling sad and lonely all on your own?' She would then prepare a fresh drink of sweet plantain and corn and serve it to me in a banana leaf. When she was working far away, she would send a child to bring me food and to keep me company. I was very grateful, for the days I spent sitting in my corner were interminable.

I also found it strange to find myself at the centre of attention because of my periods. Both men and women were evidently delighted to see me obeying their ancestral custom and, as they were passing my house would exclaim: 'So, you are making dirt!' The headman let me know of his approval and explained with a smile on his face, 'In this way, people live well. If the woman walks around when she is making dirt, she does not know how to behave properly and becomes an angry person. We men get headaches, we fall ill and we cannot work any more.' People's attitude towards me helped me realise that the state of a menstruating woman is a matter of public interest. It is openly discussed by everyone and affects all the activities of her household and in the community.

Menstrual symbolism and practices

In *Blood Magic*, Buckley and Gottlieb (1988:51) critically assess previous anthropological approaches to menstrual symbolism which narrowly focus on notions of female pollution and subordination to men. The authors demonstrate that 'the significance and value of menstruation in any given culture must be determined *in situ* and cannot be ascribed on the basis of an a priori scheme'. Menstrual ideas and practices do not exist in isolation but rather occur within religious, political and reproductive contexts. Thus situated within a wider framework, they manifest culturally specific understandings of female creativity, health, leisure, gender relations and empowerment. Attitudes towards menstruation are not merely abstract symbols but part of people's lives, affecting their relationships and emotions. The same applies to the Airo-Pai symbolism and practices.

The religious basis of Airo-Pai menstrual ideas is inscribed in their mythology and cosmology. Menstruation is loaded with ambivalent values and a myriad of meanings which reflect the full complexity of Airo-Pai understanding of the relationship between spirits and people. In mythical times, menstruation originated when the highest divinity, Moon, had sexual intercourse with his wives and by this rendered them capable of procreation. Each month when a woman menstruates people say that she 'sees the moon', as in the myth. For this reason the Airo-Pai refer to Moon as 'our father' (*mai jaquë*), indicating that the god is the first to render all women fertile by bringing about their menses. The flow of menstrual blood is conceived as a cyclical purge of body 'dirt' which is a prerequisite to bearing a child, and like all forms of purging, is seen as highly beneficial.

Nevertheless, menstrual blood is abhorred by Moon and the other divinities, who are said to be fundamentally angry at it and to refuse any rapport with women whilst they are menstruating (cf. Payaguaje, 1990:15; Cipolletti, 1988:64; Bellier, 1991:157; Langdon, 1974:97). Menstrual taboos are generally expressed in terms of the fear people feel at the divinities' fury at menstrual blood. Typically, both men and women say that they feel 'fear of anger (*cadaye*)' at the thought of transgressing menstrual restrictions. Menstrual blood is also said to attract blood-feeding spirits which inhabit the other world and are harbingers of death amongst humans. Since menstruating women are perceived as, on the one hand, in need of protection from harmful spirits, and, on the other hand, as possessing the potential to arouse divine wrath, women of a reproductive age are discouraged from practising shamanism, which is conceived as a means of communicating with both divinities and spirits. Men, who are ritually initiated to shamanism as part of their puberty rites, are also expected to refrain from physical contact with menstrual blood which will contaminate them with a specific illness. Their heads would suffer, they explain, because the head is the bodily site of shamanic visions and other-worldly communication. Menstruation thus ruins a shaman's capabilities. Minor contamination causes headaches in men, but more serious contact causes severe nose-bleeding and even death by haemorrhage.

When a woman menstruates she is also considered to be vulnerable to character failures, such as irritability. Women who break their menstrual seclusion are associated with the red deer (*mazama americana*). This solitary and nocturnal animal has scum in the mouth and 'jumps from one side to the other, going nowhere', they explain. Similarly, a restless woman 'talks too fast', criticising others and alienating her spouse and relatives. During her menstrual seclusion, a woman is encouraged to remain sitting still inside the house so as to protect herself from all bad influences. Physical tranquillity is conceived as the best prophylactic against any possible harm, both physical and moral.

In remaining secluded, women also protect their husbands' health and capability as shamans. Generally people are rather strict in their observances. Nevertheless, during my fieldwork, men regularly complained they had headaches and claimed they had been contaminated with menstrual blood. 'I hear a jaguar roaring in my head,' explained Eugenia's husband one day, 'I have been sitting too close to my wife and now my head is aching. Give me a tablet.' To my surprise, I learnt that aspirin was an appropriate medicine for minor exposures to blood. Major contamination, it was explained, requires shamanic treatment.

The complex menstrual symbolism I have only briefly sketched above sustains the ritual celebration of female puberty at the onset of the first menses and the monthly practice of menstrual confinement. Whilst the rites of the first menses are key to the achievement of womanhood in Amazonian, as in other parts of the world (cf. Lutkehaus and Roscoe, 1995), women's monthly seclusion is a less dramatic but equally important routine.

Monthly seclusions alter the rhythm of daily life and bring about changes in the division of labour. Long-term gender relations and emotions are thus brought into play. Each time she menstruates, a woman interrupts her daily chores, rests and remains at the receiving end. She is fed and looked after by others. If she has an unmarried daughter who is not menstruating, her daughter cooks for her, otherwise her husband cooks and does the housework. There is no shame in this for a man. Quite the reverse, men are particularly proud of their cooking skills, although their recipes are less elaborate than their wives' and they rarely bake manioc bread. Since they have little time left for hunting in remote places, they catch small fish in the nearby rivers. Even when hunting, they avoid killing big prey because it is thought that the animal's bleeding could cause menstruating women to haemorrhage.

Even though women are discharged of their usual responsibilities, they do not emphasise the positive aspects of their leisure, but rather their feelings of sorrow, loneliness and hunger. During the rest of the month, they take snacks at any time and have complete control over food distribution. Therefore, they deeply dislike being left alone at home, unable to feed themselves and dependent on others. At the same time, they regard their husbands' acts of care as concrete manifestations of love and are always deeply moved when they speak of them. 'My husband cooks for me when I am alone on my own,' explained Eugenia, 'he looks after me well.' This type of statement is a characteristic expression of marital love. Women stress their own vulnerability and their husbands' devoted bestowal of care.

Pregnancy and couvade observances

Like menstruation, pregnancy also extends to a woman's partner. The creation of a foetus is a long process which is thought to require repeated sexual intercourse to accumulate sufficient amounts of male and female sexual fluids (Belaunde, 1994:103). As is the case amongst other Amazonian groups, repeated sexual intercourse is needed to 'make a child', as they say. Fidelity is encouraged for both genders, but it is not uncommon for women to have sexual access to their husband's brothers, and vice-versa. Nevertheless, unlike some groups, the Airo-Pai do not generally acknowledge multiple paternities in the making of a child's body. Children are said to be the offspring of one man, usually the mother's husband (cf. Bellier, 1991:193; Lagrou, 1998:71; Pauli, 1999:193; Vickers, 1989:220).

Pregnancy is acknowledged around the third month, when it shows a little and the woman's appetite is 'spoiled', they explain. From that moment onwards, the expecting couple and their young children eat from separate dishes lest the pains of pregnancy be passed on to others, particularly the elderly and the sick. Since a pregnant woman can cook only for herself and her husband, she cannot take part in the mutual exchanges of cooked food which typically take place between the women of the community before each meal.

During pregnancy, both parents are subjected to a series of dietary and physical restrictions which highlight the existence of a bond of substance between parents and child. In particular, the father's behaviour is said to affect the well-being of both the mother and the child. His responsibility becomes particularly important towards, during and after the delivery. For instance, he should not build any structures or tie strong knots, nor should he bathe in the river against the water current because this could cause delivery problems. He should not use fish poison, because the mother's milk would dry out. He should not kill or eat certain animals, such as the peccary, which might contaminate the child with parasites, or the boa or jaguar which might take spiritual vengeance. He should avoid making loud noises, digging big holes or kicking things vigorously, lest the baby becomes unsettled and jumpy and cries angrily. During the delivery and the following days, the father should cease working entirely and remain still in his hammock with a necklace of bells by his head. Men do not mimic the birth. Rather, like women during their menses, they are required to remain still in order to prevent any possible harm, protect the mother from haemorrhages and the newborn from wasting away with colic, diarrhoea and incessant crying. As an informant explained: 'It is better to take precautions than to cause the death of children.' (Payaguaje, 1990:89).

Men do not help during childbirth because they fear contamination by the mother's blood which is equated with 'dirt' and menstruation. A woman gives birth outside the settlement, in her garden, alone or with the help of a female relative. If experienced, she cuts the umbilical cord herself and buries the placenta on the birth spot. During and after childbirth, she remains in a hut in the garden until the post-partum bleeding stops. After a few days of rest, her husband is expected to take on all household tasks and provide his wife with safe food. This is food which is bland in taste and is made with vegetables such as cooked plantains and flesh from animals which are considered to have little blood such as larvae (*calandra palmarum*) and small fish (*astronotus ocellatus*). The husband fetches and prepares the food but sends a child or a female relative to take it to his wife. Women are particularly moved by the memory of the time spent alone with a newborn baby. Their husbands' provision of a diet of small fish, which is considered a delicacy, brings about a heightened awareness of their own vulnerability and their husbands' bestowal of care and expression of love towards themselves and their babies.

The couple interrupt most post-partum restrictions after three vomiting sessions, which take place when the baby's umbilical has fallen. Both parents, and all those who live in close contact with them, take part in these early morning vomiting sessions which are induced with *mañapë* roots (unidentified). It is said to clean their stomachs of the 'dirt' accumulated during pregnancy. As we can see, husband and wife act together throughout gestation and birth and they involve the rest of the community in the process.

Birth spacing

As long as the child is breastfeeding, both spouses are expected to maintain sexual abstinence to avoid another pregnancy and to spiritually protect the child's growth. Children are breastfed for a year or so, until they start to walk. It is understood that when a woman becomes pregnant again her milk turns bad and the baby must be weaned and consequently may suffer malnutrition and die. Repeated pregnancies are also detrimental to the mother who becomes exhausted, loses weight and wastes away. Men are held responsible for any unwanted pregnancies. The consensual practice of contraception based on sexual abstinence is key to the couple's family planning and long lasting union. A man's love for his wife, expressed verbally as 'looking after' her, is effectively manifested in his controlled sexuality (see Belaunde, 1997 for an in-depth study of Airo-Pai contraception).

Men and women have explicit ideas about family size and spacing. They say that the ideal number of children is three and that a woman should not become pregnant until her last child is capable of eating and moving around independently (cf. Vickers, 1989:224). Long birth spacings are necessary to provide an adequate upbringing for young children, who are bestowed with the undivided attention of their parents. Closely spaced children are said to suffer, cry and develop angry characters. Birth spacing is therefore required both to secure the good health of the mother and child and to provide an appropriate environment for childrens' social and affective development.

In spite of growing pressure from surrounding Quichua and Spanish-speaking populations, amongst whom many and closely spaced children are the norm, most Airo-Pai couples practise birth control. Very few women have more than five children, and birth spacing is generally longer than three years. Such a collective decision to hold on to their fertility observances reflects the Airo-Pai's desire to perpetuate the very roots of their self-perceived cultural and ethnic identity. If they were to adopt their neighbours' ways, they would quite simply cease to be Airo-Pai and become either Quichua or colonists, they explain. This would also deeply affect, according to them, the affection shared by spouses and the emotional growth of children.

Neglecting one's spouse

Neglect of their spouse's needs during menstruation and other critical moments, whether by men or by women, is seen as a clear sign of a lack of interest in the relationship. Neglect of pregnancy and birth observances have even more drastic consequences, for they often entail the death of the child. Pregnancy during lactation often ends in the baby's death by malnutrition, and neglect of couvade may end in infanticide. Although I did not come across any cases, women say that if a man does not acknowledge his paternity by obeying pregnancy observances, the mother may provoke an abortion or kill the baby at birth. Women explain that unhappy mothers act out of anger because the father's neglect means that he wishes the child dead.

Nevertheless, marital problems due to perceived neglect on the part of either spouse are common, especially amongst young people before they have children. Women, in particular, explain that when newly married they were often uncomfortable and sad because they felt their husbands were unwilling to provide food for them, build a new house and spend time with them. There is a recurrent pattern in young people's life episodes. Usually, one or the other spouse decides to return to his or her parents' home. After a time away, which can be a few days or a few months, some young people return to their spouse. Others separate for good. The incidence of separations due to this form of neglect or other incompatibilities between spouses is very high. In the community of Huajoya, for example, out of forty-four adults, thirty-one had been separated at least once and then married somebody else with whom they remained and had children.

Sometimes marital problems occur after the birth of a child, as I observed during my fieldwork. A couple who had a year-old baby broke up publicly during a manioc drinking party. The husband, who slept in his wife's parents house, took away his mosquito net and bedding. Although he was the one to leave, she complained that he had 'thrown her away', because, she said, he did not provide for her and her daughter. She angrily complained that her baby would be cold at night and soon die. In typical Airo-Pai manner the young man's mother attributed his behaviour to his immaturity. 'My son does not know how to think yet,' she lamented. In the end he returned to his wife's house, explaining that he wished to raise his child and see her grow up. On the eve of the reunion, everybody kept off the river shore while the couple bathed together as a public manifestation of their decision to remain together. The following week, they left for a hunting expedition and returned with timber and materials to build their own home.

Conclusion

Menstruation, couvade and birth spacing are inseparable aspects of Airo-Pai fertility regulation. It could be argued that the general idea emerging from this chapter is that these practices restrict and render women dependent upon men. I agree, but this is only part of the picture. The reverse side of women's culturally constructed vulnerability is men's responsibility for, and active participation in, women's fertility processes. An anthropological examination of women's autonomy narrowly understood as lack of dependence on others would preclude an understanding of how both genders manage their reproductive lives together (cf. Rao, 1998:9).

Overing (1986:141) argues that gender analysis often hides a catch-22 and assumes that '... male obligations give men status and female obligations constrain women'. With this pitfall in mind, I take my cue from my Airo-Pai informants and suggest that these cultural practices are equally constraining on both genders and their aim is not to maintain women's subordination but to foster the couple's love and the well-being of their children. As Gow (1991:121) has demonstrated for the Piro, the language of helplessness and vulnerability is key to Amazonian constructions of affection and kinship. Long-lasting bonds of love are conceived as resulting from cumulative acts of feeding and the bestowal of care, especially towards young children who are regarded as particularly vulnerable. The relationship of marriage, he argues, allows the spouses to satisfy each other's desires for food, objects and sex, and to engage in relations of caring through the making and feeding of children. Amongst the Airo-Pai, caring and the language of vulnerability extends to the spouses, especially during key periods of their reproductive life when their shared desire for children binds the couple together. Like Hampshire, Hawkins, Russel, Unnitham and Zahida in this book, the Airo-Pai case shows the critical importance of a culturally specific desire for children in fertility decisions.

Another theme to emerge from the Airo-Pai ethnography is the fine line existing between indigenous understandings of love and anger in association with fertility practices. Menstrual blood, the first source of fertility, is perceived as arousing divine anger and endangering women, who become irritable if they transgress their menstrual seclusion. Similarly, newborn babies cry angrily if minor couvade restrictions are not properly followed by their fathers. They grow up to be irate individuals if they are born too close together and are unable to receive individualised attention. Finally, neglect of fertility practices by either spouse results in the angry break up of the couple. Such a prevalence of anger should be understood with relation to the close association existing between death and anger amongst Amazonia peoples (cf. Belaunde, 2000; Ellis, 1997:107; Lagrou, 1998:197). Whilst the observance of fertility practices feeds the couple's love and parenting, the anger attached to their transgression prefigures the conflicts and death of children this may bring about.

A critique of demographic theory emerges from the Airo-Pai material and complements the alternative theoretical and methodological views put forward in this book. Demographic transition theory tends to assume that modernisation means a shift from natural to controlled fertility (Henry, 1961). This approach leaves little room to societies such as the Airo-Pai and other Amazonian groups (cf. Hern, 1994) amongst whom integration into the national society implies the abandonment of fertility regulations. Although currently the official policy of the Peruvian state promotes modern reproductive health and family planning, this policy has little influence upon remote communities in the Amazon. As shown by other contributors to this book, reproductive changes in multi-ethnic areas do not respond to central planning but rather to processes of inter-ethnic communication, inter-marriage and changing cultural identities. Understanding changing reproductive trends at the local level requires an examination of the collective and personal motivations sustaining not just contraception, but all significant fertility practices, including menstruation, couvade and post-partum observances.

Carter (1995:60) has argued that the distinction drawn in demographic theory between natural and controlled fertility ultimately rests upon the contrast between culture and agency, which he shows also reproduce deeply embedded presuppositions about the uniqueness of modern societies. In demographic theory, premodern societies are characterised by natural fertility because fertility regulations, when they exist, are specified by taboos. Allegedly, in this context fertility is channelled by unchallenged cultural norms rather than individuals' motivation, choice and agency. By contrast, in modern societies the practice of controlled fertility rests upon the active decision-making of individuals rather than cultural rules. Following Carter, I argue that this dualistic framework hinders rather than illuminates an understanding of reproductive behaviour in both so-called premodern and modern societies. The status of agent, and what constitutes a decision, is always culturally produced (cf. Rao, 1998:6). The notion of the rational economically-minded decision maker is as restrictive to a study of reproductive behaviour in modern societies as the idea of the overpowering culturally ruled community is to the Airo-Pai (cf. Russell, Price, Hawkins and Unnithan-Kumar in this volume). In both cases issues of personal choice are inextricable from the complex inter-play of cultural considerations, inter-personal relations and emotions.

Acknowledgements

I am extremely grateful to the people of Huajoya who received me generously and helped me with my research. I hope that this paper is a faithful translation of their ideas.

CHAPTER 7

Looking for a Child: Coping with Infertility in Ado-Odo, South-Western Nigeria

Andrea Cornwall

> If you have money but have not given birth to a child you have done nothing
>
> – Yoruba proverb

Having children is so central a part of women's and men's lives, identities and relationships in south-western Nigeria that no one would choose to be childless. For those who are unable to bear children of their own, everyday struggles become all the more difficult and peace of mind is ever more elusive. Marriages flounder, rocked by pressure from relatives to produce offspring; intimate relationships remain fragile and uncertain without the anchor of co-parenthood. For men, the failure to become a father is barely imaginable. For women, impaired fertility eats into their energy, money and peace. Some move from healer to prophet to herbalist to hospital, desperately seeking some resolution, driven by hope and despair. Some seek new partners, hoping that the next relationship will prove to be the one that can give them a child. And others simply remain and endure, while their husbands take new wives whose fecundity becomes a boast that makes the pain of infertility all the more searing.

Yet while infertility can have devastating consequences in a cultural context where children are so desired and cherished, women who are unable to conceive or carry a child of their own to term are rarely totally bereft of children. Their experiences, I suggest in this chapter, offer important insights into the relational dimensions of reproduction and to what it means to be a mother. It is with these experiences that this chapter is concerned. In it, I draw a distinction between mothering, motherhood and being a mother.

Mother*ing*, I suggest here, constitutes a cluster of social practices in which virtually all women, irrespective of their fertility, engage in at some stage in their lives. Mother*hood* is both an experiential state and a social status. In this context, it is tied not only to having borne children, but to having brought into the world children who survive to adulthood. The appellation 'mother of many children' denotes an esteemed social identity in itself, irrespective of whether or not these children are raised by the woman who gave birth to them. 'Mother' is a relational identity, one that is used idiomatically to describe relations of dependency, care and guidance in other spheres, and one that can come to denote relationships between women and the children of others. But it retains a particular salience in binding a woman to a man and his kin. Only by becoming a mother is a woman regarded as a 'wife' by a man's family; only through biological reproduction are ties created between a man and a woman that provide a semblance of security, and the possibilities of maintenance. A man's love for his wife, many women told me, was often expressed most directly through the way he treated the children they had together, affirming the bond between them as mother and father.

In this chapter, I address these different dimensions and explore the strategies and tactics that women who experience impaired fertility may draw upon to recoup identities as mothers. My focus is on the social and experiential dimensions of infertility, rather than on its perceived causes and treatment options for impaired fertility, which I discuss elsewhere (Cornwall, 1996). I begin by setting infertility in the broader context of reproduction, parenting and parental identities in Ado-Odo, a small town in the South-Western corner of Nigeria. I go on to explore in more detail the relational implications of being unable to bear a child. My focus is primarily on women's experiences of infertility. This is less a deliberate choice than a consequence of the fact that while I knew dozens of women who had experienced primary or secondary infertility, I knew of only one man – and he was disabled. As I go on to discuss, the very possibility of male infertility is so disruptive to men's sense of themselves, it is barely possible for them to countenance it. Yet, as I suggest here, men's reactions to the experiences of wives who look for a child are significant in other ways.

Situating infertility

Children play a major part in the constellation of factors that make a good life in Ado-Odo, a small town of around 30,000 people in the agricultural hinterland of metropolitan Lagos. The struggle to support children and to educate them well occupies the energies of many townsfolk. Trade, farming and the processing of farm products dominate the town's economy, alongside a range of service professions catering for local demand. Almost every trade has an association, and almost everyone belongs to some kind of informal organisation where mutual support can be sought. Dozens of religious institutions co-exist with little friction in a population that is about equally Muslim and Christian, with a few, mainly older, followers of Yoruba indigenous religion. Herbalists and healers of all religious persuasions are scattered throughout the town, and serve as the principal source of assistance to women and men who experience sexual and reproductive health problems. Children are at the heart of everyday life in the town, part of every domain of social life; a concern with having and sustaining children permeates almost all of the town's social institutions.

What, then, of those who are unable to bear children of their own? As Okonofua et al. (1997a) point out, the social dimensions of infertility are a sorely neglected subject in an already sparse literature. Given policy concerns with high fertility, it is perhaps not surprising that within the substantial demographic literature on south-western Nigeria so little attention has been paid to women's struggles to have children. Yet infertility is widely regarded as one of the most pressing problems faced by Nigerian women (Okonofua et al., 1997a). Substantial numbers of women and men in this region suffer some degree of infertility, with estimates ranging up to almost a third of the female population (Caldwell and Caldwell, 1983; Okonofua et al., 1997a).[1] Sub-fertility has long been of concern in

1. There are no reliable recent figures on the incidence of infertility in the Ado area. Data from other parts of the country tends to converge on combined primary and secondary infertility rates of around 30 per cent (Okonofua et al., 1997a). The authors of the 1991 WHO report on infertility note the difficulties in accurately assessing primary infertility in particular, pointing to the incidence of under-reporting in the data and suggesting that fosterage and adoption practices may mask actual numbers. As I go on to note, this would certainly be the case were a demographic survey to be conducted in Ado.

Ado, and the area immediately around Ado has been highlighted as a region of relatively low fertility (Retel-Laurentin, 1974; Caldwell and Caldwell, 1983). In a small demographic survey conducted in one quarter of the town, I discovered that almost half the women aged 40 and over in my sample had three or fewer children, 9 per cent had only one child and 9 per cent had no children at all.[2] Given a relatively high rate of divorce and separation it would be problematic to infer fertility problems in every case. In a context where fertility continues to be valued, however, these findings do indicate levels of sub-fertility and infertility that are worrying.[3]

Epidemiological studies have drawn attention to the relatively high incidence of gonorrhoea in the southern Nigerian population, the prevalence of reproductive tract infections and their association with impaired fertility (Adekunle and Ladipo, 1992; Okonofua et al., 1995, 1997b).[4] Significantly, healers and ordinary people alike generally failed to associate many of the conditions that are considered to be causes of infertility with sexually transmitted disease of any kind, and few draw links between gonorrhoea and subsequent fertility problems in women.[5] While younger women might be suspected of having 'spoiled their insides' by having abortions, most infertile women remain the objects of blameless pity.[6] More often, causation is attrib-

2. These data are presented with the following reservations. First, the size of the sample is very small, consisting of only 109 women. Secondly, due to the extreme insensitivity of directly asking women whom my assistant, Dorcas Odu, and I suspected not to have any children of their own directly, we used a variety of questions to determine whether a woman had children and how many she had. In some cases, we also asked neighbours whom we knew well, to triangulate these women's answers. While I think this improved the quality of the data, it may also have led to inaccuracies. Conducting such a survey after a year of close acquaintance with many people in the sample, however, certainly improved my feel for potential inaccuracy.
3. Ideal family size in Ado is roughly between 4–6 children. Asking about ideal family size, however, often produces the 'it's up to God' response that Lockwood (1989) reports from surveys elsewhere (see also Caldwell, 1976). It would be rare for women to choose to have less than four children.
4. See also Frank (1983) and Meheus et al. (1986) for comparative African data.
5. Space precludes a fuller discussion of the medical anthropological aspects of the categorisation and treatment of conditions associated with infertility. What is, however, significant is the high proportion of cases dealt with by healers of all persuasions that related to infertility, and considerable diagnostic variance between them (see also Buckley, 1985; Erwin, 1993).
6. Anecdotal evidence would suggest relatively high abortion rates amongst younger women in Ado; in a self-completed, anonymous survey conducted amongst 100 school-age youth, 26 per cent of women reported having had an abortion (Cornwall, 1996). Although rates are difficult to estimate see

uted to the malevolent intentions of others – especially co-wives, but also members of a woman's own family – and thus separated almost completely from any suggestion either that it may be the man's problem, or that he may be implicated in any way in having brought about a woman's infertility by his sexual behaviour.

Clinical work would suggest that in cases of infertility, almost half of the time the problem lies with the man.[7] Although *ato idomi*, watery sperm, is recognised as a possible cause of infertility, in most cases the presumption is that a failure to conceive is a woman's problem, and that she is the one who needs to do something about it. Men's families, and particularly their mothers and sisters, are quick to reject wives who fail to reproduce and to encourage sons to find another woman. 'There's no marriage without a child', people in Ado say. Most contemporary marriages begin with pregnancy, and few last in the absence of children. Claims can be made on a man, and on his family, once there is a child; a child creates ties that bind. Irrespective of whether or not they cohabit, women remain 'wives' to the families of their husbands once they have children and can continue to maintain relationships of co-parenthood with men long after divorce or separation. Women who are unable to bear children are often placed in a doubly fragile position: neither are they recognised as wives within men's families, nor do they have any security in their relationships with men (cf. Brandon, 1990). A wife without children lives in fear of the day her husband might bring home a pregnant second wife, or the day her husband's family persuades him to send her away. A wife without sons fears for her future, as well as for her present.

Okonofua and Ilumoka (1991) for comparative data on Nigeria. Abortion certainly accounts for a proportion of infertility cases, especially where it is self-procured and results in sepsis, and the risk to fertility and indeed of mortality from unsafe abortion remains high (ibid., 1991). See Renne (1996) on attitudes to and methods of abortion in Ekiti, which are very similar to those used in Ado.

7. Alemnji and Thomas (1997), for example, found that around half of the men in a study of couples with infertility were infertile (46 per cent primary infertility, 54 per cent secondary infertility). The higher levels of secondary infertility were related to the incidence of infection. Other studies confirm higher levels of infection-related infertility in men than amongst other populations (see, for example, Ogunbanjo et al., 1989). The implications for HIV transmission are beyond the scope of this paper, but would indicate the usefulness of a strategy focusing on prevention of *infertility* as a route to increasing condom use amongst men in HIV prevention.

Experiences of infertility

Writers on infertility in south-western Nigeria have portrayed infertile women as figures ostracised by others in the community, set apart from the flow of everyday social life and often stereotyped as 'witches' (Morton-Williams, 1956; Caldwell and Caldwell, 1983; Okonofua et al., 1997a). Caldwell (1976), for example, reports a survey that sought to quantify responses to questions like 'a woman who has not given birth to a child may as well never have been born'. The answers indicate that the vast majority of people agreed. Indeed, the picture that is painted is so bleak that I wondered when I first read about the subject how such women survive at all. Yet the realities of living without any children of one's own are rarely described in the literature.

In Ado I came to know a number of women who were unable to bear a child. At first, they were not easy to identify. Most failed to match up to the picture painted in the literature. Some had children around them who called them 'mother' and appeared to be, to all intents and purposes, their own children. Several were very popular and gregarious people, a far cry from the image of sour, crabbed women with lives indelibly scarred by the failure to do what every woman should do. Some had succeeded in business and had brought up foster children in the process, for whom they had catered as any mother might. Older women would tell me of how these children would send them money and look after their needs; while I knew women with adult sons who would mutter about being neglected, and quietly confide in me that their sons gave them no support at all. I also came to know many women who searched for children, some of whom suffered strings of miscarriages and others who went years without conceiving, seeking in increasing desperation any form of treatment they could find. Others had moved through a series of relationships, looking for the man who could give them a child.

Infertility is rarely talked about openly. There is no Yoruba term that describes a man who is potent but infertile. The term that is used is *okobo*, glossed as impotent, a word laden with shame. Healers thrive on treatments for a 'weak or dead organ'. I rarely heard the term for a woman who suffers primary infertility, *agan*, used: it is one that carries pain, as well as shame, and would be whispered in private rather than used to describe someone in public. Herbalists, healers and prophets would spend hours telling me about sexual and reproductive health problems. But women were guarded about these matters, which were never the topic of the conversations I would have with groups of women about sex, men and other intimate issues. It is considered rude in the extreme to ask a woman how many children she has, for fear that she has none; raising the subject, without invitation, of a woman's experiences of infertility would be seen as callous. But, over time, women came to tell me their stories as they told me about their lives.

As I came to know more and more women who had experienced reproductive difficulties, I began to realise that it was only those women who had nothing else going for them who seemed to be set apart. The ways in which people related to women who had no children of their own seemed to depend on their conduct and status. People would sometimes say how popular a certain woman was, adding that she had no child of her own. Indeed, one of the infertile women I came to know well held high ranking positions in the mosque and the market, and was universally liked. The perceived cause of childlessness among these women was only remarked upon when suspicious incidents gave rise to speculation about ulterior motives.[8] For most of my time in Ado, I shared a house with a woman who was constantly trying to become pregnant. Her own grief and anxiety was barely ever on show, but her absence at family occasions and her treatment by her husband's kin gave me insights into experiences shared by other women, no matter how successful and popular they were.

Here, then, were women who managed to make do despite having no children of their own. And, having managed to cope with their situation, they were both admired and also sympathised with, and very rarely ostracised. Rather than being excluded by others, some actively excluded themselves from occasions such as family gatherings. This was explained to me in terms of the pain they would suffer at seeing others with their own children, that they would feel sad and lonely – not that others would not want them there. Here too were women who desperately searched for a child, spending every last penny they could find on treatments, leaving relationships, doing whatever they could to find a way of becoming pregnant before their time ran out. Hearing their stories, and situating these women within the domains of association in which women cluster in Ado, made me all the more aware of issues of contingency and agency. It impressed upon me the importance of not simply taking reproduction for granted, and of looking more closely at the strategies and tactics that women make recourse to in their quest for

8. In eighteen months of ethnographic fieldwork, I only once came across of an infertile woman who was ostracised on suspicion of having used *aje*, 'witchcraft', after a string of deaths in the family.

money, children and peace of mind (Cornwall, 1996). It also threw into sharper relief what it means to be and become a parent. It is to this that I now turn.

Being a father, becoming a mother

Fatherhood exists almost independently of any engagement with, or even maintenance of, a child. Simply by having impregnated a woman, a man becomes a father – and remains 'the owner of the child', irrespective of whether he makes any contribution to the child's upkeep. Men retain entitlements to children they have fathered that they can activate at any time; and through children who are publicly acknowledged as a man's offspring, women are able to make claims on men as the fathers-of-their-children. A child without a recognised father is stigmatised and bullied, and can turn against its mother in anger and shame. Having a father, then, is as important for children as having children is for men, whether or not the two have any contact.

Once men have had a cluster of children, they are secure in their identities as men. Several men who talked to me about the experiences of wives they had married who failed to have children spoke of how important it was for the woman to become pregnant. Some had gone to considerable lengths, and great expense, to seek treatment for the woman. It seemed that this was more to secure the child that would make their wives happy, and make them stay, than because they themselves wanted more children. Pressure on men to become fathers can be extreme. As I go on to illustrate, relatives can deploy various strategies to try to force the issue if a man holds on to an apparently infertile wife.

Fathering is something that was not often spoken about and men often play a relatively minor role in the everyday lives of children. The significance of fathers, it seems, lies in who they are, rather than what they do for their children. And the 'benefits' men enjoy are not necessarily the 'intergenerational wealth flows' Caldwell (1976) talks of – as several men pointed out to me, mothers are the ones to whom children usually pay most attention to as they grow older – but reside in other, less tangible, attributes that come from occupying the subject position 'father'. A father who can boast of many children pursuing important careers can gain both status and satisfaction. One elderly chief, for example, used to tell me about his wives in terms of the 'fruits' they had borne him: daughters and sons in whose glory he basked, and whose achievements became his own success story.

Women too benefit from being known to be mothers, and, as I suggested earlier, the linkages with men and their families that come about by virtue of being a mother to a man's children are in themselves potential sources of support (see Guyer, 1994; O'Laughlin, 1995). Yet while motherhood offers an ascribed status, when children talked of their mothers, they spoke about the things they *did* for them: about the practice of mothering. Akanmi, in his forties, told me: 'We usually love our mothers more than the fathers. Fathers don't have the time to listen, while mothers will always be enquiring after what you do, giving advice and listening to us'. The kinds of 'maternal thinking' (Ruddick, 1980) I saw in Ado situated being a 'good mother' in demonstrating love materially, by providing for children, training them well, giving them what they needed and securing for them promising futures.

In Ado, as elsewhere in south-west Nigeria, women are rarely completely dependent on men for their livelihoods. Pooled household income is so rare as to be remarkable (Guyer, 1981; Fapohunda, 1988). Women's activities as traders, farmers and in food processing not only supplement but sometimes sustain their hearth-holds.[9] Women's networks spread beyond the families of their kin and affines to other domains: market, savings, religious and other social associations provide conduits for flows of resources and assistance, as well as arenas for influence in which their agency as social actors is largely independent of their status as wives or mothers. In many of these arenas, the idiomatic use of the term 'mother' evokes a relationship that is available to all women, no matter their status. In the market where sellers are referred to as *Iya Alata* (literally mother of pepper), *Iya Aląsọ* (mother of cloth) or *Iya Ẹlẹfọ* (mother of vegetable), women's social identities as traders are constructed as a relationship of love, care and influence. In the numerous tailoring institutes and hairdressing salons dotted around town, women become 'mothers' to their apprentice charges as they train them, like children, to survive alone in the adult world.

Just as women seek influence in these arenas not simply for opportunities for earning more money, women love children not merely as objects that are 'useful to invest in' (Bledsoe and Isiugo-Abanihe, 1989:443) but for the joy, companionship and support they enjoy from them: as *their* people. And their relationships are not merely ascribed, but actively made through maternal practices. Although residence is generally patrilocal and kinship is notionally

9. I use Ekejiuba's (1995) term 'hearth-hold' here to denote the functional irrelevance of conventional models of the household in this cultural context.

patrilineal, children can choose to affiliate themselves more with their mother's family as they get older. Men may have exclusive rights over their children as their 'owners', something that can bind women into relationships they would otherwise wish to be out of. And men's families may make claims on children whom men have fathered. But the agency of children themselves, and the possibilities open to women for actively crafting relationships of intimacy through maternal practices is extremely significant, and especially so for women who fail to bear their own children.

Holding close, holding dear and holding on

Scheper-Hughes (1992) cites Ruddick's (1980) understanding of mother love in terms of the 'metaphysical act of "holding" – holding *on*, holding *up*, holding *close*, holding *dear*' (1993:361). Despite the universalistic tone of Ruddick's formulation, a position that Scheper-Hughes offers a compelling critique of, the notion of 'holding' is, I suggest, valuable as a lens through which to look at women's experiences of reproduction in this setting. 'Holding close', 'holding dear' and 'holding on' offer a way of exploring the kinds of affective relations that women form with children over time, whether or not they are biological mothers.

It is apparent from studies of fosterage in this and other West African settings (see Schildkraut, 1973; Brydon, 1979; Bledsoe and Isiugo-Abanihe, 1989) that 'holding' children, as in physically catering for and nurturing them, can come to play a crucial role in the coping strategies of women with impaired fertility. For some women, like Talilatu, fosterage offers a way not only to cope with, but to overcome many of the hardships of impaired fertility. Through active mothering, the relationships that are formed can effectively become as intimate and lasting as the relationships that 'real' mothers have with their children, as Talilatu's story shows:

Talilatu was born into a poor family, one of a number of sisters and brothers whose parents had neither the money nor the inclination to send to school. To this day, she can't read and write: but, she proudly notes, she has sons who calculate her profits and losses, and keep her books in order. From small beginnings, Talilatu has managed to successfully identify a number of niche markets and diversify into a range of goods, bringing her prosperity. At the same time, she has earned respect from market women and other townspeople for her industriousness and entrepreneurial nature; she is a popular, much liked woman, who appears at every major ceremony as a celebrated guest. Yet Talilatu has never carried a child to term.

Her first marriage, to an older man her parents chose for her, lasted for five years. She described how at first she was grudgingly accepted by his two other wives, then how they began to turn against her. It took two years before she had her first miscarriage. It was when she suffered her second miscarriage that she decided to go, suspecting that they had used something on her. She then met another man while travelling to a nearby market. He was a driver, and he also had other wives at home. With that man she didn't even get pregnant once. He soon lost interest. She went back to her father's house, bought herself a plot of land and began, slowly slowly, to build herself a house.

It was when she moved into that house that she met her third husband. He had other wives at home and visited her regularly. Still she didn't get pregnant. He was so concerned that he took her here and there to herbalists, spending so much money on her. But still no pregnancy. [Her ex-husband, whom I knew well, confided in me that their relationship had ended when he caught her in bed with another man whom, he thought, she had got involved with to get pregnant. He felt so insulted by this, after all his efforts, that he left her].

By this time, her business had grown so much that she was able to branch out into transport. It was then that her sister begged her to take one of her children to raise. Soon she had a house full of children, sent to her by her family. She put all of them through school, and then through university, sparing nothing to give them whatever they wanted. And they kept on coming back to her, their 'mother'. She sent one to the USA for study and often talks about her trip there; another is at medical school, others are completing their examinations for university entrance. Since that third husband, she hasn't remarried: 'why bother myself', she would say, 'I have my sons, what would I need a husband for?'

Talilatu attributed her failure to carry a child to term with her first husband not to biology, but to the malevolent intentions of his other wives. Denying her children by him was the surest way to break the bond between her and their husband; co-wives are often the first in the line of suspicion in cases like this. With her second husband, the relationship simply fell apart when she failed to produce a child. Doing nothing, spending no money, making no effort, is equally a way to kill a relationship in a context where money and love are intertwined so closely (Cornwall, 1996). But in situations like these, women may not hang around. One older man told me of the 'countless' wives he had in late middle age. Each had come, stayed for a while, failed to get pregnant, and left. 'I married them for enjoyment, not issue, as I had so many children, so I didn't bother to do anything for them or take them anywhere [for treatment]', he said. He didn't want to waste his money, he added, as he saw it as their problem. For their part, they simply moved on to another man or, like Talilatu, found other ways of having access to children.

As well as the insult of her taking another lover, it was also perhaps the implication of diminished potency that drove Talilatu's third husband away. Speaking about his experiences, the hurt of seeing the love he poured into their relationship spurned in such a tangible way welled up in his eyes. For him, fatherhood was less important than Talilatu's need to become a mother – he already had ten children – and it was this need that connected him to her above and beyond simply producing children. Out of his love for her, he wanted to be able to give her a child.

Talilatu eventually found another way of becoming a mother, by actively mothering the children of others. Women in her position can come to be known as the 'mothers' of children whom they have brought up as their own, with whom there may be greater intimacy than with the child's biological mother. What, it may be wondered, has biology got to do with it if foster children can come to care as deeply for their other mothers as 'biological' children? Esther Goody (1982), writing about northern Ghana, argues that the primacy of identities through birth, the very tenacity of the bond between biological parent and child, accounts for the maintenance of affective ties between 'real' parent and child in the midst of considerable fluidity in child-rearing arrangements. But structural explanations deny the children themselves agency in making their own ties and their own choices, and, like economistic arguments, fail to capture the dynamism and particularity of relationships that are created over time rather than simply given (see Oppong and Bleek, 1982).

Goody's (1982) analysis suggests that no matter who cares for the children on a day-to-day basis, biological parents can continue to 'hold on' to their children in the longer term. But as Bledsoe and Isiugo-Abanihe (1989) suggest for Sierra Leone, these relations can be strategically built up and built on by the women who care for other women's children. In Ado, I sometimes heard stories of children choosing other mothers – begging their mothers to let them go and live with a sister or a friend, who would sometimes continue to bring them up until they were ready to leave home. When I asked women about this, they said that this is the choice the child has made: what could they do to stop them? By caring for other mothers' children, these mothers-of-choice were not only 'holding' children, but actively creating the basis for 'holding on' to them.

In Talilatu's case, the fluidity of kinship linkages and the agency of the children themselves also came into play. The sons of her sister chose to identify themselves with their maternal line and with her as their mother of choice. They remained members of their father's lineage, but did virtually nothing to maintain relationships. There might come a time in the future when it would be expedient to revive them, but as they passed through school and university, Talilatu was for them the mainstay of support that they needed. And it was Talilatu who boasted of their successes, and enjoyed the times when they crowded the house with visitors and went out into the town as *her* successful sons.

Waiting it out

For a few women, then, fosterage and the ability to attract children of friends and close colleagues, provides a way in which women without their own children can become mothers of others. But this is not available to all women. For a precondition of fosterage is to be seen to have the means to bring up a child more successfully that their 'real mother', or to have relatives who are struggling with a large brood of children. Afusatu had neither. Afusatu never sought to move, but stayed and stayed, hoping and praying, until she was too old to bear a child. She never knew what the problem had been: she was not aware that she had experienced any reproductive ailments. She just waited until her time was up.

As I sat talking to Afusatu, a petty trader in her late fifties, a small child came to sit in her stall with a tiny bowl of beans. We fell silent as he began to eat. Afusatu gazed at him tenderly as he lapped up the beans, scraped the bowl clean, and scampered off to join his friends. When he'd gone, she told her story. Children would come to play with her, she said; and she liked them to come, so that they would enjoy together and they would keep her company. But later on they'd go back to their homes and she would be alone.

That's how she spent most of her days: alone. She'd returned to Ado when it became obvious that she was never going to get pregnant. To her father's house. But then he had died and she had nowhere else to go. She was the only child of her mother; she had no helper. So she'd stayed there with his co-wife and her daughters, with whom she had a tense relationship; one marked by fear of them, and by avoidance. She told me, sadly, of all the years she had spent hoping and praying that she would be given a pregnancy by Allah. No herbs, no doctors, she said, only Allah. But Allah had not provided her with the child she yearned for. She'd waited and hoped and waited and hoped until the blood that came every month started to trickle away, leaving her bit by bit until there was none again. And then she knew for sure that she would never have a child.

Not only did she have no child, she also had so little money that the shelves on her stall were virtually bare. As we talked, she began to complain, with anger and hurt, about those women who could just become 'sugar mummies'; not those glitzy middle-aged cash madams who take younger lovers, but older women who tempt children, she said, to come to them by giving them fine things and making the children love them as if they were their real mothers. Those women steal the children from their real mothers and they go on to cater for the foster mothers and neglect the real mother, leaving her to suffer. That, she said with aching sadness in her eyes, was something very, very bad.

Afusatu sought no means, apart from prayer, to tackle her infertility; her husband simply did not care, relying on other wives to give him children, and they left her alone while he was alive. She was left with no security and no one to care for her. Fate had dealt her a bad hand, and there seemed little that she could to do lever herself out of a situation of desperate powerlessness. Afusatu's misery was compounded by her poverty; and her rage was directed at those who had the means to overcome some of the most potent and painful aspects of their infertility. For money would enable such women to have children to hold, to educate and train properly, and give them some of the things that their biological parents might not be able to afford.

One of the women's associations in Ado is called *ọmọ ni bori owo*, 'children are more important than money'. This in itself tells only part of the story of the relationship between having money and holding children. Children may be more important than money, but money offers women without their own children a lifestyle that makes them attractive foster parents. In Afusatu's perception, women with money can attract children to them to whom they become mothers-of-choice. And such women can not only hold these children close and dear. They might also be able to hold on to them, to continue to be cared for by them in the twilight of their lives as Talilatu might well expect to be.

Between these two cases, both extreme examples, lies a spectrum of possibilities and experiences. Many women wait, like Afusatu, and carry on trying. Some eventually find the child they crave. I knew women whose lot continued to be infertile unions until they were surprised by pregnancy after years of trying; for others, phantom pregnancies lasting years at a stretch masked their hopes as well as their disappointment until a child finally emerged. Others pour their energies, like Talilatu, into their work and their social networks, and into relationships with the children of relatives and friends, whom they may not foster, but to whom they become loved and valued 'aunties'. Of those women who are able to hold onto their relationships with their husbands despite their infertility, few trust friends or relatives enough to really share with them their pain.

But few men are willing or able to wait this long. Monogamous marriages are quickly dissolved, or transformed with the arrival of a pregnant new wife. Even where the man puts up a fight against his relatives' insistence on him taking another wife, conflicts within the home often force the infertile wife out. In a situation where male infidelity is so usual as to be the norm, accidents can happen. In one case, Dele, a man in his thirties, loved his wife so much that he stopped speaking to the relatives who were trying to disrupt his relationship. A random act of everyday infidelity resulted in him getting another woman pregnant. He tried to get her to abort, he rejected her, she tried to pin the pregnancy on another man; none of these tactics worked. His family ended up holding a naming ceremony in the absence of the father to claim the child as theirs. As the ceremony ended they marched on his house and emptied his wife's possessions into the street, claiming to have found conclusive evidence that she was using *juju* to 'poison his mind'. Still he stood by her. Two years later, he had still not accepted the child as his. His wife, meanwhile, finally became pregnant and gave birth to a son.

Waiting it out and battling to maintain a relationship against all odds is fraught with precisely the contingencies that reveal the embeddedness of would-be parents in social relations that can eclipse their agency as individuals. Afusatu's experience vividly illustrates the powerlessness many women experience in similar situations. Waiting is the only option that seems open to them. Although there are men who have little empathy for their wives and offer no support, not all are heartless bystanders who simply seek out another woman if their wives fail to match their expectations. Like Dele, they too may find their agency diminished by those around them who attempt to take charge of the situation for their own ends. In a sense, they too are 'holding': holding on to relationships in situations where the failure of a woman to become a mother places both at risk of others' interventions.

To have and to hold

In the absence of effective biomedical treatment and the reproductive technology that might make a difference (Okonofua et al., 1997a), and in a context where so many women search for a child, the scale of misery caused by reproductive health problems that interfere with fertility is immense. For those women who are unable to bear their own children, 'holding' provides a way to recoup some of their hopes and enjoy the experiential dimensions of motherhood – holding close, holding dear – that might otherwise be denied to them. If reproduction is cast less as a patterned set of choices than as a contingent process over time, through which people cope with uncertainty and the unforeseen consequences of other actions (Cornwall, 1996), then 'holding' can be seen as an unpredictable process over time, with hoped for, but ultimately unforeseen outcomes. 'Holding on' – both to children and to intimate relationships – becomes a process that remains fraught with uncertainties, yet one that mirrors in crucial respects the processes of mothering through which biological mothers create and sustain relationships with their children.

As the examples I draw on in this chapter show, impaired fertility may be perceived as a consequence of fractures in social relations as well as a cause of them. And yet many women who suffer these fractures can go on to recuperate their hopes for a good life, seeking status and success in other domains and drawing on their networks of kin and friends for support, and for access to children. If a woman fails to have children of her own, then there are still ways to salvage her situation. But fosterage is a fall-back position, and one that is both contingent and uncertain: for the doing of mothering requires resources and becomes all the more imperative when a child can turn round to say 'you are not my real mother'. Figuring children's agency into the picture, and looking at relations of mothering not as ascribed by kinship but actively made and remade through social practices, offers a different perspective on fertility.

Talilatu's case illustrates the ways in which mothering practices can create the possibilities for women to assume the social identity of 'mother' and enjoy some of the experiential, and material, benefits of motherhood. For women of Talilatu's generation, marriage is so closely tied to reproduction that when she failed, in each relationship, to become pregnant there seemed no reason to continue with the marriage. And, with the means to support herself, she could see no reason to bother herself with men again. Like other, older women she laughed at the thought of remarriage. That these sons now chose her as their 'mother of choice' was an important dimension to her story; her connectedness with others, through membership in multiple associations that create a web around her of people for whom she is also 'mother', is another.

Afusatu's story, however, shows the contingencies involved. It situates mothering in terms of material, as well as social practices.

But Afusatu lacked more than money. She lacked a sense of her own agency, shouldering the burden of childlessness in all its senses with recourse only to Allah. Her husband, like many other polygynists I knew, made no attempt to help her; she had no family to speak of who could 'help her to forget'. And she had no children around her for whom she could become a 'mother of choice'. She excluded herself from everyday sociability, spending day after day alone in the makeshift shelter from which she carried out her petty trade. She was not avoided so much as left to fend for herself. One of the few people I knew with no social network at all, Afusatu had few means to gain opportunities of mothering, let alone access to becoming a mother of others.

Despite the possibilities that exist for women to achieve mothering through fosterage, to enjoy some of the experiential dimensions of motherhood and to build up client bases as 'mothers' to unrelated others, all women long for their *own* children. As Okonofua et al. note, 'many couples foster children to provide social security for such children rather than to resolve the social and psychological problems associated with infertility' (1997a:207). The longing for a child that women experience is something that no rationalising explanation can ever make sense of. I knew women who severed links with their families, left relationships with men that other women would dream about, and put themselves through abject poverty in order to try to find, by any means they could, a way of having their own children. Interpretations that focus on the value of *children* alone fail to fully account for the depths of suffering that women go through in their struggles to become mothers. And this may be because their focus is on children, rather than on what it means to be a mother.

Note

I am extremely grateful to all those women and men who shared such intimate, and difficult, aspects of their experiences with me. My grateful thanks go to my assistants, Dorcas Odu and Adebowale Akinsowon, for helping me to make connections with people and to understand more closely the issues involved. I am indebted to Mary and Tokunbo Akinsowon and J. D. Y. Peel for their support and care, and to the Economic and Social Research Council and the Simon Population Trust for funding the research on which this chapter is based.

CHAPTER 8

The Meaning of Children in Hong Kong

Diana Martin

It might reasonably be supposed that something as fundamental as the way parents regard and value their children would be much the same the world over. However, as field and historical studies show, this is far from being the case. At different times and in different places, children are accorded a different value which influences, sometimes vitally, the way that they are treated by their family members and by the wider society. To take a very obvious example, it is well known that in Chinese society in the past, and to some extent today, girls are explicitly valued much less than boys. This has not been true to the same degree in European societies.

The historian Alan Macfarlane has argued that the average English couple, from the late Middle Ages onwards, did not regard children as essential, so that by contrast to other cultures, the wife's inability to conceive was not a reason to dissolve a marriage. Children, he maintains, were regarded as pets (1986:59). They were luxuries (ibid.,:56) to be enjoyed and played with by those who could afford them. Since they did not add to the family purse but rather drained it, it was preferable not to have too many. The factors that contribute to these different attitudes are grounded in the wider social structure, the political and the economic system which all determine the kind of family system that prevails in any given place.

In this chapter, I shall argue that, for social and historical reasons, the predominant traditional Chinese attitude to children, especially male children, is that they are essential, in that they are of potentially great value and usefulness to the family. This value is on two levels: the economic/practical and the ritual/religious. Economically and practically, male children are precious as future income earners and as carers of their aged parents with whom they are culturally obliged to remain in the family home. In ritual/religious terms, it is male children who will continue the family line and whose wives and children bear the responsibility of making offerings to the recently dead and to the ancestors, maintaining their graves and keeping them supplied with all that they need in the next world.

I also argue that despite their value, or maybe because of it, children are in and of themselves less important than the adults who gave them life and whom they have a lifelong duty to respect and obey. In other words, children are valued for what they will become and what they will do rather than what they intrinsically are. Hence it is fair to say that attempts to understand and appreciate the particular nature of childhood are not well developed.

My sources of information for this paper are my own doctoral research on pregnancy and childbirth among the Chinese of Hong Kong, which I conducted largely by means of interviews with mothers and hospital personnel in Hong Kong in the early 1990s. This research took place in the context of my living, working and raising my children in Hong Kong from 1977 to 1997. In the late 1980s my family and I became involved with the International Social Service section of the Social Welfare Department as volunteers visiting and taking an interest in children who were being adopted. My views are therefore also informed by my visits to two children's homes and discussions with social workers. In addition I draw on the many observations made by anthropologists, historians and others who have researched various aspects of Chinese family and social life.

The Chinese family

In Chinese society, the focus within the family is on the family unit, its functions and its continuity rather than on the individuals within it (see Baker, 1979). The younger generation's needs are subsumed in those of the older generation, and the individual's in those of the family. The Chinese family was a religious unit as far as the worship of the ancestors was concerned; it was also an economic unit with a common purse and holding common property. In theory at least the family was synonymous with the household which was symbolised by the sharing of a common stove. The earnings of all its members went into the common purse and added to its wealth. To an extent this remains the case in Hong Kong and is reflected in the fact that government statistics of income generally refer to household income. Such a system can probably only function where there is a clear and immovable hierarchy and this is indeed the case. The Chinese family is hierarchical and the emphasis is mainly on the needs and demands of its senior members. Thus children defer to parents, younger siblings to older siblings and wives to husbands. In ancient times the important relationships were codified by Confucius as the 'five relationships' (*wu lun*): emperor/subject, father/son, husband/wife, elder brother/younger brother, friend/friend. As Catherine Pease points out, although these relationships were supposed to be reciprocal, 'in practice the sense of obligation extended more upward than downward' (Pease, 1995:285). Until recently, family members called each other by kinship terms precisely delineating their place in the family and kinship hierarchy. Parents traditionally had more or less absolute rights over their children and their children's earnings when they started to take up outside employment. Until the last fifty years or so, marriages were arranged for the children without their consent and without consulting them. (I was struck by the response of an elderly informant from southern China whom I had asked what would have happened if she had refused to marry the man her parents had chosen. Her eyes opened wide and she said 'It would never have occurred to me to refuse.' Her response was not untypical, although I have also been told of daring escapes across the border to Hong Kong in order to avoid marriage.)

The absence of any kind of community-based responsibility for the old made the family unit of central importance. It was essential that children be obligated in perpetuity to their parents in return for the gift of life and the care invested in them. This sense of continuing obligation to the older generation is the cornerstone of Chinese family life. The concept of filial piety (*xiao*) is arguably one of the most important precepts of Chinese society, thought to lead to behaviour that is socially beneficial. It refers to the duties that adult children, as opposed to small children, have towards their parents.

The most basic consideration for the family is, of course, survival. This can be taken both in the worldly sense – to have the means to eat, to have shelter and to be free of sickness (which in a China frequently beset by droughts, floods, rapacious landlords and political instability could not be taken for granted) – and in the long-term sense of the spiritual survival of the patrilineal family of ancestors over many generations. Children, therefore, belong to the family unit in which they are supposed to remain in the case of divorce or death of a parent.[1] Hence, in the Chinese patrilineal and patrilocal family system sons are ritually important as only they can continue the family line. This is one reason why daughters are traditionally valued much less than sons. Since daughters marry 'out', often relocating to another village, a married daughter's obligations are to her husband's family. She can thus neither look after her parents in their old age nor worship them after their death. (There is evidence that this is changing in Hong Kong and urban China as daughters make increasing inroads into the labour force). There is an old Chinese saying that daughters are 'goods on which one loses money'. Anything that has been invested in a daughter – money on education, time and effort in the teaching of skills etc – will merely benefit another family once she reaches the age of marriage. As is well known, in the bad old days of dire poverty, men sometimes sold their daughters or even wives (see Pruitt, 1945). Female infanticide was practised although the scale is not known. Even today in China there are more abandoned female babies in orphanages than male ones.

As historians have shown (Stone, 1977; Macfarlane, 1986), such a family set-up is entirely different from that which has prevailed for several hundred years in England where, for various reasons, the rights of individuals, including children, were well developed. Children there were free to keep their own earnings, to marry as and whom they pleased, and were not obliged by law or custom to maintain their elderly parents which was the responsibility of the parish and the community. Given this very different perspective, it follows then that the particular developmental and psychological needs of children as they are seen by western psychologists, have little resonance in the Chinese context.

In my view the Chinese family can be characterised as parent-centred rather than child-centred. Chinese children receive care from their parents on the tacit understanding that they will eventually repay them by looking after them in their old age. The British and American model is predominantly child-centred, so that westerners repay their 'debt' indirectly by raising and looking after the next generation of children. The value of adult independence makes many old people in Britain reluctant to rely on the younger generation for support. Although the attitude is changing in Hong Kong, older people regard it as their right to be looked after by the generation they have brought up.

1. Several elderly widows told me that they could not have remarried because taking their children with them would have deprived them of their family line (*heung dan*).

So, if the Chinese family is parent-centred, it follows that parents may have specific, defined reasons for wanting children. This is borne out by the findings of Jack and Shulamit Potter who conducted research in a village in Guangdong province in southern China during the 1970s and early 1990s. They find that the peasants explicitly see in children the answer to their need for care in old age, 'rather than thinking of themselves as assuming responsibility to care for another' (Potter and Potter, 1990:225). Margery Wolf (1970) has argued that Chinese mothers (who have entered the family as outsiders) have their own agenda within the strongly patrilineal and patrilocal ethos. She maintains that they consciously set out to create strong emotional ties with the sons they raise, and who with their wives will remain in the family home after marriage, so as to ensure a comfortable old age for themselves. Even if the requirement to take care of the elderly is now no longer so prevalent in the city of Hong Kong, there is a residue of it. Many young people both before and after marriage contribute a substantial proportion of their salaries to their parents, whether or not they co-reside. Partly for cultural and partly for economic reasons (the very high price of accommodation in Hong Kong) most young people live at home until they marry – usually in their late twenties – when the ideal is now to set up on their own, at least by the time they have children.[2] Nowadays this financial contribution is made by daughters also, both married and unmarried.

Chinese history and mythology abound with inspirational stories of filial piety, the highest and most essential of virtues, and of children making all kinds of sacrifices for their parents. There is a famous tale of a young man who voluntarily lay down in his parents' bedroom to let the mosquitos sate themselves on his blood. When they had had their fill, his parents could go to bed and sleep in peace. Another story tells of a daughter who cut off her little finger which she boiled in medicine to help her mother recover from an illness. Her act of filial piety was noted by the gods and her mother recovered. In modern Hong Kong, children are urged to do well at school (there is nine years free schooling) so that they can get good jobs and help the family financially. This pressure starts early so that many children take tests at the age of two to enable them to enter a good kindergarten.

If children are valued for what they can do for the family and for their future potential, rather than for what they intrinsically are, it follows that not a great deal of attention will be paid to the

2. In cases where the elderly co-reside with their children this is now more likely to be in the home that is rented or owned by the younger generation.

child's point of view. Their lives will be organised very much for the convenience of the older generation – a fact evident in much of the writing of historians and anthropologists.

What we might now regard as a rather callous attitude towards children has been true in the past in many cultures in times of high infant mortality. Also, of course, before the advent of efficient contraception, babies arrived whether or not they were wanted or could be afforded. The historian Edward Shorter (1982) has drawn a most unpleasant picture of what pregnancy and childbirth could involve in Europe before modern times. Maternal death rates were high, complications and sickness were likely, and many women suffered from lasting complaints as a result of problems in childbirth. There is evidence in many of the historical writings about Europe that, before the decline in infant mortality, small children were regarded as just passing through, their hold on life tenuous. This is true of China as well, and in more recent times. It also the case among the poor in present-day Brazil where infant mortality is high (Scheper-Hughes, 1992). People and cultures formulate different strategies on both a societal and personal level to cope with the pain of losing children.

In Chinese society the strategy was to deny full personhood to children. Thus their deaths could, at the level of society and of ritual, be treated far less seriously than the deaths of adults. Anthropologist Emily Ahern, who worked in Taiwan (Ahern, 1973), relates how children who die are considered not to have been true children of the family at all. The dead child is thought to have been the soul of someone to whom the parents owed a debt. When the debt is paid in terms of the care invested in the child, it dies. As a consequence of this belief, children were not given proper burials like an adult but something much more perfunctory.

A few years ago a young Hong Kong Chinese woman of my acquaintance, married to an Englishman, had the misfortune to give birth to a stillborn baby. Whereas the young couple wanted to give the baby a funeral, the wife's mother hoped that the hospital could 'just get rid of it'. Going further back, although the dissection of dead bodies was culturally repellant to the Chinese because of the need to keep the body whole after death, it was apparently acceptable to let western doctors dissect the corpses of children – as Tucker (1986), quoting Dr Kerr's 1867 report for the missionary-run Canton Hospital, has noted. The view of children as transient and incomplete adults is understandable at a time when their lives were indeed fragile and vulnerable to the host of infectious diseases which were not yet curable. In addition, there is a notion in Chinese society of *yuan* or roundness, meaning that to live a complete life a person should become adult, marry and produce descendants. Thus those who die prematurely are thought to become wandering ghosts who may cause trouble for the living. The practice of ghost marriage in which two dead children are married to each other when they would have become adult is one way of settling the ghost of a dead child (Martin, 1991).

Nowadays, because of medical improvements, better education and increased affluence, the state of affairs in Hong Kong is quite different. Infant mortality is now low by world standards – currently standing between 4 and 5 per 1,000 live births, which is lower than in the USA or Britain. In addition, the fertility rate is now about 1.3 per woman *(Hong Kong Social and Economic Trends 1982–1992*). In everyday terms, this means that nearly all families are composed of one or two children. Ironically, the Family Planning Association's 'Two is Enough' campaign of the 1970s, combined with the aspirations to middle-class affluence in capitalist Hong Kong, has brought about the ideal that has been coerced in China. In Hong Kong, as in China, this constitutes a dramatic and sudden change as the parents of today's young children are likely to have five to seven siblings themselves. In terms of family form, more than 61 per cent of Hong Kong people now live in a nuclear family (ibid.). So the family of parents with one or two children is now both the norm and the ideal. Although, from anecdotal evidence, there is still a lingering preference for sons over daughters, it is evident from the low fertility figures that modern couples no longer 'keep on trying' in the hope of having a son. There are other priorities now, such as ensuring a good standard of living for all the family. It is thought necessary to keep a close eye on children's educational standard to make sure that they succeed at school and can get well-paid jobs. The widespread availability of contraception, and of abortion (to which there are almost no cultural or religious objections) means that nearly all children are wanted. But can this be taken to mean that children are valued and cherished for their own sakes? Can it be claimed that their specific emotional and psychological needs are understood and catered for? We shall now look into these questions.

An infant's needs

My interviews with pregnant women and newly-delivered mothers lead me to conclude that the requirements of an infant and small child are viewed as being primarily physical. Thus the infant is seen to need food, warmth and a clean environment. As I have argued elsewhere, the mother does not seem to be regarded, nor does she regard herself, as the indispensable provider of these needs (Martin, 1997:199). Nor do many mothers feel that it is up to them to do so. For rather than experiencing the birth of a baby as a beginning, the new mother considers it as 'a project finished' (in the words of an experienced Hong Kong Chinese midwife who had also practised in Britain in the early 1980s).[3] The nine-month period of symbiosis for which she is solely responsible is over. The responsibility can now be shared with others. Another midwife (a Cantonese-speaking Malaysian Chinese, who had also practised in Britain, Australia and New Zealand) claims that young Hong Kong mothers say that they do not need to learn to look after a baby as their mother-in-law will do it for them.

It is not considered particularly important who carries out the tasks of ensuring that the baby's physical needs are met. Any competent person will do. It could be the mother or father, it could be a grandparent, paid baby-minder or domestic helper, it could be a series of nurses in the hospital where the baby is born. In my experience of maternity wards, and from discussions with maternity personnel, little appreciation is shown of the possible emotional needs of infants, or of the need to create a bond between mother and baby. One woman obstetrician in charge of a maternity ward in a charity-supported hospital told me she regarded 'bonding' as something that was 'up to the mother'. This view was echoed by a northern Chinese woman whom I met in Oxford in 1992. She had had her first baby in a hospital in northern China and her second a few years later in the John Radcliffe Hospital in Oxford. Her comment on her experience in Oxford was about 'this bonding thing'. It was all right, she said, but 'it wasn't really necessary'.

There is at least one private hospital in Hong Kong where the mothers are not allowed to touch their babies for the five days of their stay in hospital. The mother is given a polaroid photograph of her baby. She is also allocated four set times a day when she can view the baby in the nursery for neonates. She stands at the glass door to the nursery while the baby, in his or her cot, is wheeled up to the other side of the door. After a few minutes the two of them go their separate ways. If a woman gives birth by caesarian section in this hospital she is confined to bed for two or three days. As hospital rules do not permit that the baby is brought to her in her

3. A Chinese-American woman anthropologist said to me 'Once the mother has had her baby, her job stops there' (Linda Koo, personal communication, 1993).

room she does not see the baby until she is able to get out of bed and go downstairs. If the mother is breastfeeding her baby she is allowed to come down at four set times a day and to feed the baby in a little room off the baby nursery. Feeding on demand is not a possibility in this hospital. Moreover, every baby is 'topped up' with bottled milk by a nurse after breastfeeding.

Child-minding and the continuity of care

The financial need for many mothers to return to full-time work means that baby-care needs to be found. In the course of interviewing new mothers I found that those who are in low paid jobs are unlikely to return to work because they cannot afford to pay a baby-minder. Nevertheless these women claim that they would rather return to work, expressing the view that looking after a baby is a very hard shift, for twenty-four hours a day, about which there is nothing enjoyable.

When I conducted my research in 1992 and 1993, a daily baby-minder cost HK$2,000–2,500 per month.[4] A weekly baby-minder, who takes the baby in overnight from Sunday to Saturday, cost HK$3,000–4,000 per month plus the cost of milk and disposable nappies. Average household income at the time was circa HK$ 11,000 per month. For some reason it seems to be much easier to find someone to take care of the baby for a week at a time. The baby returns to live at home between the ages of two and three when it is old enough for kindergarten. Mothers I have talked to claim that the toddler has no problems of adjustment. However, this could well be a matter of perception. Esther Goody, who writes of European children returning home after two years with a wet-nurse with whom affective ties may well have been created, comments: 'While ... difficulties may well have occurred, but not been recorded for the twentieth century analyst, it would appear that this was not *seen as a problem* at the time' (1982:25). The same could apply to present-day Hong Kong families who place a child in someone else's home. Further research is needed.

A report on child-minding in Hong Kong, conducted in 1986 by the Family Welfare Society, found it 'disappointing' that many parents whose children were in weekly care did not appreciate the need to visit their small children, to maintain their relationship with them, to take them home at weekends. I would suggest that this apparent neglect occurs because it is thought that small

4. There are roughly HK$ 11 to 1GBP.

children do not have much awareness of who is looking after them. The same is found of women in Beijing who say that 'At that age children don't notice who they are with' (Wolf, 1985). Hence continuity of caretakers is not thought to be important and a sudden break is not perceived as detrimental to a child's sense of security or general well-being.

The view that the need for continuity of affection is low on the scale of the child's needs persists well beyond toddlerhood. I met a young boy of eight who was being considered for overseas adoption. He was a normal child and the reason that he had become available for adoption at such a late age was that he had been cared for by a child-minder all his life. His mother, a single woman, had paid the child-minder's fees for the first year. After that she had stopped paying and had, in effect, disappeared. The child-minder, an elderly woman, had continued to look after the boy out of affection. However, she had eventually become too infirm to continue and had contacted the Social Welfare Department. I asked if the boy was continuing to see the old lady while waiting to be adopted by a family from overseas. I was told he was not as in their view it was better for the boy to have 'a clean break'. It seemed to me that unless the relationship between the boy and his carer had been in some way unhealthy, it was very sad and potentially damaging for the boy to be cut off from the person who had been a mother to him for eight years. Such an action implied that the trained social workers thought that the discontinuity would not hurt the child emotionally.

It is also assumed that a mother's/parent's attachment to their children can be weak as the following can illustrate. A social worker told me about a two year old boy in a children's home (whom I met) who had been placed there by his father after the separation of his parents. His mother, who visited him frequently, wanted to reclaim him but for some reason was unable to prove that she was the mother. As the mother of small children myself at the time this situation seemed to me heartbreaking and I asked the social worker what she thought the mother could do about this. Her reaction was 'Oh, she'll forget about him'.

I would suggest that, in the past, the prevalence of the Chinese extended family (whether sharing a household or not), with its multiplicity of caretakers, has meant that these caretakers, as far as daily routine functions are concerned, were regarded as more or less interchangeable. In Hong Kong there are many adults who were born in China but were sent to Hong Kong as children to be raised by grandparents or uncles and aunts. This is a common tale. Currently, some couples who emigrate to Canada or the USA leave the baby or toddler in the care of grandparents until the parents are settled. The woman from northern China who had had her second baby in Oxford had left the first in China until she and her husband had settled in Oxford. The grandmother brought the toddler to join them in England at the age of two and a half.

Barbara Ward, who conducted studies among the Hong Kong boat people (the Tanka fisher people) from the 1950s till the 1970s, has written incisively on the subject of attitudes to children. She compares the English and Chinese views on children's sensitivity, comparing the fuss made of English children when they fall over with the lack of fuss made by Chinese parents at the same very minor injuries. She finds the Chinese and English interpretations of their different behaviour to be of interest. The English parents express the view that children feel pain more keenly because they have not yet learnt to control their reactions. Of the Chinese response Ward writes:

> The Chinese villagers I know say: because he is a child he does not *feel* pain as badly as an adult would, so there is no need to fuss. Once I asked a woman how she *knew* that children felt pain less than adults do. She said: 'But of course you don't feel pain so badly when you are a child; if you did you would remember, but look at this' – she showed me some deep scars on her chest – 'that happened when I was about two years old and it was very serious as you can see, but I can't remember anything about it. So it can't have hurt very much' (Ward, 1985:176). The fact that people cannot subsequently remember, on a conscious level, physical pain or trauma undergone as a small child is taken to mean that they were unable to feel pain at the time it happened.

Ward also found that no activity undertaken by children was taken seriously, other than their schoolwork, the end product of which was clearly improved employment prospects leading to increased wealth and status for the family. Thus among the people with whom Ward lived it was always justified for an adult to interrupt or disrupt the activities or games of children. Another anthropologist, Jack Potter, confirms this observation from his work among southern Chinese in rural Guangdong (Potter, 1993:personal communication). In my own experience, a woman university professor from Beijing, who stayed in our house for nearly a year in 1988, told my eight-year-old daughter that her drawing was 'not very good'. Such a blunt and frank comment (from a normally kindly person) suggests two things. The first is that she was judging the drawing by adult standards, the second that my daughter's feelings would not be hurt, or should not be hurt, or that it did not matter if they were hurt.

Instrumentality

If people are likely to have children for a specific purpose (often, as we have seen, to look after them in old age) then it might follow that children are also seen as expendable if there are too many, or if the circumstances are unfavourable. That people might be inclined to abort an unwanted girl is certainly the view of the government hospitals where ultrasound scans are performed. A young woman doctor in a new government hospital told me with evident distress that she had learnt that a patient whose ultrasound scan had indicated that she was carrying a girl, had gone to China to have an abortion. Now they will not divulge the sex she told me. However, figures in Hong Kong do not support the idea that the aborting of female foetuses is widespread. According to the *Summary Results of the Hong Kong 1991 Population Census*, the ratio of males to females under the age of fifteen in the years from 1981 to 1991 has fluctuated from 1,079 per 1,000 in 1981, to 1,088 per 1,000 in 1986, to 1,084 per 1,000 in 1991 (1991: 35). In China the figures tell a different story as the sex ratio there can cause alarm in some areas leading to fears of female infanticide (Wolf, 1985:270). However, it is also possible that girl babies are simply not registered or are abandoned.

There are in addition some cases of girls – now women – who were given away at birth or soon after. A Hong Kong woman (now aged about forty-five) who is a good friend and who assisted with my research, providing me with many valuable cultural insights, told me that she had been the third child and second girl in her natal family. She had hence been given away to a childless older couple. The only reason she knew her history is that when she was thirteen her natural mother had come to find her. I have heard a similar story from other adult Hong Kong women and the topic would benefit from systematic research.

The most extreme case that I have come across of the conceiving and bearing of a child for a specific, and in this case short-term, purpose was that of a senior obstetric nurse who had recently become a convert to breastfeeding.[5] Having bottle-fed her two children some years previously in the 1970s, she told me that she had decided to become pregnant again specifically in order to breastfeed her baby. That way she would have a better understanding of the feeding method she was promoting and her own

5. For various reasons the practice of breastfeeding was very uncommon at the time that I did my research and for some years before that. The reasons and issues are discussed in Chapter 5 of my doctoral thesis (Martin, 1994).

example would lend weight to her arguments. She did in fact successfully breastfeed her daughter for over two years, she told me with evident pride. She continues to promote breastfeeding and to run courses to teach other nurses to assist mothers in its practice.

Parents and children

There is considerable concern at present in Hong Kong about the relationship between the generations, particularly between children/adolescents and their parents. On a journalistic level, there were many articles on this topic in the Hong Kong *South China Morning Post* in the early 1990s. A study was conducted in the spring of 1994 by Helen Ho Kit-wat and Tse-man Hong of the Hong Kong Polytechnic (now Polytechnic University) which suggests that many parents do not talk to their children and many children do not turn to their parents for help. The number of calls from desperate young people to Hong Kong's telephone hotlines is witness to the fact that many young people feel they have no one to turn to. The factor that is always blamed by journalists and researchers is the Hong Kong lifestyle. The interpretation is that it is because Hong Kong people are so hard-working and so keen to aspire to better their families financially that there is no time or energy left over to spend with the children. A prominent social worker in Hong Kong, Susannah Tsoi, who gives courses in parenting skills told me that she thinks that people try to compensate materially for the time they spend away from their children. Thus at weekends they buy them toys and treats and hope, in this way, to make up for the time and attention that they have not given to their children. She laments the fact that there is very little in Chinese for parents to read about how to be parents and is herself trying to improve the situation. She also is of the opinion that because many Hong Kong parents shared their parents with many other siblings, they do not think that their children need intensive parenting. One can add that they do not have a model of intensive parenting.

In spite of Tsoi's views about the need for more active parenting, she has no strong feelings about bonding or breastfeeding, not seeming to regard these as relevant for the subsequent parent-child relationship.

It is notable that there is a good deal of physical distance between parents and children in a Hong Kong Chinese family. Although parents have plenty of physical contact with very small children, inasmuch as they are carried around a great deal, this is discouraged after the age of five or six, or when the child no longer needs to be carried. The continuing emphasis on family hierarchy is one possible explanation of this restraint, and the lingering effect of the extended family with the need to inhibit incest as another. It is an area which would merit more investigation.

Given the continuing lack of emphasis on the individual, and especially the individual child, the parenting of infants and small children can be characterised as protective, and then later as the child is expected to take on more responsibility for his/her actions, as directive. In western culture, the ideal style of parenting could be characterised as interactive. These are of course best thought of as emphases rather than as absolute categories. An example of directive behaviour in infancy is shown, however, in the common Hong Kong way of toilet training. Beatrice Kit-May Hung, in her research on early mother-infant interaction, describes how a mother makes certain different sounds (a hissing or a humming sound) when she wants the infant to urinate or defecate. The aim is that eventually the baby will respond (like the dogs in Pavlov's famous experiment) and perform on demand. Hung comments that unlike the British or American idea which is that training is to help the toddler control his/her own body functions, the Chinese idea is that the mother determines when these should happen (Hung, 1983).

Conclusions

Hong Kong society has undergone tremendous changes in the past forty to fifty years. It is now an affluent, sophisticated and highly urbanised society. It ranks fourth among the world's most competitive economies and the average annual per capita income is higher than that of Britain. Many of the parents of today's children are themselves the children of immigrants from rural China. The dramatic drop in family size and change in family relationships have far-reaching social and emotional consequences. Even though the prevalent family form now bears a resemblance to that in many western countries there are still fundamental differences, as outlined above. There is little reason why traditional attitudes to children should change in one generation, when many of these appear to be still highly functional. The relative absence of a high level of adolescent rebelliousness or defiance of parental authority would also seem to testify to the success of traditional child-rearing practices. It has not traditionally been the

Chinese way to reach down to children to try to understand their sensitivities, insecurities and all the other particular needs of children as they are perceived in the western psychological tradition. Hence the Hong Kong family remains parent-centred, and the majority of children remain relatively obedient to their parents and committed to fulfilling their parents' expectations.

Part Three

POLICY AND VULNERABLE GROUPS

CHAPTER 9

Some Reflections on Scientific Conceptualisations of Childhood and Youth

Jo Boyden

Introduction

In the late twentieth century young people have become a major theoretical and empirical concern internationally, attracting considerable research and policy interest. Developmental psychology, paediatric medicine, demography and education have been in the forefront of this work, generating major literatures and theoretical models and a multitude of specialised professional organisations for the training and care of the young. Economic and social research has proved far more reticent, with the sociology and anthropology of childhood only recently becoming established as notable academic fields, and economics tending still to render young people insignificant in its analyses, emphasising their cost to society not their contributions. Nevertheless, even with this spate of new research, the focus is normally on the more established, incontrovertible category of childhood, youth retaining a liminal status in most academic disciplines. Thus, expertise in developmental psychology, nutrition and physical health generally centres on children under five, while the main focus in regard to education, learning and socialisation is middle childhood, research with youth having been confined mainly to culture, life style and aspects of health.

The recent upsurge of academic and policy interest in young people is no accident, but is motivated by compelling social forces. First, young people under the age of twenty now represent around 50 per cent of the population in many parts of the world, leading to a consideration of demographic change, and the implications of population growth for public services and the labour market. In rich industrialised countries we find a very different trend, in which the ageing of the population has fuelled a powerful emotional attachment to childhood. This is reflected in the rise of childhood sciences like paediatrics and educational psychology and the emergence of a myriad of child guidance and monitoring systems (Zelitzer, 1985:3). Second, the widespread ratification of the UN Convention on the Rights of the Child has generated considerable momentum among rights activists, practitioners and policy-makers to develop effective policies for young people based on valid and appropriate information.

An increased research focus on youth specifically is linked both to its emergence globally as a significant social category and to a concern to inculcate in the young high moral and social values. At one time young people (particularly girls) reached social majority at an early age and adolescence was regarded as no more than a brief interlude between puberty and marriage. As the average age of menarche has begun to fall, and with an increasing trend towards later marriages, however, this period has been extended and a large number of people now exist in the world who are post-pubertal but excluded from adulthood (WHO/UNFPA/UNICEF, 1989). Beyond this, much of the recent attention to youth has been due to extensive media coverage and research implicating young people disproportionately in some of the world's gravest social problems, such as unemployment, crime and political violence, this being a source of moralising discourses in many quarters. Thus, while the health problems specific to youth were given little prominence in the past because this age group is generally less vulnerable to disease than others, the situation has now changed and the health, especially reproductive health, of young people has become a major area of attention (Mensch, Bruce and Greene, 1999). This is due in part to concerns about youth sexual behaviour, teenage pregnancy and the high prevalence and transmission of the HIV virus among urban teenagers particularly. It is also linked to the understanding that lifetime habits in matters such as diet, health-seeking behaviour and fertility are commonly founded early in life. For example, those who start having children early generally have more children, and at shorter intervals, than those who embark on parenthood later, this being an issue of population growth, maternal health, and the survival, care and even education of children (WHO/UNFPA/UNICEF, 1989:7).

Powerful practical considerations such as these help explain why so much of the research on childhood and youth is applied. These practical priorities have produced certain distortions, however, for the goal of understanding how young people become healthy, successful, fully integrated adult citizens seems to override interest in childhood and youth as valid life experiences in their own right. For young people, however, this orientation has direct consequences because there is often a serious lack of fit between the research paradigms and their actual life-worlds, undermining research evidence as a credible basis for youth policy.

Even with the present efforts in anthropology and sociology to treat young people as authentic subjects of research, scientific conceptualisations of the younger generations are often bedevilled by adult-centric thinking. Due to weak theory and a shortage of valid empirical information, much of this thinking is sustained by popular stereotype. Within the literature, young people are variously revered and feared, and very often problematised as beings in need of protection or control. Mostly it is children who are seen to merit protection, since views of children tend to be permissive and benign, whereas youth are more likely to invoke adult alarm and restraint. Along with concerns about violence, crime, and subversive youth cultures, sexuality and reproduction are the spheres of youth activity and attitude that provoke the greatest moral panic and receive the greatest attention from researchers. In this chapter I argue that this kind of pejorative imagery is largely an outcome of modern perspectives on human development, for while this process is seen to encompass youth and stop at adulthood, the empirical and theoretical effort in this field has focused on early childhood. Middle childhood and adolescence tend to be regarded merely as periods of consolidation, expressions of social competence in this age group being perceived as a social threat rather than resource.

Orthodox perspectives on human development

In the discourse on generation, children and youth normally share certain critical features. Both tend to be understood as immature beings in a state of development and training for competent adulthood and social majority. Consequently, they are distinguished both by what they lack in relation to adults (power, abilities, responsibilities and so on), and their special needs (Woodhead, 1997). They are also linked conceptually and analytically in the sense that childhood is the foundational class from which youth emerges: childhood conjures up the criteria that demarcate immature from mature beings, and as a relational category, youth is a mere refinement of that central project.

Especially influential in shaping these research understandings internationally have been theoretical and clinical studies in developmental psychology conducted largely between the 1960s and 1970s. Although developmental psychology has in many respects moved beyond the thinking of that period, other disciplines tend still to be embedded in historical paradigms. The accepted scientific wisdom is that childhood and youth are natural life stages derived from a universal biological condition. Human competence is understood to be, above all, a function of age, the overall developmental trend involving transformation from simple to complex and irrational to rational behaviours, an immature child to mature adult, dependent childhood to autonomous adulthood. The model most widely endorsed in research holds that this process is made up of a sequence of fixed stages, each one of which has certain defining features and developmental expectations and builds on the accomplishments of the previous stage. Within this paradigm, the work of Jean Piaget has been the most influential.

Many contemporary societies endorse stage theories of human development, these in some cases encompassing the afterlife (Serpell, 1996). The predominant model internationally has known origins in medieval Europe in medical works, didactic literature and moral treatises (Shahar, 1992). Shulamith Shahar has shown that European childhood was at this point divided into three developmental stages: *infantia* (birth to seven years); *pueritia*, seven to twelve for girls and seven to fourteen for boys; *adolescentia*, twelve or fourteen to adulthood (ibid.:22). The post-adolescent period was usually recognised as distinct from adulthood and denoted *juventus*. Each phase was marked by certain developmental outcomes – emphasis often being given to moral and cognitive development. Although childhood was generally short at this time, for men in certain social groups the passage to full social majority could be quite protracted – extending to the late twenties or early thirties – depending on completion of apprenticeship, study, or military training, joining the knighthood, marriage, and/or financial independence and the acquisition of land (ibid.:28). Women, on the other hand, tended to marry very young (at puberty) and girls were almost entirely disregarded in discussions about adolescence.

Many contemporary European and North American ideas about the development of young people mirror the thinking of earlier times, with important implications for the way scholars conceptualise the young. First, the focus has been on learning how the foundations for future adaptation are laid, privileging adulthood as the end point of development rather than giving worth to childhood and youth experience (Burman, 1994). This focus has legitimated an emphasis on early childhood, which is taken as pivotal in the development of the fully functional, healthy and resilient adult. According to the scientific perspective, then, adolescence is not a transformative phase, but a crystallisation or consolidation of earlier childhood patterns (Garbarino, 1999). Yet, this is in stark contrast to ethnographic evidence that reveals that puberty is a significant transition in most societies, often marked with formal rites of passage and in some cases signifying the end of childhood, especially for girls (Mensch, Bruce and Greene, 1999). While early childhood may establish the pattern for many aspects of development, especially in adverse situations, an ecological view of development that respects social and cultural context and also takes account of individual agency would suggest a far less deterministic model. Moreover, this inordinate research focus on early childhood has diverted attention from the social and moral competencies of adolescents and youths, as I show below.

Second, although depicted as universally valid, the developmental pattern marked out by stage theories happens to draw on normative ideas about childhood, for much of the empirical evidence in developmental psychology in the 1960s and 1970s was based on clinical investigations with middle class children in industrialised countries. These children lived with their parents, attended school and did not work, their lives not being very typical of the countries they came from, let alone other countries and cultures. As a consequence, ideas about development in young people that are represented as universally valid 'scientific truths' often draw on normative representations that have little relevance to the majority of the world's young (Nsamenang and Dawes, 1998).

Third, one of the central preoccupations of developmental psychology has been to establish environmental factors that are most conducive to normal development in children. Piaget, for example, recognised that caretaker relationships and other environmental factors are of great importance to young people's physical and mental growth. However, while certain physical elements – food, fluid and rest for instance – are indispensable to well-being, formulations of normality in childhood and youth are very variable according to context, and young people grow, indeed flourish, in a wide variety of circumstances and conditions (Dawes and Donald, 1994:21). When scientific assumptions of normality are projected as a universal standard, they have the effect of pathologising those young people whose achievements and life courses are divergent. Again, I will return to this issue later.

It turns out that a unitary view of development conceals major differences between young people in terms of social power, expectations and experience. Gender, for example, interacts with, and radically transforms, the experience and outcome of childhood and youth (Mensch, Bruce and Greene, 1999). Gender roles during the early decades of life can be highly prescriptive, determining behaviour, dress, education, work and practically all other matters, gender disparities commonly becoming far more pronounced in mid-childhood and especially after puberty (Blanchet, 1996). As in medieval Europe, in many contemporary societies the age at which childhood ends is prescribed by gender, girls generally passing into adulthood and marriage before boys. Distinctions in the treatment of boys and girls are often justified by ideas about innate biological or psychological difference. In Bhutan, for example, girls are perceived to be weaker and softer than boys, having before them a life of struggle (Wikan, 1989).

In many societies, gender discrimination results in girls being cast in a subservient role and subjected to a range of taboos that put severe constraints not just on their personal autonomy, but also on their health, education, income and occupational mobility. For example, they may be required to leave school early, or excluded altogether, while their brothers attend full-time. After puberty, the regulation of girls' sexual behaviour and fertility is frequently a major social concern and leads to their confinement to the domestic arena. Bhutanese parents prefer their daughters to stay at home with them because they show greater tenderness and are softer at heart than sons. Girls, it is believed, must help with the care of younger siblings, housework and looking after the elderly and should not be further burdened by schooling. But gender roles within childhood are not necessarily fixed, and can be affected by birth order and sibling group composition (Punch, 1998).

Orthodox scientific accounts tend to regard such cultural and social expressions of childhood and youth as little more than digressions from the underlying biological and psychological trend. But several eminent scholars in a number of disciplines have advanced a very different perspective. Historically, within the discipline of psychology, stage theory received its greatest challenge from Lev Vygotsky, who called attention to the essential role of culture and society as indispensable elements in the growth of the human mind. In anthropology, Margaret Mead questioned a unitary view of human development by highlighting that there are many different kinds of youth, that young people in different cultural contexts are raised in very different ways and with very different expectations and outcomes. For his part, the social historian Philippe Ariès suggested that the concept of childhood itself is not universal, but in Europe at least was invented gradually over the course of the fifteenth to eighteenth centuries. Even though the assertion that medieval Europe ignored childhood has been refuted by several people, the social construction of generational categories is now a well established axiom in research.

Alternative development paradigms

While in orthodox thinking universal biological and psychological structures were seen to prevail in human development, today greater stress is placed on both relational and genetic factors. Moreover, the search for common patterns of growth, development and socialisation has led to an increasing appreciation of differences. It is now widely accepted in the scientific community that young people do not develop in a predictable pattern towards a fixed end point. Biology and culture, working together, generate both differences and commonalities of human development. There are genetic influences for diversity just as there are genetic bases for human similarity, both of which are necessary and both of which mesh with culture to ensure survival of the species (Wilson, 1998).

Advances in genetic research have helped provide a better understanding of the forces influencing individual variation in human competence. At the present time, this research emphasises that individual children achieve the ability to perform various tasks at very different rates according to their genetic make up, and that shared features of the gene pool account for developmental variation as well as similarity. Thus, cognitive capacity and growth is not uniform, and young people have multiple and varied intelligences that are not merely, or even principally, a function of age or stage of development.

However, as important as it is to recognise the practical implications of variation in the patterns of young people's native abilities, it is the social aspect of human development that has attracted most attention. Following Vygotsky, researchers have been examining the ways in which society and culture function as indispensable elements in cognitive processes. As Vygotsky pointed out, the very acquisition of language is an intensely social act that consists of structuring the self through a set of social codes. There is no essential separation between the individual and the social, for one cannot become an individual without becoming social (Cole, 1992:731–2).

Following this tradition, there is an established literature in North America in particular that holds that children learn the cultural repertoire of adult society through a process of apprenticeship. It maintains that human beings are co-operative problem solvers and development consists of learning how to solve effectively the problems of everyday life within a cultural and social context. Hence, as Barbara Rogoff puts it, 'it is essential to consider the role of the formal institutions of society and the informal interactions of its members as central to the process of cognitive development' (1990:11). Moreover, each community tends to define child development in terms of the basic skills required to survive and succeed in that society, these circumstances determining to a large extent the course of development (ibid.:12; Super and Harkness, 1996)

Cultural values with respect to the social integration, capacities and vulnerabilities of young people are highly variable and, to a significant degree, define the opportunities for and constraints to their development. This is illustrated by Jean La Fontaine's (1998:114) comparison of ethno-theories in Africa and Europe concerning the integration of the young. In the former, children are prized for the social and cultural continuity their existence ensures, while in the latter they are cherished as embodying progress, a better future. Such values influence both the goals of child socialisation and the expectations of children in terms of behaviour and achievement. Where family continuity and integration are important social attributes, emphasis is likely to be placed on competencies such as respect for others, social responsibility, sharing and reciprocity (Chisholm, 1996; Serpell, 1996; Rabain, 1979, cited in ibid.:133). Thus, in many parts of rural Africa, children's filial duties are expressed in multiple obligations to family that override all other duties, endure throughout life, and are spiritually endorsed (Armstrong, 1994:5). Where children represent future progress, on the other hand, the emphasis is on the development of a sense of individuality, personal achievement in school, sports and other arenas and social and economic autonomy in adulthood (Woodhead, 1998).

But such normative codes are mere abstractions without reinforcement through example and habitual practice. So, for instance, the Wolof in Senegal use teasing and other forms of social pressure to teach children from the very first years of life to share food and other resources, joint, mutually interdependent activity being a highly valued behaviour (ibid.). Similarly, in societies that give value to family continuity and integrity, children's work plays an important role in the accomplishment of domestic chores and in many cases also contributes significantly to family income. In contrast, in northern industrialised settings, young people who work tend to do so for their own learning and material gratification, the more important work of childhood in such contexts being schoolwork (Manning, 1990; Mansurov, 1993). From these examples, it becomes clear that development is contextualised by the environment in which the young are raised, with implications for the specific competencies they develop.

The social marginalisation of young people

The notion of development as guided apprenticeship in adult culture brings to the fore the process of socialisation, which is another core concept of research on young people, with strong foundations in child psychology, anthropology, sociology and education (Mayall, 1994; Caputo, 1995). Socialisation is understood as the fundamental process whereby societies sustain themselves through the generations; adults imparting meaningful cultural messages to the young, who become successful, well-adapted citizens largely through assimilation and conformity (James, Jenks and Prout, 1998:23).

Much prominence has been given in the socialisation literature to formal sites of learning, such as the family, the school and other specialised institutions. Some attention has also been paid to informal learning in traditional settings where community elders or specialist narrators convey to the young knowledge of the genealogies of important families, myths of origin, land inheritance and major events such as battles, invasions and famines. Consideration has also been given to rites of passage through which young people assimilate adult knowledge and skills in relation to work, endurance of hardship, warfare, sexual conduct, spirituality and so on. And there has been some research on play and work as contexts for learning gendered adult roles, the latter being identified as fostering technical skills, fortitude, the capacity to solve problems and manage dangerous situations, sociability, interdependency and a sense of self-efficacy (Peacock, 1992; Bunster and Chaney, 1985; Briggs, 1986). As in the child development literature, in all this research there is an underlying assumption that stability and continuity in nurture and care are essential ingredients in effective socialisation and adaptation among young people.

Nevertheless, this kind of socialisation research has come under increasing criticism for a number of reasons. First, the tendency, particularly in anthropological research, has been to conceptualise society as embodying a coherent system of norms and values that are consistent over time, highly formal and the subject of widespread consensus. It is suggested, however, that the human condition is not a matter of homogeneity and equilibrium, but inherently precarious and perilous, involving uncertainty, ambiguity and contingency. Most social groups, even small, comparatively isolated ones, manifest varying, competing and sometimes dissenting ideas (Allen, 1989:48; Youniss and Yates, 1994; Reynolds-White, 1998:18–19). Hence, young people do not receive societal values as consistent messages and growing into adulthood entails a high investment in rational thought, the continuous evaluation of options, making choices and negotiating decisions with other actors (Youniss and Yates, 1994).

Second, early socialisation studies in particular tended to consider young people not as agents in their own lives and development, but as passive objects of adult training who merely assimilate, learn and respond to adult initiative (Hardman,1973:87; Caputo, 1995).

> The traditional view of socialisation sees adult behaviour, in the context of a society and culture, as an independent variable, based on a fixed set of rules, roles and modes of conduct which children must assimilate before they become significant social actors. The role of child is the role of learner; sociologically, unless he [sic] is a 'delinquent', the child is passive. Thus, child culture is seen as a rehearsal for adult life and socialisation consists of the processes through which, by one method or another, children are made to conform – in the cases of 'successful socialisation' or become deviants, in cases of 'failed socialisation'. (Schildkraut, 1978:109–10)

This perspective renders childhood and youth insignificant in relation to adulthood, the ultimate goal of socialisation and development, and reflects the widespread rejection of young people as competent social actors (ibid; Youniss and Yates, 1994). There are numerous and subtle ways in which young people have been trivialised in such research, not the least being the conception of play as imitative rather than creative social action (James, Jenks and Prout, 1998:93). Another example is the tendency to characterise youth cultures as reactive rather than transformative

(Comaroff and Comaroff, 1999). Similarly, discourses about young people's work often depict vital economic tasks within the household or on the farm as leisure activities, 'hobbies' or 'apprenticeship', as if they contributed solely to the entertainment or learning of the young and not to family or personal maintenance (Boyden, 1997; Zelitzer, 1985).

This indicates how research, as a basis for analysis of childhood and youth, privileges the formal and socially legitimated mechanisms through which societies train their young, and overlooks whole dimensions of young people's action and lives. Seldom have children and adolescents been considered in their roles as carers of younger siblings or incapacitated adults, educators of peers, freedom fighters, rights advocates, community volunteers, or political activists. And an emphasis on family and education as the most appropriate sites of learning and socialisation has led to the neglect of work as a research topic, even though it defines the life experiences and opportunities of millions of young people throughout the world today. Indeed, the association between childhood, youth and school on the one hand, and adulthood and work on the other, is so strong in modern thinking that entry to work has become one of the major thresholds of social majority. Indeed, even without proper empirical evidence as to the effects of work on the young, retaining young people at school and out of work is an active policy objective in many places that both prolongs childhood dependence and denigrates young people's existing contributions and competencies.

The end of the age of innocence

One of the major effects of gaps in the research is that scientific conceptualisations of childhood and youth often appear more consistent with popular stereotypes than with sound human development theory. Striking, for instance, is the tendency to hinge distinctions between childhood and youth not on integrated notions of development but on one particular aspect of development – sexual maturity, normally associated with puberty. Striking also, as Karen Corteen and Phil Scraton (1997:82) observe, is that while in most dimensions – for example, cognitive, social and physical – the process of development is viewed as gradual and continuous, sexual maturity is normally regarded as an abrupt transition. Thus, pre-pubescent children are rendered asexual beings, this setting them apart from adolescents and youths, whose burgeoning sexuality is widely admitted, if not socially accepted (see Montgomery this volume; Kitzinger, 1997).

This, Corteen and Scraton (1997:76) highlight, represents one of the greatest ambiguities of modern ideas about human development, in that children who are socialised into gender-appropriate roles from birth are expected to remain sexually naïve into adolescence, and often beyond.

Historian Hugh Cunningham has shown how in Europe this kind of sentimentalised account of childhood fits powerful social and religious values that were first articulated historically under the influence of Christianity, movements such as the Renaissance, the Reformation and Counter-Reformation and Enlightenment, and the work of romantic writers like Locke, Rousseau and Wordsworth (Cunningham, 1991; 1995). Early attitudes towards children were moulded by the Christian concept of original sin, the view being that children were 'born with an inheritance of sin and wickedness and so were believed to be in the same danger of hell as adults' (Hoyles, 1989:22). The Puritans advocated the use of chastity belts, straightjackets, clitoridectomy, deliberately painful circumcision and the attachment of toothed rings to boy's penises to prevent masturbation, as means of controlling children's sexuality. Modern perspectives retain anxieties about sexual experimentation among children, but the greater inclination is to celebrate and ideologise their innocence and purity. In Europe, this romantic outlook originated largely with the idea that children are closer than adults to nature and God, and that childhood should be a time of carefree happiness (Cunningham, 1991; 1995).

As far as most adults – and indeed most researchers – are concerned, the notion of children as pre-sexual beings seems to rest comfortably with the prevailing image of their innocence and vulnerability. But scientific perspectives on adolescents and youth are far more ambivalent, reflecting the liminal status of this social category in the modern world. While youth is classified as post-pubertal, and so tangibly different from childhood, it fails to meet the social and moral criteria believed to characterise adulthood and so is distinguished by its exclusion from adult freedoms, obligations and spheres of influence. Accordingly, youth participation in sexual (especially homosexual) activity, political processes, armed combat, and many forms of work is severely constrained. This hints at another of the more salient features of modern cultural and scientific representations of youth development: the separation between puberty as a physiological event and the acknowledgement of reproductive majority. Thus:

> ... although the appearance of secondary sexual characteristics, and changes such as the onset of menstruation may 'mean' that

> children are reproductively mature in a physical sense, most social groups require further social proof of reproductive responsibility, such as the skills or means to support the next generation' (Ennew, Gopal, Heeran and Montgomery, 1996b:45).

Hence the widespread regulation of reproduction and sexuality well beyond puberty, boys often having to wait long after physical maturity before being recognised as men, and girls entering womanhood at around the age of menarche, but only though marriage and the control of their reproductive potential by their husbands. In fact, with recent demographic and social trends, a growing number of young people globally with reproductive capability are regarded as having insufficient moral and social competence to assume adult reproductive roles (WHO/UNFPA/UNICEF, 1989). Taboos regarding youth sexuality and punitive treatment of young people place those who digress from accepted sexual norms in danger of exclusion from school and/or home (see Price, this volume). Early childbearing in girls is particularly abhorred as a source of family humiliation, affected girls often resorting to the sex trade as the only means of economic survival, and is punishable in some societies by death. On the other hand, in some parts of sub-Saharan Africa a growing number of young men are forced to remain in suspended minority status, since they are not allowed to marry without proof of economic solvency and yet cannot find jobs. Denial of youth sexuality also results in widespread ignorance among the young of the risks associated with unprotected sexual activity (WHO/UNFPA/UNICEF, 1989:10). Such circumstances undermine the social integration and self-efficacy of the young and also provoke adult disquiet about youth alienation and insurrection.

Demonising the young

Attempts to acknowledge and legitimate the cultures of the young were made some time ago by the Opies in their work on children's songs and games and by the Centre for Contemporary Cultural Studies at the University of Birmingham, which in the 1970s and 1980s produced a number of studies of youth subculture and class from a Marxist perspective. Even so, most research on this subject has focused on urban, western, male youth (Wulff, 1995:2). Moreover, as a liminal category, youth tends to invoke considerable adult ambivalence. While youthful energy and enthusiasm is commonly revered and harnessed for social and health projects, there is a darker side to scientific and popular representations of youth. This emerges in discourses about young people consuming illegal substances, violence in school, promiscuous or pregnant teenagers, delinquents, youth gangs, political agitators, football hooligans and the like. Thus, as Christine Griffin (1993), for example shows, research in Britain and the US tends to conceptualise young people as deficient (and hence in need of education), delinquent (and hence in need of control) or dysfunctional (and hence in need of therapy). Wendy and Roger Stainton-Rogers (1992:183) detect a strong gender bias in such discourses, female adolescents commonly being seen as inherently 'troubled' and males as 'troublesome', or often both at the same time. Such stereotyped conceptualisations highlight the systematic demonisation of youth, in effect proclaiming deviance as the most critical feature of this life phase (Sommerville, 1982). Of all groups, street and wandering youth are possibly the most reviled, for they are often isolated from the sites and agents of socialisation legitimated by mainstream society, while at the same time showing a propensity for criminal activity. Young people such as these, who step outside the societal boundaries set for childhood and youth, are commonly censured or criminalised and become the fodder for research that is both highly patronising and judgmental.

In Europe notions about young people's innate capacity for evil appear to have earlier roots even than ideologies of childhood innocence. Cunningham argues that in ancient Rome and Greece children were characterised mainly by their deficiencies. In classical Athens, for example, they were regarded as 'physically weak, morally incompetent and mentally incapable' (Golden, quoted in Cunningham, 1995:26). Physical correction was widely endorsed as a means of suppressing the wayward tendencies of Europe's young, the Latin word for 'teaching', *disciplina*, having the same meaning as punishment. Christian ideas about original sin further fostered a concern about children's propensity for wrongdoing.

The family was the main agent of socialisation and control in Europe and during the sixteenth and seventeenth centuries the young were regarded as the property of their parents and denied a will of their own. Fathers determined their sons' occupations and their childrens' marriages. The law provided positive reinforcement for parental authority in the form of severe sanction by the state for filial recalcitrance, including, in some instances, the death penalty. Work was one of the main instruments of child discipline and reform at this time. Thus, English children over the age of five and below fourteen who were orphaned or found living in idleness or begging were bound into agricultural service or a craft to inculcate in them a sense of virtue and industriousness and discourage laziness (Zeitz, 1969:9; see also Fyfe, 1989). By the nineteenth century there was a strong tendency in some quarters to view young people as 'a social problem', a potential or actual threat to the social order. This reflected growing anxieties about civil disobedience, hooliganism and juvenile crime in urban areas and led to the development in several countries of systems of juvenile justice (Morris, Giller, Szwed and Geach, 1980:3; Pearson, 1985).

The influence of medical psychology in early social research in industrialised countries played its own part in these moralising discourses. For a long time scholars interpreted social phenomena such as delinquency or homelessness as the result of individual psycho-pathology or a lack of thrift rather than macro-structural conditions (Younghusband, 1981). Welfare practice was built on moral rearmament and the strengthening of character, and policy on the task of counteracting idleness, seen as tantamount to crime, the focus being on vagrant, homeless or indigent families (Zeitz, 1969; Pearson, 1985). State regulation and control of young people was seen as an essential antidote to families unable or unwilling to act as effective agents of socialisation.

Today, moral panics about the young commonly focus on three perceived global trends. The first is a decline in gerontocratic values in society and the associated loss of control over value formation in the rising generations. This line of thinking resonates with orthodox ideas about young people as the passive receptacles of socialisation, incapable of forming their own judgements. Countless young people today are growing up in the social and economic turmoil accompanying rapid urbanisation, migration, industrial expansion, globalisation of culture and economy, extensive tourism, the spread of the mass media, political and demographic transition, and other forms of structural transformation (Borland, Laybourn, Hill and Brown, 1998:7). Such trends are thought to be associated with a decline in the guidance and control exerted by religion and family, lone migration by young people to cities, consumersim and the breakdown of law and order in cities. Much attention is also given to the pervasive and pernicious influence of both the media and international companies in creating and promoting urban youth movements and subcultures, with media images of violence and sex depicted as shaping aberrant youthful values, attitudes and practices.

A second trend, linked to the decline of senior generations as role models, is inter-generational conflict, perceived to be a growing problem, especially in urban areas. Here, the contexts of rapid change create a disjunction between generations within the family and community, in that the young often have access to the trappings of modern culture while the adults close to them do not. Believing that their parents and other older family members inhabit a world that favours past tradition over future progress, exposure to globalised norms is thought to lead the young to rebel against family guidance and authority. But economic factors are also held to be contributory, in that survival in urban communities means family members may be highly dispersed for much of the time, both geographically and within the labour market, having little contact with each other. Also, as women enter the formal labour market in increasing numbers, so mothers are less involved in child-care. All in all, the concern is that adults today have less control over the young than in the past, while at the same time the networks through which young people can communicate and learn from their peers are growing in number and potency.

Of course, peer influence during adolescence and youth is regarded as resoundingly negative, for the young are considered inappropriate role models and commonly thought to foster behaviour in peers that is inherently risky or seditious. It is often observed, for example, that sexual behaviour and reproductive patterns in young people are highly susceptible to social influence, the implication being that in the face of peer pressure young people feel compelled to engage in unsafe, promiscuous sexual activity to conserve popularity and self-esteem (WHO/UNFPA/UNICEF, 1989:8). The repercussions for girls are seen as particularly grave, for their social status often depends on fecundity.

A third trend is the rising social and economic exclusion of youth due to the decline of appropriate role opportunities. Southern countries with relatively large youth populations, yet very limited school places and slow growth in, or even decline of, jobs and economic possibilities, confront the gravest problems. In such situations youth survival and social mobility are extremely precarious. Social crises noted as being associated with this trend include high crime rates, as in some parts of the United States where crime has become a route to social acceptance among young people in black communities, and even armed conflict, as in parts of Africa, where for lack of anything else to do, many young men drift into military life. Thus, with such trends in mind, the adult case for moral panic about youth appears quite convincing. Yet this case rests on the notion that young people are inherently susceptible in the face of contradiction and change, a notion that needs greater appraisal.

Young people as social agents

There now exists a large and growing body of scholars who are deeply critical of the way orthodox research has tended to trivialise childhood and youth, and who offer a far more optimistic view of youth competence and morality. Within the child development literature strong evidence is provided of individual agency, in that even from the first days of life babies are found to be fully active in defining the environment for their own development. Rogoff, for example, stresses individual effort as essential in growing up, along with social heritage and social engagement. She clarifies the process by quoting Wartofsky:

> ... the child is an agent in its own *and* the world's construction, but one whose agency develops in the context of an ineluctably social and historical praxis, which includes both the constraints and potentialities of nature and the actions of other agents. Nurture, in short, is both given *and* taken; and so is nature. (Wartofsky, in Rogoff, 1990:25)

Within the sociology and anthropology of childhood, especially under the influence of social constructionism, research attention in Europe in particular has now shifted to young people's own perspectives, with emphasis on their creative participation in learning and action (Mayall, 1994). Scholars in this tradition conceive of the young as developing primarily through 'a world of meaning created by themselves and through their interaction with adults' (James, Jenks and Prout, 1998:28). Young people learn about the social world, it is suggested, through 'a creative, often transformative engagement with the social and institutional structures of which it is composed. In this sense, children's socialization and their part in processes of cultural reproduction involve no passive mimicry' (ibid.:89). This perspective has produced a spate of studies in the past few years, distinguished by their sustained concentration on young people as competent social agents.

In this literature it is held that engagement with the complexities of life involves young people organising, making sense of and interpreting the world about them, interpreting and managing competing or even conflicting societal values, defining their roles and identities, resolving crises and working collaboratively with others (ibid; Punch, 1998; Baker, 1998; Woodhead, 1998:24; Hutchby and Moran-Ellis, 1998:8). Some doubt has even been cast as to whether, in order to flourish, young people really do need enduring security and stability in their social milieu. Recent research has spawned new insights into how the young perceive and process discontinuities, inconsistencies, and indeed outright conflicts in their environment. Ideas emphasising the value of stability in the development and well-being of children have given way to a far more dynamic view, which emphasises the active, constructive nature of human development.

In general, it transpires that young people have considerable inner resources for coping with contradiction and that fears of permanent psycho-social stunting by change, confusion and misfortune may be somewhat overblown. Change, contradiction and even crisis are argued to be normal – a healthy part of childhood and youth – and not inherently unnatural or undesirable (Diggins, 1994:223, quoted in Reynolds-Whyte, 1997:18). Even when confronting extreme adversity, such as sexual abuse or armed conflict, many young people are highly adaptable and creative, devising coping strategies that reduce both exposure and psychological impact (Kitzinger, 1997). Many find ways of coming to terms with deeply disturbing or threatening circumstances (Garbarino, 1999). Sometimes in the most acute situations it is the young and not the adults who are the mediators of meaning, action and resilience (Youniss and Yates, 1994; Boyden and Gibbs, 1997; Hinton, 2000).

Conclusion

Research on demographic trends, fertility, reproductive health and sexual behaviour among the young has revealed important insights into certain specific aspects of youth experience. However, it has failed to provide a holistic understanding of young people's lifeworlds and has privileged adult judgement, perspectives and interests over those of youth. Only in a limited number of quite recent studies have young people been treated seriously as social agents and their views and ideas accepted as sound testimony of the experience of childhood and youth, no longer viewed merely as preparatory stages in the production of the adult. Such research provides new insights into the processes of socialisation and development, in which the social and moral values and competencies of young people are found to be quite similar to those of adults.

This raises the question as to what underlies the prevalent demonising discourses about young people. In this complex, demanding, and sometimes confusing world, the extension of childhood dependence and training into the teen years is probably inevitable. However, in the absence of sound empirical data and an adequate, integrated theory of human development and socialisation beyond the early years of life, young people expressing their agency, whether through political activism, sexual experimentation, independent work, or other means, is condemned by adults as sinister or perverse. Even while the UN Convention on the Rights of the Child advances young people's right to take part in processes and decisions affecting them, societies commonly resort to a range of protective and exclusionary policies to control and constrain their young. This is a continued source of frustration among young people, for although sexually mature and socially and morally competent, they are in this way cast as outsiders in opposition to adult society. To date, research has done little to provide insight into the lives of young people or counteract pejorative social stereotypes, suggesting that if youth policy and societal practice are to become more sensitive to the actual circumstances and concerns of the young, the research community needs to advance new theoretical paradigms and empirical evidence.

CHAPTER 10

YOUNG PEOPLE'S SEXUAL AND REPRODUCTIVE HEALTH: TOWARDS A FRAMEWORK FOR ACTION

Neil Price and Kirstan Hawkins

Introduction

Until the full extent of the HIV/AIDS pandemic became evident, the health needs of young people in developing countries[1] had been largely overlooked by health policy-makers. The reliance on mortality as the main indicator of health status meant that young people were seen as the most healthy age group, and consequently given low priority in health programmes (WHO/UNICEF, 1996). However, in recent years there has been a growing recognition that, because of a combination of biological, social and economic factors, young people face a range of health problems. International attention is currently focused on the high incidence of sexually transmitted diseases (STDs), including HIV among young people, on the persistence of high age-specific fertility rates among the under twenty-year-old population cohort,

1. In the absence of a suitable generic term for what was formerly called the Third World, the chapter uses the terms poor countries, pre-industrial and industrialising countries, developing countries, and resource-poor settings interchangeably. No wider meaning is implied in any of these terms.

and on maternal mortality and morbidity related to early childbearing and high rates of unsafe abortion.

Recognition of the importance of young people's reproductive and sexual health,[2] has been articulated in two major international conferences. The 1994 International Conference on Population and Development (United Nations, 1994:7.47) highlighted the special sexual and reproductive health needs of young people. The Fourth World Conference on Women (United Nations, 1995:para. 106 ff.) established that young people have a right to sex education and modern contraceptive services, and that young women have the right to continue in education after childbirth. Both conferences emphasised the threats posed by HIV and AIDS in developing countries, as young people – particularly young women – are the most vulnerable to infection. Young people's need for information about sexual and reproductive health before they become sexually active is now widely recognised following these international conferences. However, it is also accepted that it is difficult to meet unmarried young people's sexual and reproductive health needs, not least because of political sensitivity, moral opposition, and religious and legal constraints.

Within the international health policy discourse, ambiguity surrounds definitions of the group interchangeably labelled adolescents, youth, young people and young adults. Adolescence is the transition from childhood to adulthood, encompassing the 'development to sexual maturity, and to psychological and relative economic independence' (International Planned Parenthood Federation, 1994:5; see also Boyden, this volume). The age range inherent in such a definition is clearly imprecise, as the length of the transition varies between and within cultures. In some cultural contexts, the ascription of adult status (i.e. the end of adolescence) is less to do with age than passage through specified socially

2. The concept of reproductive health, as used throughout the following discussion, is derived from that contained in the Programme of Action agreed at the International Conference on Population and Development (United Nations, 1994, para 7.2): '...a state of complete physical, mental and social well-being and not merely the absence of disease or infirmity, in all matters related to the reproductive system and to its functions and processes. The term therefore implies that people are able to have a satisfying and safe sex life and that they have the capability to reproduce and the freedom to decide if, when and how often to do so'. We also adopt WHO's definition of sexual health as: '...the capacity to enjoy and control sexual and reproductive behaviour in accordance with a social and personal ethic; freedom from fear, shame, guilt, false beliefs and other psychological factors inhibiting sexual response and impairing sexual relationships; freedom from organic disorder, diseases and deficiencies that interfere with sexual and reproductive functions.' (WHO, 1994c).

recognised transition rituals, notably initiation, marriage or childbirth (see Montgomery, this volume). The World Health Organisation (WHO, 1986), in an attempt to overcome this ambiguity, employs an age-based classification in which adolescents are defined as those in the age group ten–nineteen, youth in the age group fifteen–twenty-four, and young people as those between ten and twenty-four. In the international health policy and programme literature, young adult is a term often used to cover the period of adolescence and early adulthood (however defined). Age classifications are of limited utility (Boyden, this volume): the defining characteristic of young people is that they are socially liminal. In many sub-Saharan African societies, for example, a teenage woman who is married and has children will be considered an adult, whereas an unmarried male in his early twenties attending high school or college is unlikely to be considered locally to have reached adulthood. In such cultures the concept of adolescence is a relatively new phenomenon,[3] a consequence for many young people *inter alia* of decreasing age of puberty, postponement of marriage, and the extension of schooling. In many societies, the rites of passage and ritualised age-set traditions which once represented a recognition and regulation of the transition from child to adult have broken down. The result throughout the industrialising world is an extended period in which young people are developing physical and emotional maturity and self-reliance, whilst lacking the status and resources of adults.

Throughout this paper, the term 'young person'[4] is adopted to refer to those in the age group which spans the period before the onset of puberty up to early adulthood, as defined locally. This definition recognises that action to help the development of sexual maturity and identity, and to educate about sexual and reproductive health, will often need to take place before puberty. Many children in poor countries are involved in sexual practices at very early ages. But differential needs are influenced by factors other than age alone: class, ethnicity, education, gender, residence (rural/urban/street), parenting and kinship patterns and social

3. Indeed in many cultures, there is no term for adolescence. Kambou et al. (1998:114) note that young people in Lusaka, Zambia use the terms boy/girl and older boy/older girl to refer to the age groups covering respectively the period from pre-pubescence to late teens, and late teens to late twenties. '*Mutsikana* is used to refer to girls aged 10 to 20 years, who are subsequently called *bakulu* (older girl)…' (ibid). A *bakulu* becomes an *amai* (woman) only when she is thirty years of age or older (by which time she is also expected to have given birth).
4. The sex-specific terms young men and young women are also used.

networks all shape experience, ultimately influence sexual and reproductive behaviour, and determine the demand and need for services, support and information.

This chapter offers a framework of action to improve the design, implementation and evaluation of young people's sexual and reproductive health programmes. After exploring the causes and consequences of young people's sexual and reproductive behaviour,[5] the chapter critically reviews policies and programmes in resource-poor countries to offer lessons on the most appropriate strategies and approaches, before concluding with a set of recommendations for addressing young people's sexual and reproductive health needs.

The context and outcomes of young people's sexual and reproductive behaviour

Context

People under twenty-five years of age represent over half of the world's population (United Nations, 1997). In the developing world as a whole, the population of ten–nineteen year olds is currently estimated at 914 million, or 20.2 per cent of the population of all ages (Bongaarts and Cohen, 1998:99).

Many young people in developing countries face conditions of increasing poverty. Lack of employment opportunities and increased pressure on land in rural areas have led to migration and the breakdown of kinship structures and mechanisms through which young people traditionally received sex education. As societies urbanise and local economies become monetarised, education has become increasingly important, with far greater numbers of young people in poor countries completing primary and secondary schooling than did their parents. However, in high fertility societies strong normative pressures for early childbearing coexist with conflicting pressures for women to take advantage of educational opportunities (Price, 1996; Gage-Brandon and Meekers, 1993). In poor families, priority is often given to educating boys, with the result that the proportion of women with secondary education remains low in many high-fertility

5. Most of the empirical data presented in this chapter are for the countries of sub-Saharan Africa (and parts of South Asia and Latin America). While most developing countries for which survey data exist have experienced some decline in 'adolescent' fertility over the past ten years, this is not the case for much of sub-Saharan Africa, where over 50 per cent of the population is currently under eighteen, and where globally the highest rates of STDs and HIV exist among young people.

settings: in sub-Saharan Africa for instance, only 40 per cent of women aged fifteen–nineteen have received any secondary school education (Alan Guttmacher Institute, 1997; World Bank, 1995 and 1996).[6] Poor health outcomes and low use of preventive services, such as family planning, are associated closely with illiteracy and low educational levels, while lack of employment and economic opportunities are associated with risk-related sexual behaviour, such as young people's engagement in unprotected sexual intercourse, and sexual activity for economic gain. A study undertaken in a peri-urban compound in Lusaka, Zambia (Kambou et al., 1998; Shah et al., 1999) reports that girls from livelihood-insecure households use sex as a form of currency with which to barter for essential items such as clothes, medicines, accommodation, bus fares, school fees etc. (Kambou et al., 1998:115–17).

In addition to the demise of traditional indigenous authority structures and socialisation practices, recent data reveal decreasing ages of puberty and rising ages of marriage (Bongaarts and Cohen, 1998; McCauley and Salter, 1995; Zabin and Kiragu, 1998:213). In Kenya the age of menarche dropped from 14.4 years in the late 1970s to 12.9 years in the 1980s. Gray (1983) suggests that improved health and nutrition may be determining factors in the earlier onset of puberty. The median age of first marriage is rising in most regions of the world (West Africa and South Asia are exceptions, see Singh and Samara, 1996). The trend is associated with urbanisation – in rural areas in poor countries, women continue to marry earlier than their counterparts in urban areas. The timing of marriage is the most significant proximate determinant of young people's fertility, consequently around 24 per cent of rural women in the developing world begin childbearing in their teenage years compared to about 16 per cent of urban women (McDevitt, 1996:v–vi) There is no universal trend in change in age of first intercourse, which has increased for women in many parts of Latin America[7] and South-East Asia, but has declined for sub-Saharan Africa, where half of women aged fifteen–nineteen had ever had sex in eleven of seventeen countries for which data are available, with Cameroon and Cote d'Ivoire recording levels of 70 per cent (Blanc and Way,

6. School enrolment ratios have risen substantially in most developing countries over the past twenty years, with the exception of sub-Saharan Africa where enrolment ratios fell during the 1980s (McDevitt, 1996:v–vi)
7. However, Vasconcelos et al. (1995) report from a school-based study in Brazil that 36 per cent of young women had their first sexual experience before the age of thirteen.

1998:107)). These changes mean that, for many young people, the period of transition between the onset of physical maturity – and sexual development – and entry into adulthood is lengthening. With marriage in most pre-industrial and industrialising countries remaining the defining institution of adulthood, first sexual intercourse is increasingly occurring before marriage, often in contexts where young people have little or no access to quality sexual and reproductive health information and services (see Senderowitz and Paxman, 1985).

The social, cultural and economic context which shapes marriage patterns, school enrolment and urbanisation, also creates gender differences in sexual experiences, expectations and the ability to adopt safer sexual behaviours. A common manifestation of gendered ideology is for young women to be labelled promiscuous if they suggest condom use (Berglund et al., 1997; Cash and Anasuchatkul, 1995; Hughes and McCauley, 1998; Paiva, 1993; Stewart and Richter, 1995; Russell, this volume). The power imbalances characteristic of gender relations are cross-cut by conditions of poverty, placing many girls and young women at very high risk of unsafe sexual activity. Sexual activity for economic gain (as a livelihood strategy) and sexual coercion underlie many poor young women's sexual experiences (especially their first or early sexual experiences, see Weiss et al., 1996:7, Bongaarts and Bruce, 1995:72, Boyer and Fine, 1992). There has, for instance, been a rise in many parts of sub-Saharan Africa in the numbers of 'sugar daddies', older men who seek out girls for sex in exchange for gifts or money (De Bruyn, 1992; Gorgen et al., 1993; Schoepf, 1994). Such gendered contexts limit young women's ability to protect themselves from unwanted pregnancy, STDs and HIV/AIDS (Weiss et al., 1996:7). Young men in many societies face conflicting messages between sexual abstinence (predominantly from religious and state institutions) and sexual activity as a proof of manhood (from peers, and increasingly the media). Peer pressure among young men is one of the most important determining factors in their sexual behaviour (Barker and Rich, 1992; Berglund et al., 1997; Bezmalinovic, 1997), and many young men describe feelings of insecurity and self-doubt if they are not in sexual relationships (Keller, 1997:25).

Social and health outcomes

The sexual and reproductive health of many young people is undermined by lack of access to information and services: many sexually active teenagers use no method of family planning (Curtis and Neitzel, 1996). There are few data on contraceptive use and prevalence among young men in poor countries because most surveys focus exclusively upon women. In sub-Saharan Africa, the proportion of women aged fifteen–nineteen who reported that they were using family planning methods ranged from 2 per cent in Tanzania, Niger and Senegal to 23 per cent in Cameroon. In Asia, the Near East and North Africa, in which surveys are limited to ever-married women, the proportion of young women reporting current use of contraception ranges from 1 per cent in the Philippines to 34 per cent in Indonesia (Demographic and Health Survey data, reported in Blanc and Way, 1998:110). Although the contraceptive prevalence rate for married women aged fifteen–nineteen for all developing countries is around 17 per cent, in almost all cases unreliable methods are used. In Ghana, contraceptive prevalence among sexually active unmarried teenage women is 17.5 per cent, but only 0.9 per cent for modern methods (Ketting, 1995:30). Bongaarts and Cohen (1998:103) report that young people are particularly unlikely to use contraception the first time that they have sexual intercourse. The adverse consequences of coerced and/or early engagement in unprotected sexual relations can be summarised as follows:

Early pregnancy/childbirth: Despite global trends showing increasing age of marriage, there remain regions where early (often coerced) marriage is the norm for young women, notably in South Asia and West Africa where age at marriage shows little sign of increasing. Over half of women are married before the age of sixteen in the Indian states of Madya Pradesh, Bihar and Uttar Pradesh, and 40 per cent in West Africa. Fifteen million women under twenty years of age in the developing world have children annually, representing 20 per cent of all births each year. Singh (1998:121), presenting Demographic and Health Survey data, shows that between 10 and 15 per cent of young women had given birth before the age of fifteen in Bangladesh, Cameroon, Liberia, Mali, Niger and Nigeria. For the West Africa and South Asia regions, between 50 and 70 per cent of women are mothers by the age of twenty (in Bangladesh, Cameroon, Liberia, Mali and Niger this figure exceeds 65 per cent, see Singh, 1998:121; Bongaarts and Cohen, 1998:101). Pressure on young women to prove their fertility before marriage (Barker and Rich, 1992; Gage, 1998:159; Price, 1996; Price and Thomas, 1999) remains evident in cultures which value high fertility, where early childbearing is a characteristic of family building (see Price, 1996, 1998; Price and Thomas, 1999; Singh, 1998:133), and in societies in which kinship or other structures provide for child-shifting (or fostering). For instance, in matrifocal societies, such as the former

British colonies of the Caribbean and (increasingly) urban sub-Saharan Africa, teenage mothers are able to rely upon their own mothers or other female kin for childcare while they complete their education or engage in wage labour (see Price, 1989; Preston-Whyte, 1994; Ingstad, 1994). Nevertheless, as many as 60 per cent of pregnancies to women under twenty in poor countries are unintended (Weiss et al., 1996:3). Early pregnancy and childbirth are of particular concern in terms of the health and social impact on young women and their newborn. Teenage childbirth – especially in poor countries – is associated with higher morbidity and mortality for both mother and child (United Nations, 1989; Govindasamy et al., 1993). In poor countries, girls aged ten–fifteen are five times more likely to die in pregnancy or childbirth than women aged twenty–twenty-four. Between 30 and 40 per cent of babies born to under-sixteen-year-olds in poor countries are premature, have low birth weight or are still-born; infant mortality is 30 per cent higher for infants born to women aged fifteen to nineteen than for those born to women twenty years or older (McCauley and Salter, 1995:15; Alan Guttmacher Institute, 1998). Zabin and Kiragu (1998:219) report that infants born to young women in Sudan are 64 per cent more likely to die than those born to women in older cohorts.

Box 1

Reproductive and Sexual Health of Young Women in Uganda[8]

In Uganda, the median age at first marriage for women (including customary and 'informal' unions) is 17.5 years, although one in six women currently aged 15–19 were married before age 15. The median age at first sexual intercourse is 16 years; but by age 15, 30 per cent of women have had sexual intercourse. Use of modern contraception for family planning, and condoms as prophylaxis against STDs including HIV, are both very low among women under twenty. A child born to a Ugandan woman under 18 years of age is 85 per cent more likely to die before age 5 than a child of a lower-risk Ugandan mother.[9]

8. The data in this box are derived from the Uganda Demographic and Health Survey (1995) and Price (1997).
9. The risks are those associated with the mother's age, parity, and her latest birth interval (see Uganda, 1995:104).

Unsafe abortion: The accuracy of abortion data in developing countries is poor, as both women and providers are reluctant to discuss the subject (often because of its illegality). However, it has been estimated that five million teenage women undergo abortions each year, of which two million are performed under unsafe and unhygienic conditions (Noble et al., 1996; World Health Organisation, 1994a, 1994b). Abortion is riskier for young women because they are more likely than older women to resort to unskilled practitioners and to delay seeking a pregnancy termination (Singh, 1998:132; Gage-Brandon and Meekers, 1993). It is estimated that over a third of all women seeking hospital care for abortion complications in poor countries are under twenty (Noble et al., 1996), with much higher incidence in sub-Saharan Africa, where young women aged eleven–nineteen account for between 39 and 72 per cent of all abortion-related complications in the region (Centre for Population Options, 1992). In hospital studies in Kenya and Nigeria women under twenty represented over 50 per cent of abortion complication cases (Kinoti et al., 1995). Other hospital studies report even higher figures: Zambia 60 per cent, Uganda 68 per cent (Zabin and Kiragu, 1998:222), and Tanzania 71 per cent (Jutensen et al., 1993:21–2). Young women who undergo unsafe abortions risk short-term morbidity from infections, perforated uterus, cervical lacerations and haemorrhage. Longer-term health implications include increased risk of ectopic pregnancy, chronic pelvic infection and infertility. The combined health risks associated with pregnancies going to term (in the absence of adequate antenatal and delivery care) and unsafe abortions mean that the teenage maternal mortality ratio[10] in poor countries is two to four times higher than for women twenty years of age and over (Alan Guttmacher Institute, 1997). A study in Zaria, Nigeria found maternal mortality among women under sixteen to be six times that for women aged twenty–twenty-four (Zabin and Kiragu, 1998:216). Similar findings have been reported from Ile-Ife, Nigeria (Okonofua et al., 1992), and from Cameroon and Ethiopia (Zabin and Kiragu, 1998:216).

Sexually transmitted diseases and HIV/AIDS: Fewer than 10 per cent of unmarried sexually active teenagers in developing countries report using condoms (Blanc and Way, 1998: 114). Young people currently account for more than two out of every three new STD

10. The maternal mortality ratio is the risk of pregnancy-related death, expressed as the number of women dying of pregnancy-related causes per 100,000 live births.

cases; half a million youngsters are infected daily.[11] Over 50 per cent of the incidence of HIV worldwide is among people under twenty-five years of age (UNAIDS/WHO, 1999b; WHO, 1998:4–5), with six million young people (predominantly in South-East Asia and sub-Saharan Africa) currently infected (UNAIDS/WHO, 1997). In parts of sub-Saharan Africa, teenage girls are now five to six times more likely than boys to become infected with HIV (see UNAIDS/WHO, 1999; Kambou et al., 1998:112, for Zambia; Price, 1997, for Uganda). In the Masaka District of Uganda, the prevalence of HIV in girls aged thirteen–nineteen is twenty times that of boys in the same age group (Grunseit, 1997:25). On average women become infected with HIV five to ten years earlier than men (World Bank, 1994). These gender-based differentials reflect the persistence of low female status, the associated trend of older men engaging in sexual relationships with young girls, and the greater biological risk of HIV infection from vaginal intercourse for women than men, given the same exposure to infected partners (see Barongo et al., 1992; Konde-Lule et al., 1997; Nunn et al., 1994; Preston-Whyte, 1994).

In addition to the poor health outcomes inherent in early (and unprotected) sexual intercourse, there are a number of other social, economic, emotional and health risks faced by young people.

Sexual abuse: Sexual abuse is 'a violation perpetrated by someone with power over someone who is vulnerable' (Stewart and Richter, 1995:17), and includes rape, domestic violence, sexual assault or harassment and incest. The sexual abuse of young people is a worldwide problem, and contributes to early and involuntary entry into sexual activity and unwanted pregnancy. Thirty-three per cent of women in one US study who became pregnant as teenagers had experienced coerced sexual intercourse (ibid.). In Nigeria, 20.6 per cent of university women surveyed said they had been forced to have sex (Weiss et al., 1996). Population Council data from six countries in the Americas indicate that half of all reported rape and sexual assault victims are under the age of sixteen, and that up to 78 per cent of victims knew the perpetrator (cited in Stewart and Richter, 1995:18). The problem, however, is not limited to young women and girls: a Canadian study revealed a third of all young males had experienced some form of sexual abuse (Stewart and Richter, 1995). In situations of extreme poverty, marginalisation or conflict young people's vulnerability to sexual abuse increases significantly (for studies of street children see Anarfi, 1997 on Ghana, and Raffaelli et al.,1993 on Brazil).

11. Figure derived and extrapolated from data presented in WHO, 1998:6.

Female circumcision: Often performed as part of the rites of passage marking the transition from childhood to adulthood, female circumcision (also known as female genital mutilation (FGM) or female genital cutting) is imbued with cultural and symbolic meaning related to aesthetics, sexuality, fertility and maternal and child health. Globally, it has been estimated that two million girls are subjected to FGM each year (World Bank, 1998:2). A recent review of the findings from selected Demographic and Health Surveys shows that in Egypt, Eritrea, Mali and northern Sudan over 90 per cent of women have had some part of their external genitalia removed (Carr, 1997); whilst Toubia (1996) reports that 98 per cent of females have undergone the procedure in Djibouti and Somalia. FGM has no hygienic rationale,[12] and its impact on the health of young women includes haemorrhage, urinary tract infection, septicaemia, tetanus, pelvic infection, dysmenorrhea, dyspareunia and infertility (as a consequence of the procedure); it is also associated, as a result of childbirth, with still-born or brain-damaged babies, urinary and rectal fistulae and other maternal morbidities, and maternal mortality (see Koso-Thomas, 1992:25–8).

Poverty and social exclusion: Their demonstration of sexual activity puts young people at risk of social exclusion or rejection, including expulsion from school and home (Gage-Brandon and Meekers, 1993; Barker and Rich, 1992), which for a young mother has a spiral effect on health and well-being and the welfare of her child. Studies in Chile, Barbados, Guatemala and Mexico show that the poorer a woman, the greater the negative health, social and economic impact of early childbearing (Buvinic, 1998). The poorest among young people also face an increased risk of abusive, exploitative and unsafe sexual encounters (Gage, 1998:163): in poor countries the link between transactional sex and poverty is well established (Barker and Rich, 1992; Berglund et al., 1997; Wood et al., 1998; Montgomery, this volume).

Review of policy and practice

The growing interest among international development assistance agencies, indigenous non-governmental organisations, and researchers in the sexual and reproductive health of young people in developing countries has been translated into an increasing

12. Unlike the circumcision of male infants or young boys, which has hygiene benefits (notably in reducing future risk of HIV infection).

number and diversity of programmes supported through a variety of agencies. However, few programmes have been subjected to rigorous evaluation. This section provides an overview and critique of current policies and programme approaches, and where appropriate indicates lessons learned.[13]

School-based programmes

The importance of the school setting for prevention and education programmes is increasingly being emphasised (Mensch and Lloyd, 1998). The United Nations Joint Programme on AIDS (UNAIDS) is now focusing on school-based STD/HIV prevention and promotion as a key component of national programmes to improve the health and development of children and young people (UNAIDS, 1997). Nonetheless, there are significant institutional, political, religious and cultural barriers to implementing school-based programmes which are highlighted in the discussion below along with the strengths and limitations of approaches undertaken in school settings.

Family life education and population education: In-school education is frequently a starting point for government programmes addressing young people's reproductive health. Typically, school-based programmes in developing countries have adopted population education and family life education (FLE) approaches (see Meekers et al., 1995; McCauley and Salter, 1995; UNFPA, 1998), perceived to be the least controversial interventions. Population education, with its exclusive focus on demographic and environmental issues, does not address sexual or reproductive health. FLE typically emphasises normative social values, although its content, quality and scope vary considerably in different countries.

In many countries in Asia, FLE evolved from a population education base, yet FLE remains a sensitive subject in the region and is taught superficially and theoretically (UNFPA, 1997:25). Generally, no coverage is included of critical issues such as STDs, AIDS and gender. Although FLE has been taught in Sri Lanka since 1973, the focus remains almost exclusively on population dynamics, with the concept of family planning mentioned but with no reference to contraception. Experience in Thailand shows a discrepancy between policy and practice: although the curriculum specifies more sexual

13. Because of the shortage of published evaluations of young people's health programmes this chapter draws heavily on the extensive fieldwork and consultancy undertaken by the authors for and with international donors (DFID, EC, World Bank, USAID, UNFPA) and international NGOs, such as IPPF, CARE International and Marie Stopes International.

and reproductive health content than in other Asian countries, in practice these issues are rarely taught due to cultural sensitivity and inadequate teacher training (UNFPA, 1997:26). Kenya's FLE efforts date back to the 1980s (see Meekers et al., 1995; UNFPA, 1997:27), since when pilot materials and curricula have been developed. These materials include reference to STDs, but not to contraception or sexuality: 'Students report that they do not receive the most relevant information nor skills to practise safe behaviors' (UNFPA, 1997:27). Despite the conservative nature of the programme, a presidential decree has prevented implementation of the curriculum on a national level. In contrast, in many Latin American countries sex education has been introduced into the school curriculum. Following an extensive media campaign during the late 1980s, Colombia introduced a national sex education programme in 1993 (see Saavendra, 1996), which takes account of social and cultural diversity through regional programmes, and which emphasises reproductive health, gender and sexuality (UNFPA, 1997:26; Birdthistle and Vince-Whitman, 1997:54).

Box 2

School-Based Family Life Education and Population Education: Major Shortcomings

Lack of clarity in curricula allows individual teacher discretion in what is taught; teachers are ill-equipped for teaching sensitive issues

Lack of importance accorded to the subject by students and teachers because it is not assessed or examined (Mensch and Lloyd, 1998:180).

Over use of didactic teaching methods and over emphasis on demographic topics (notably population growth and dynamics).

Failure to take account of young people's expressed needs and fears, notably sexuality and gender relations.

Coverage only of the norms and values of 'responsible parenthood': premarital abstinence, delayed marriage, and family planning within marriage (Mensch and Lloyd, 1998:180; Price et al., 1993), with an emphasis on 'conventional' family forms (often the nuclear family).

Taught at secondary school, by which time attitudes about sex roles have been formed, and many young people have left school (and are sexually active).

Sex Education and HIV/AIDS Education: There is increasing focus from agencies such as UNAIDS on the need for formalised provision of sex education. However, formal sex education for young people has had a chequered history in industrialised as well as developing countries. Sex education is far from being a homogenous or unitary concept in substance and approach. The diversity of interpretations of sex education is reflected in the wide range of curricula, teaching approaches and terminology (Grunseit, 1997).

AIDS education is only effective if it begins in primary school and is developed in a comprehensive and systematic way, taking account of the physical, emotional and social changes that the school child undergoes (Hubley, 1997:20). As programmes become more sophisticated, the emphasis has shifted to integrating HIV/AIDS education within a comprehensive school health education approach. Some countries (e.g. India) have developed guidelines on teaching about AIDS in the school curriculum. WHO have collaborated with UNESCO to run international workshops and have coordinated the development of curricula, teaching guides and educational materials on HIV/AIDS (Hubley, ibid.).

There are few published examples of evaluations of school AIDS education programmes in developing countries. AIDS education is typified by the limitations of FLE, notably the proselytising tone and content of the approach, which emphasises abstinence and knowledge (at the expense of prevention skills). Consequently, increased levels of knowledge of HIV/AIDS through the school curriculum have had little impact on teenage STD rates, although when linked to peer programmes and services, AIDS education appears to increase condom use and reduce the numbers of sexual partners (Barnett et al., 1995).

There is no evidence to support arguments made by advocates of population education/FLE that sex education promotes sexual activity and experimentation. The box below summarises the conclusions of a review of nineteen published evaluations of sex education programmes mainly from Europe and the US, but also including Thailand and Mexico (Baldo et al., 1993).[14]

School-based health services and health education

School clinics, which include reproductive and sexual health counselling (and services) as part of a wider programme of school-based health services, are rare outside North America and Europe (some are found in Latin America). Such clinics, particularly those

14. See also Grunseit and Kippax (1993) and WHO (1993a), which review the findings from 1,050 published articles on sex education programmes.

Box 3

Evaluation of School-Based Sex Education Programmes

Sex education does not lead to earlier or increased sexual activity.[15]

In six studies, sex education led either to a delay in the onset of sexual activity or decrease in overall sexual activity.

In ten studies sex education increased the adoption of safer sex by sexually active youth.

Programmes promoting both postponement and protected sex among sexually active youth are more effective than those promoting abstinence.

Programmes are more effective when given before young people become sexually active and when they emphasise skills rather than knowledge.

distributing condoms and supplying other contraceptives, have met with opposition (notably from parents and religious institutions). Evaluations have shown them to be highly successful in reducing pregnancies and in increasing condom use; and no link has been established to increased (or earlier entry into) sexual activity. Schools with poor linkages to wider health services have little impact on the health of schoolchildren (Cohen, 1996). Conversely, linking school health and sex education services to out-of-school family planning services has been shown (in a US study) to increase contraceptive use among those who are sexually active (Koo et al., 1994).

School-based health education presents a special challenge to policy makers, in that it necessitates the development of strong linkages between two government sectors: health and education. Where health education includes sexual health and AIDS education, the challenge increases. School health education interventions are being supported by the United Nations through the School Health Initiative (WHO/UNESCO/UNICEF, 1992) and through the School-Based Interventions (UNICEF, 1997). However, few studies have been conducted on the impact of health education in developing countries, and few reliable data exist on the effect that such programmes have on the health behaviour of

15. However, a recent review by UNAIDS (Grunseit, 1997) acknowledges that sex education is associated with girls having first sexual intercourse at slightly earlier ages in some settings.

young people. Evaluations to date (see Barnett et al., 1995:5) show limited public health benefits of school health education, that at best health education improves health knowledge (but not behaviour), and the few examples of a clear effect on health behaviour and health outcomes are from programmes in which there is a strong link between the school and wider health service provision.

Non-governmental community-based programmes

In developing countries, most community-based/outreach programmes seeking to reach young people with information and services, are small-scale initiatives by non-governmental organisations (NGOs). NGOs are often perceived by governments to be better placed strategically to offer information and services to young people where there is evidence of public resistance. However, some outreach approaches have included broad-based media efforts or have been linked to government programmes.

Youth Centres: The multi-service youth centre model, offering counselling, health education, health services, recreation and income generating activities, is predominant in Latin America. This broad-based/ holistic approach emerged in recognition of the economic and social contexts of young people's sexual and reproductive health. Many of these programmes are now downplaying the role of fixed location activities, and expanding their community-based components (Senderowitz, 1997a), as a result of the high running costs of fixed-service sites and the apparent lack of impact in reaching target populations. An evaluation of Centro de Orientacíon para Adolescentes (CORA) in Mexico City, which has served as a 'model' multi-service centre for young people, revealed that the centre attracted only 16 per cent of its target population. CORA has now shifted to peer promoters to reach young people in schools, factories and the community with information and condoms (Birdthistle and Vince-Whitman, 1997:56; Senderowitz, 1997a:18).

The youth centre model has influenced many NGO programmes in Sub-Saharan Africa, where the approach appears to have been replicated on the basis of scanty evidence of effectiveness (Senderowitz, 1997a). A recent evaluation of the Family Planning Association of Kenya (Erulkar and Mensch, 1997), which operates two centres, found the approach was not cost-effective as the centres were under-utilised for reproductive health services, and used predominantly by older men (outside the target ten–twenty-four age group) for recreational purposes, creating an intimidating environment for young women. The evaluation concurs with similar findings emerging from youth centre programmes in other parts of Africa, which indicate high costs per young person reached with services resulting from low utilisation.

Peer Programmes: Peer approaches use informal networks of young people to provide information, counselling, referral and condoms in clinics, schools, factories, military bases, bars, sports events and on the streets, through trained youth volunteers.[16] The approach is particularly successful in identifying and contacting difficult-to-reach groups such as street youth, young people involved in commercial sex, and those not reached through schools. Peer approaches have the advantage of providing services by young people of similar age and background and therefore starting from young people's concerns and perceptions of their own needs and reflecting young people's own culture and social environments.

The Gente Joven programme run by the Mexican NGO, MEXFAM, is a well-established peer education programme. Recognising the limitations and resource implications of the youth centre approach, MEXFAM – through trained high school volunteers who provide condoms and information on sexuality and reproductive health to their peers – has successfully taken its activities to places where young people already meet: schools, existing recreation centres, meeting points for street gangs etc. (Juarez, 1993:31). In northern Thailand, a programme set up in the dormitories of unmarried female migrant workers (aged fourteen–twenty-five), which trained peer leaders and used a variety of popular media (comics, romance novels) led to increased condom use and better negotiating skills (Cash and Anasuchatkul, 1995). There are very few peer education programmes in sub-Saharan Africa (Kenya, Ethiopia, Nigeria, Tanzania and Zambia are the exceptions). Two of the more successful and innovative are implemented with support from CARE International. CARE Kenya's CRUSH project (Community Resources for Under-Eighteens on STDs/HIV) is an innovative way of providing sex education to under-eighteen-year-olds through the use of interactive educational methods combined with peer education, which has led to positive behavioural changes among participating young people toward STD/HIV prevention (Chege et

16. Peer approaches include information-giving (*peer educators*), facilitating decision-making (*peer counsellors*), encouraging contraceptive use (*peer promotion*), and providing contraceptives (*peer distribution*). Frequently these terms are used interchangeably, and programmes have been found to suffer from lack of clarity among peer workers of their different roles and responsibilities (UNFPA, 1997).

al., 1995 cited in Senderowitz, 1997a:22–3). CARE Zambia's PALS project (Partnership for Adolescent Sexual and Reproductive Health) has successfully utilised peer educators in the integration of youth-friendly services at government clinics and health posts (see below).

Despite the proliferation of peer approaches there has been little systematic evaluation of them, and as a result there is little information on which to base conclusions about the extent to which peer approaches succeed in improving young people's sexual and reproductive health. Informal assessments indicate that young people prefer to talk to their peers rather than to adult educators and counsellors. However, peer approaches should not be viewed as a panacea for meeting all young people's needs. Peer approaches appear to be most effective when they are based on realistic expectations, include continuous training and supervision, focus on providing information and are linked to service delivery programmes. Providing information alone is insufficient to generate change in sexual and reproductive health outcomes: successful peer programmes appear to have made the link between information, counselling and service provision (Senderowitz, 1997a). The main findings of small-scale evaluations of peer programmes are summarised below.

Information, education and communication (IEC)

The mass media (music videos, popular songs, radio and TV soap operas, magazines and posters) and community media (drama contests, school events etc) have been under-utilised in developing countries as channels for reaching young people with reproductive and sexual health information (UNFPA, 1997).[17] There are few evaluations available on the impact of information campaigns and mass media on behaviour. One review (Johns Hopkins School of Public Health, 1995) concludes that successful IEC approaches base their messages on careful needs assessment and research, use a variety of media, involve young people in the design of messages and the choice of medium, use information to link young people with services (IEC appears to be most effective when the main message is promotion of services), address gender-specific issues, and develop a broad base of support (from parents, families, teachers and community leaders).[18]

17. UNFPA (1997) urges caution, as broad-based media approaches have inadvertently created a backlash over adolescent sexual and reproductive health issues in some countries.
18. Pearson et al. (1996) report remarkably similar findings from a review of UK approaches.

Box 4

Key Lessons from Peer Programmes

Peer workers need a clearer understanding of their tasks and responsibilities.

Peer educators are effective in reaching young people with information, but behavioural change is probably greatest among peer educators themselves.

Peer counsellors and promoters need enhanced counselling skills to be effective in empowerment, referral and contraceptive distribution.

Greater attention needs to be given to protecting young people in vulnerable situations.

Gender issues need careful consideration: peer approaches are more effective in reaching young men; peer pressure is a more significant factor in sexual behaviour of young men than it is for young women.

Effective peer strategies require a long-term investment as participation is transient with a high turnover.

Continuous training and supervision is essential: successful peer programmes involve regular feedback from peer promoters/educators to programme managers.

Young people should be involved in the selection of peer workers.

Successful peer programmes have links to service delivery sites, which are physically accessible, free or affordable and provided at times which do not conflict with work or school.

Facility-based service delivery approaches

Health promotion and awareness activities directed at young people continue despite the absence of accessible services. Sexually active youth are thus made aware of how to avoid pregnancy or STDs, without the means to do so. Government, non-governmental, private and indigenous health sectors have important and complementary roles to play in meeting the health needs of young people. To date public sector efforts in implementing youth-focused health services have been minimal in developing countries, although some governments have begun pilot testing activities with NGO involvement (Senderowitz, 1997b; 1999). Providing services to young people (especially the unmarried) presents a particular challenge to the public sector. Even where there is governmental support for the provision of contraceptive advice and services to young unmarried adults, young people are reluctant to use public facilities. The main factors are: lack of privacy and confidentiality; fear of a judgmental and unsympathetic reception; implicit policies restricting services (to the unmarried or childless); physical distance to service providers; lack of knowledge about how to access services; lack of services targeting young people's needs; poorly trained service providers; inadequate primary health care, and legal constraints (including the need for parental consent for contraception, prohibition on abortion etc.) (Senderowitz, 1997b:16; 1999). Young people's health-seeking behaviour thus leads them to private practitioners, traditional healers, peers, herbalists, pharmacists and unlicensed drug sellers.

Even where there are no legal restrictions on the provision of sexual and reproductive health services to unmarried young people, discriminatory service provision – by marital and/or fertility status – continues to be the norm in many Asian and African countries. For example, in Kenya young unmarried women who have given birth, had an abortion, or been treated for an STD are considered high risk (and 'adults'), and are thus able to access contraceptive services, whereas unmarried 'adolescents' (defined locally) who have not proven their fertility will often be denied services (Price, 1996). Similar practices are reported by Gorgen et al. (1993) and Boohene et al. (1991) for Burkina Faso and Zimbabwe respectively. Brown et al. (1987) report that although in Zambia a husband's consent to practise contraception is not embodied in law, custom means that a woman will often be denied access unless she can document such consent.

Gender-specific issues need to be taken into account in the provision of services for young people. Young women are particularly vulnerable because of the asymptomatic nature of many STDs and because in many cultures female sexuality is a taboo subject. Unwanted pregnancies and STDs among young women may also be the result of coercive or abusive sexual relations. We have already noted that HIV prevalence rates are much higher among young women than young men.[19] High prevalence rates in men over twenty-five years of age confirm that young women are being infected by older men (Brabin, personal communication, 1997; see also Grunseit, 1997). Recent research in Nigeria

19. Age specific data from Zambia and Uganda analysed by the Liverpool School of Tropical Medicine (LSTM) indicate that HIV prevalence accelerates rapidly in the 15–19 age-group among young women, reaching a peak in women in the 20–24 age group (L. Brabin, 1997: personal communication).

conducted by the Liverpool School of Tropical Medicine indicates that in some settings non-sexually transmitted vaginal infections are more prevalent than STDs (with the exception of chlamydia (which is largely asymptomatic). These data suggest the need for greater attention to treating reproductive tract infections (RTIs), and a dispelling of the assumption that all young people seeking treatment and screening services are sexually active (Brabin, personal communication, 1997). Other unmet needs include menstrual management,[20] which has been given no attention in discussions of delivery of reproductive health services to young women, yet may serve as an effective entry point for such services.

Collaboration between the public and nongovernmental sectors

Currently, most youth-friendly services that exist in poor countries are stand-alone projects run by NGOs. They are usually located in urban areas and reach only a limited number of young people. Although replicating successful stand-alone initiatives should be part of an overall strategy to expand the availability of user-friendly health services to young people, it is vital to improve the responsiveness of public sector health care delivery systems to young people. A rare example of a district-level public sector health initiative is the Youth Friendly Health Services project in Lusaka, Zambia, implemented by a consortium of NGOs in conjunction with the health department of the district council, and supported by UNICEF (UNICEF, 1997). CARE Zambia's PALS project, based on lessons learnt from the UNICEF-supported initiative, has been effective in sensitising and training health care workers, and through the posting of peer educators/youth counsellors at government health centres (working in 'youth-friendly corners') has bridged the gap between young people and health care providers.

The youth-friendly approach

Evidence from Scandinavia and the Netherlands shows that a non-problem-orientated approach by policy makers and health professionals to young people's sexual health and sexuality, combined with good access to counselling and services, leads to extensive use of public sector services, and to the lowest pregnancy, STD and abortion rates among young people in the 'developed' world (Santow and Bracher, 1999; Jones et al., 1985).

20. LSTM's Nigeria data indicate that over 12 per cent of girls suffer excessive blood loss during menstruation, leading to anaemia; and lacking the means to manage blood flow, many girls are forced into absence from schooling during very heavy flows.

Box 5

Young People's Reproductive and Sexual Health Service Delivery Approaches

School health services: Although they include routine visual and auditory check-ups, vaccination, diagnosis and treatment of common illnesses, few school clinics include reproductive health services. Quality and content vary greatly.

Public sector health services: There are few examples of 'youth-focused' clinics, those that exist tend to be provided at a particular location on a specific day.

NGO programmes: providing services from youth centres, using peer educators to fulfil the function of promotion and referral, are often under utilised and costly.

Condom social marketing: Although some campaigns have successfully targeted young people and proved effective at making condoms available, the approach rarely includes counselling, information, or referral for STD diagnosis and treatment.

Private sector services: Private practitioners are often a preferred source of services for young people due to increased confidentiality and privacy. However, cost of services is a major barrier to many young people.

The emerging consensus is that the most appropriate and sustainable approach to reaching young people with sexual and reproductive health services in developing countries is through 'mainstreaming' youth-friendly services within the existing health service delivery structure (UNICEF, 1997). In poor countries, the greatest barriers to young people's use of public sector services are lack of privacy and confidentiality, negative attitudes of providers, and inappropriate clinic opening hours (UNFPA, 1997). Tailoring existing services to make them youth-friendly does not necessarily require significant additional resources, but does require services which have '... attributes that attract youth to the facility or program, provide a comfortable and appropriate setting for serving youth, meet the needs of young people, and are able to retain their youth clientele for follow-up and repeat visits' (Senderowitz, 1999:11). Box 6 reflects the emerging consensus on the components of truly youth-friendly services.

Box 6

The Components of Youth-Friendly Services

Services geared to the specific needs of different groups of young people.

Young people involved in service management/monitoring (see Russell, this volume).

Skills-based education (to enable young people to explore values and feelings) combined with access to services.

Engagement with the wider community (including parents), presenting accurate and up-to-date information about the health problems faced by young people.

Service providers and educators who have a commitment to serving young people in a non-judgmental manner (with respect for individual rights and feelings); and who are technically competent, with good communication and counselling skills, trained to deal with young people's concerns around sexuality.

Services provided confidentially and in a way which maintains privacy.

Clear guidelines and service delivery protocols which ensure quality.

A comprehensive array of health services (to meet different needs of young people).

Clear information for young people on the types of health services being provided and the way in which they are delivered, through promotional materials and peers.

Towards a framework for action

The chapter concludes with a set of recommended actions and interventions for meeting young people's sexual and reproductive health needs in resource-poor settings, based on the knowledge generated to date on the relative strengths and weaknesses of different approaches.

Use social analysis for the design of locally-specific programmes: Young people's sexual and reproductive health needs are highly culture and context specific. Interventions need to be designed using small-scale ethnographic analyses and localised needs assessments, which analyse the specific epidemiological and cultural contexts of young people's sexual and reproductive health needs (see below on vulnerability). Sample surveys of knowledge, attitudes and practice (KAP surveys), widely used for assessing health needs, fail to draw on young people's experience in the design of survey questionnaires, and deal inadequately with context, and young people's reluctance to admit to behaviour which adults censure. WHO's *Narrative Research Method* (WHO, 1993b) is an experiential needs assessment approach premised on the importance in project design of understanding contemporary patterns and determinants of young people's sexual behaviour.[21] A tool recently developed for appraising young people's demand for and access to reproductive and sexual health services (Hawkins and Price, 2000) is designed to generate data from which to build an understanding of the diverse social and economic realities in which health, sexuality, fertility and reproduction are experienced, the ways in which needs and priorities are identified, and the social dynamics of exclusion, vulnerability and marginalisation. The tool uses a peer ethnographic approach to data collection, and provides programmes and services with a framework from which to assess the appropriate means of improving the responsiveness of service delivery to the needs of different groups.

Reach vulnerable groups through an appropriate constellation of sexual and reproductive health services and information: Generalised statements have created a stereotypical view of young people's sexual activities. A large number of young people are not sexually active. The traditional distinction made between in-school and out-of-school youth has also led to a stereotyping of in-school youth as less vulnerable, and out-of-school youth as highly sexually active and prone to 'anti-social' behaviour. This false dichotomy has led UNAIDS to an approach which prioritises vulnerable groups on the basis of local social analyses and needs assessments, and which recognises that vulnerability is highly context-specific: groups identified as not vulnerable to STD/HIV infection and unwanted pregnancies may be vulnerable to vaginal infections, menstrual problems, FGM or sexual abuse. The appropriate con-

21. The method involves young men and women role-playing a story, which they consider to be typical of young people's sexual and reproductive health experiences and needs in their communities; the story is then converted into a questionnaire which is piloted before large-scale implementation. Exercises undertaken and evaluated to date by WHO reveal that the adverse social and health consequences discussed earlier stem from young people's real and perceived lack of knowledge, information, and lack of trust in and communication with adults and institutions.

stellation of sexual and reproductive health information and services will thus vary considerably according to circumstances.

Promote an integrated approach to young people's health: Increased attention to young people's health in poor countries has resulted in a wide variety of projects and programmes focusing on single health issues (such as family planning). Within the context of available resources, programmes should provide a full range of primary health care services (including reproductive and sexual health services), and also provide life skills to help young people to counter peer pressure to engage in risky behaviours. Interventions aimed at other population groups (e.g. STD/HIV prevention targeted at older men, educating parents when they visit health facilities) will impact significantly on young people's sexual/ reproductive health.

Adopt a multi-sectoral approach: Young people's sexual and reproductive health is determined by a range of interconnected economic, political, social and cultural factors. Poverty, lack of educational and employment opportunities, gender inequalities, and the lack of protection of human rights, all combine to bring about contexts in which young people experience poor sexual and reproductive health outcomes. A wide consensus has now emerged that young people's sexual and reproductive health needs cannot be addressed through a 'blueprint' or single-sector strategy or intervention. There is increasing recognition that a multi-sectoral approach (involving ministries of health, education, social welfare, youth and sport) is essential, and must take account of a range of factors including educational opportunities, the economic status of young people, protection of young people's rights, protection of young people from sexual abuse, and the provision of accurate sexual and reproductive health information alongside access to health services.

Support capacity building and partnerships: Increased interest by the international donor community in young people's health is leading to a burgeoning of projects without the local capacity to implement and monitor effectively. The limited capacity of governments to implement effective programmes through the educational and health sectors is evident. NGOs who have taken a lead in small-scale pilot approaches, are grappling with the issue of how to scale-up in a sustainable way where there is little or no government commitment. One strategic approach to building capacity in the public and NGO sector would be to support the development and implementation of standards, guidelines and protocols for the provision of sexual and reproductive health services to young people (as part of efforts to improve the capacity of NGOs/governments to develop and monitor services). In addition, training of service providers in the use of protocols and in improved quality of care is needed to improve the capacity of health staff to provide youth-friendly services. Development assistance agencies should support international collaboration through exchange visits to successful programmes, and the provision of technical assistance and information exchange through partnerships between NGOs, governments, and multilateral resource centres (such as WHO's Adolescent Health and Development Programme/ADH).

Support policy analysis and reform: A critical problem in making public sector health services youth-friendly is the existence of restrictive laws and policies. Support for advocacy groups lobbying for changes in legislation and for the subsequent monitoring of adherence to laws is recommended. Even where provision of contraceptive services to unmarried young people is not illegal, lack of an explicit policy on service provision is often interpreted by service providers as tantamount to prohibitive legislation. Support to ministries of health in the development of service delivery protocols, standards and guidelines for the provision of sexual and reproductive health services to young people, is an important strategy for improving access to services (as is the training of public sector health personnel in service delivery protocols). Such reforms will need to be accompanied by an increase in the number of public sector service delivery outlets providing youth-friendly services. Special attention also needs to be paid to policy reform and advocacy on female genital mutilation (FGM). Campaigning for greater awareness of the health implications of FGM is insufficient, as the social consequences of not being 'circumcised' are perceived by many young women in poor countries as greater than the physical consequences of undergoing the operation. The advocacy strategy adopted by the Swedish International Development Agency (SIDA) promotes FGM as a human rights issue, and seeks to establish debate among policy makers, religious leaders, men, elders, traditional midwives, health workers and school staff, and to identify alternative roles for FGM practitioners who earn their livelihoods and social status from the practice.

Strengthen monitoring and evaluation: The limited capacity to monitor progress and to evaluate impact is evident at the programme level. Managers are often able to articulate strengths and weaknesses but unable to substantiate these with documentation and data. Indeed one of the greatest shortcomings to become evident from reviews of current programmes is the lack of documented evaluation of what works (see Haffner and Goldfarb, 1997; McKaig et al., 1996). It is therefore recommended that all programmes contain activities not only for monitoring and evaluation but also for the dissemination of findings. One means of improving understanding of effectiveness is to support participatory action research and/or ethnographic monitoring (see Hawkins and Price, 2000). Investing in such approaches is likely to contribute significantly to capacity building and impact.

CHAPTER 11

Teenage Pregnancy and the Moral Geography of Teesside, UK

Andrew Russell

Introduction

'Stop Tide of Teen Births' screams the main headline of the Teesside *Evening Gazette* for 20 November 1998. Latest figures indicate, claims the article, that with 3.47 abortions for every 1000 pregnancies amongst eleven to fifteen year olds, Teesside has 'one of the highest teenage pregnancy rates in Europe', 50 per cent higher than the national average.

Such headlines, and the supporting surveys that provide such telling, but confusing statistics, highlight the problem of 'localising' national concerns in this way. The UK has the highest rate of teenage pregnancy in Europe. Does Teesside indeed have the highest rate in the UK, and if so, why? One is confronting a moral geography of blame here. Teesside is also the region with some of the poorest housing estates anywhere in Britain, with concomitant social and economic problems. One such 'problem' is a high rate of pregnancy amongst teenage girls. In the *Evening Gazette* article, the Tees and District Health Promotion officer for schools argues that:

> There has to be far more specialist help than is currently available. The people giving the advice are not skilled enough. We must educate the educators. Until we do that we will always be on the

> backfoot. Mr Mawson warned the help needed went beyond the birds and the bees. 'There should be properly trained staff to be able to fully understand what youngsters are thinking and feeling', he said. Recognition of personal, social and health education as a real subject is also essential. (Heywood, 1998:1)

Mawson's quote shows the advantages to health professionals in playing to a sense of moral panic – Teesside is portrayed as a place with a 'problem' that can only be solved with more resources to 'educate the educators'. Statistics may be massaged to highlight particular age groups, places or social categories. Thus Hartlepool is widely quoted as having the highest rate of teenage pregnancy in the UK (a claim that, significantly, Teesside as a whole cannot make) – but similar claims are also made for a number of Scottish cities, such as Dundee, and several London boroughs such as Tower Hamlets.

Teenage pregnancy is widely regarded as a social 'problem'. The government's Health of the Nation targets, introduced in 1992, aimed to halve the rates of teenage pregnancy (specifically among girls under sixteen, from 9.5 to no more than 4.8 per 1000 girls aged thirteen to fifteen) by the year 2000. However, this target has clearly not been attained, and in a survey of GPs in the Northern and Wessex regions, only 30 per cent of respondents felt that it was, from the start, realistic (Cheung et al., 1997). In fact, figures released in February 1998 indicate that on Teesside, far from declining, rates of teenage pregnancy were going up, prompting a rash of local radio and newspaper discussions around the subject of 'why', and whether sex education and family planning services were failing the needs 'of our young people'.

The project to be described in this chapter took place in the middle of this geographical context of 'blame' and 'shame'. It is based on research conducted by undergraduates on the Human Sciences and Health and Human Sciences degrees at the University of Durham, Stockton Campus (UDSC). About half of our students are from the local area and about half (not a completely intersecting group) are mature students, many from 'non-traditional' (in higher education terms) social and educational backgrounds. If 'properly trained staff' are lacking (as the *Evening Gazette* article implies), perhaps locally trained anthropologists are the people best equipped 'to be able to fully understand what youngsters are thinking and feeling'. Our degrees aim to give students a lot of 'hands on' research experience, and many of the projects and reports written by students during their course are concerned with different aspects of teenage sexuality on Teesside.

We feel that much of this work, by students who are 'of the region' and hence 'speak the language', deserves a wider audience and should be encouraged. Far from those of an anonymous researcher coming in to ask questions of a reluctant informant, the research activities to be described are frequently undertaken with friends and relatives, some of whom the researchers have known all their lives. We doubt it would be possible to collect data of such richness, diversity and depth using more conventional anthropological research methods. The project, therefore, is an experiment in research methods, in how to incorporate local-level, undergraduate research into the analysis of a social 'problem', as much as a contribution to knowledge about the 'problem' itself, teenage pregnancy on Teesside.

Anthropology and teenage pregnancy on Teesside

It is worth rehearsing the reasons why anthropology might be expected to have 'something to say' on the subject of teenage pregnancy on Teesside:

(i) Anthropologists are used to working in multidisciplinary settings in which their preference for holistic perspectives, such as a combination of biological and social research, can come to the fore.

(ii) Anthropologists have the capacity to look at a subject such as teenage pregnancy non-judgmentally, as a socially constructed as much as a social or moral problem. There is a need to question the presuppositions upon which much work on teenage sexuality is based – is it really helpful to categorise this group of the population (teenage girls) as having a 'problem', or do we need to unpick the assumptions which initially formulated teenage sexuality as a problem?

(iii) Anthropology has respect for diversity. Not all teenagers experience sexuality, pregnancy or parenthood in the same way, and nothing is achieved by treating them as a homogenous group. A more fruitful approach is to take a cultural perspective, looking at the narratives of young people in their own terms, for what they indicate about their multiple and complex beliefs and value systems, and the relationship of these systems to teenage sexual activity and pregnancy.

(iv) Anthropology also respects the 'underdog'. It seeks to give voice to the 'muted' and formalise the informal, in this case the experiences of young people on Teesside themselves.

(v) Anthropologists are used to looking at global/local interactions – in this case, the moral panic about teenage pregnancy and the policy statements which have been made about it at the national level, and the reality of life at the local level, on Teesside. They are particularly skilled at fine grained, detailed studies of local situations that can be placed against the 'nationalising' or 'globalising' tendencies of much research by disciplines other than anthropology. In this case research involves working with teenagers (of both sexes) and with the numerous professionals, their agencies and institutions, with which young people come into contact, as well as looking at what is going on at regional, national and international levels. It involves feeding the results of this wider research into the local-level research process, and looking at the results of the local-level research in this wider context to see what is distinctive about Teesside, and what is shared with other areas nationally.

(vi) Anthropologists are accustomed to methodological pluralism, and innovation/sensitivity appropriate to the group(s) being studied. One of the student projects to be discussed, for example, was conducted by someone who had established great rapport with her subjects through her involvement in a youth club. She looked at young people's perceptions of family planning service provision by encouraging them to draw maps of their neighbourhood and the places they thought they would go to for contraceptive advice.

(vii) Anthropology is inherently comparative, taking examples from around the world and using these to provide fresh perspectives on anthropology 'at home'.

(viii) Anthropology, in its applied dimension, brings evidence and ideas together and acts as a catalyst for practitioners and researchers to work collaboratively, locally, regionally, nationally and internationally. Hudson and Ineichen (1991) argue that the literature surrounding teenage sexuality and knowledge is scattered and unsatisfactory in several respects. One of our first tasks was therefore to bring together existing knowledge on the subject at national level, against which the local level reality could be compared, where knowledge is often diverse, 'muted', and non-formalised.

What is going on? Macro-level statistics

Literature reviewed by Hudson and Ineichen (1991) suggests that young people are becoming sexually active at a younger age today than in the past. This is related to a number of factors including earlier physical maturity (the average age of menarche for girls in the UK is now twelve, with the potential for fertility by the age of thirteen or fourteen), social pressures, and greater availability of contraception.

Despite this increasing sexual activity, is teenage pregnancy really the epidemic that it is perceived and portrayed as in the media (Sharpe, 1987)? National figures indicate that teenage birth rates reached a peak in 1971, when they made up 5.7 per cent of the total, and have since fallen. Burghes and Brown (1995) of the Family Policy Studies Centre, for example, estimate that there were 67.3 births per 1,000 teenage women in 1971, compared to 40.4 per 1,000 in 1992. In addition, abortion rates for teenagers grew until about 1990: there were 21,000 teenage abortions in 1971 compared to 41,000 in 1988 (Hudson and Ineichen, 1991), but by 1994 the figure had (according to the National Survey Office) declined to 28,469 (legal abortions). Rates are not evenly distributed amongst the teenage population: in the 1970s, one in four pregnant nineteen year olds had an abortion compared to three in four of those under fifteen years (Francombe, 1986). Phoenix (1991) argues that birth rates for teenagers are not much higher today than they were in the 1950s.

It is possible to argue that we now notice teenage mothers more because, while birth rates have declined overall, particularly in the twenty to twenty-four age group, and less dramatically in the twenty-five to twenty-nine years group, they have risen for the thirty to thirty-four and thirty-five to thirty-nine age groups, with the result that births to teenage mothers represent part of an increasingly bifurcated total. This is what Gillham (1997:6) calls 'part of the shifting picture that puts teenage motherhood in an increasingly distinct category' (similar arguments have been made for the US by Weatherley, 1987; Zelnick and Kantner, 1980; and The Children's Defense Fund, 1986; 1988). Popular perceptions of teenage pregnancy rates are, however, not well-attuned to general demographic trends but instead inflamed and inflated by tabloids like the *Daily Mail*, which in 1998 spoke of 'Our World Record of Shame' when newly-published figures indicated that 86 per cent of unmarried women had had sexual intercourse by the age of nineteen, prompting the conclusion that 'Britain leads the world in teenage sexual activity' (Cooper, 1998).

However, such blanket figures may obscure local or socio-economic variations (Moore and Rosenthal, 1993). Siedlecky (1984) suggests that amongst more affluent and well-educated groups, the birth rate is declining, while amongst unemployed or socially disadvantaged groups it is increasing. Links between low socio-economic status and teenage pregnancy have been observed on Tayside (Smith, 1993) and in the English regions (Wilson, Brown and Richards, 1992). On Tayside, the affluence levels of different residential areas were graded on a 7-point scale based on four variables: percentage male unemployment; percentage of inhabitants in social classes IV and V, percentage without a car, and percentage in overcrowded housing. It was found that pregnancy rates for young people aged fifteen–nineteen followed a consistent gradient, correlating with levels of deprivation across the years from 1980 to 1990. As Gillham has said, in summary, 'young women in the most deprived areas are between four and eight times more likely to become pregnant as teenagers than those in the most affluent areas. The implication is that social factors have a major impact on sexual behaviour and that teenage pregnancies have to be seen as endemic in some areas, largely because of broad social conditions' (1997:7–8; note the use of the medical term 'endemic' to describe teenage pregnancies). Similar associations between low socio-economic status and teenage pregnancy have been observed in the USA (Zelnik et al., 1981).

From the statistical data, then, it would appear that, in the UK at least, the 'problem' of teenage pregnancy is something of a social construction, but not a complete one. The fact that something is constructed should not blind us to the fact that a problem may also be 'real'. Deconstruction requires the disagreggation of people represented by the statistics into those who really do have a 'problem' and those who do not. It also requires an analysis of the social and cultural forces leading to and maintaining the construction.

Teenage mothers as a stigmatised group

'Although girls have been having babies since time immemorial, too-early pregnancy or motherhood did not arise as a *social* problem until the last few decades' (Gordon, 1997:260). In an unacknowledged debt to Margaret Mead, Gordon points out that the word 'teenage' was only coined this century. It reflects a new concept of adolescence, and a social group that we have created but remain uneasy with and ambivalent about – a halfway house between 'child' and 'adult', a 'dangerous category' as Douglas (1966) puts it. Later industrialisation has brought protracted periods of education for children and a strong identification of young people with their peers – a situation of 'intergenerational conflict' compared to an earlier pattern of integration into multigenerational groups. There is now a large gap between sexual maturity and economic independence (Weeks, 1989). The word 'teenager' has taken on a 'specific meaning; a person mature in body, often sexually active, but not economically prepared' (Gordon, 1997:261). 'Teenagers' are a problem in the dominant discourse of society, of which 'teenage pregnancy' is a part.

However, it is not just a question of dangerous cultural categories, but the way in which these are linked to a lack of political and socio-economic power. With perceived danger comes emotion, emotion that can be channelled into blame of teenagers, and teenage girls in particular, who form a powerless, 'muted' group not sufficiently articulate to reply and lacking a political voice. The discourse of blame takes many forms, and is worthy of study in its own right. It suggests widespread sexual promiscuity amongst teenagers today, their ignorance of and disregard for conventional forms of contraception, and their blissful assumption that the state will provide – indeed, the assertion that some young girls become mothers simply to 'jump the queue' in the allocation of council housing. For there is another dimension to public perceptions of teenage mothers, and one much more in keeping with general secular trends, namely that an increasing proportion of teenage births are taking place to women outside wedlock. This is a trend among women at all age levels and in fact the smallest increase in 'out-of-wedlock' births during the decade 1984–1994 was amongst those under twenty (Gillham, 1997:5). Even so, teenage mothers are regularly identified in the public consciousness with 'single mothers'. The perceived challenge that 'single teenage mothers' pose to the threatened 'status quo' of nuclear families further inflames the moralistic discourse about them. This 'moral panic' is real and, as we shall see, contributes to the feelings of shame (but also disgruntlement) felt by many teenage mothers.

Regardless of marital status, within the category 'teenage girls' an even more culpable category has evolved – that of working class teenage girls from economically deprived areas. These are the 'black spots' – Teesside has become part of what Farmer (1992), talking about AIDS in Haiti, calls 'the geography of blame', and specific communities on Teesside are widely regarded as the 'sink holes' in the area. Once communities are targeted as black spots, rather than uniting to face the problem, there is a well-documented tendency for them, and the groups of which they are composed, to react by blaming members of other communities or other groups within their community – the 'promiscuous', those who are 'beyond parental control' etc. (Given, 1998). As Gordon puts it:

> The teenage pregnancy moral panic ... is a cluster of meaning, densely packed with a variety of extreme anxieties. Because it is so packed, it is difficult to exhaust the meanings of teenage pregnancy, which could be analysed along a variety of axes: attitudes toward welfare, toward marriage, toward sex, toward abortion, toward minorities ...Teenage pregnancy may be effective as a symbol precisely because it can express so many different laments about society (1997: 264)

We might add that it is not just a cluster of meaning, but also clusters around power (or powerlessness) and place. Teenage pregnancy, as we have seen, is something that the government wants to see decrease, yet in the most powerless, deprived and (in many ways) feared parts of the country the figures move relentlessly up.

Teenage Pregnancy in a Broader Context

Part of the deconstruction of 'teenage pregnancy' lies in contextualising it as simply an aspect of teenage sexual behaviour. Moore and Rosenthal (1993) indicate that teenagers ignore sexual health measures. Between one and two-thirds of adolescents use no form of contraception. 'Why', they ask, 'are so many young people, especially males, resistant to contraception? When effective methods of contraception are readily available and the dangers of unprotected sex, both in terms of unwanted pregnancies and of potentially lethal or at least debilitating disease are known to teenagers, why are they so cavalier in their use of this technology?' They suggest a number of answers to their question: (i) lack of knowledge; (ii) lack of skill; (iii) lack of access to advice and devices, and (iv) the sporadic nature of sexual activity.

These are, if you like, the 'top down', rational, medical reasons for the failure to use contraceptives. But, as Moore and Rosenthal themselves argue, 'explanations of teenage sexual behaviour do not fit easily into rational decision-making or problem-solving models' (1993:20). There would appear to be a wide gap between intent to use a condom and actual practice. Even when all four of the above criteria are satisfied, we may well find teenagers not using contraception. This behaviour seems to be linked to socio-economic status as well as age, although research amongst undergraduate students at the University of Durham reveals many highly educated students using 'emergency contraception' after sexual activity rather than contraception prior to intercourse. We have to look beyond rational explanations for lack of contraceptive use, such as those advanced by Moore and Rosenthal, into the domain of teenage 'culture', within which our research has indicated the existence of a number of key themes:

(i) A sense of invulnerability – 'it will never happen to me'.

(ii) Fatalistic attitudes, a sense of powerlessness and of inability to change the course of life's events; a general feeling of lack of control over their lives.

(iii) Lack of confidence/assertiveness – not only in the acquisition of contraceptives, but in their use and discussion of their use (since condom use often requires negotiation).

(iv) Teenage girls are often reluctant to carry condoms in preparation for spontaneous sexual activity in case they are seen as a 'slag' (the key finding of undergraduate research carried out in Richmond, North Yorkshire).

(v) The absence of a sense of equality with partners and of equal power and control over the process of sexual negotiation.

(vi) The thrill of risk taking involved in unprotected sex – particularly amongst young men, where society 'conveys idea that "exciting" men are powerful, reckless and dangerous' (Moore and Rosenthal, 1993:80). For girls, the idea of having sex in order to 'risk all for love' contravenes parental and teacher pressure to practise safe sex.

(vii) The increasing levels of alcohol consumption amongst young people (this was an important factor in the Durham student study).

How was it for you? Micro-level perspectives

Some interesting (and again, morally charged) statistics from the Health Education Authority suggest that 'the North' has the highest rates of teenage sexual intercourse, relatively poor school sex education, and that there is a failure in the region to address the cultural norms and attitudes held about sex and contraception by teenagers (Health Education Authority, 1992). In the HEA study, 58 per cent of the northern teenagers questioned reported that they had experienced full sexual intercourse (the highest percentage in the country) compared to 48 per cent of teenagers in London. Of these, only 45 per cent of northern teenagers reported using a condom during their last sexual episode, compared to 57 per cent in London. Forty-nine per cent of northern teenage women were using some form of contraceptive pill, compared to 69 per cent in the South-West. Fifty-three per cent of those interviewed in the North agreed with the statement 'using a condom shows that you care for your partner', compared to 63 per cent in the East Midlands. Only 21 per cent of northern teenagers reported an incident where they had abstained from sex because no condom was available, compared to 29 per cent in London. Twenty-two per cent of teenagers in the North said they would be too embarrassed to suggest condom use to new partner, compared to 11 per cent in the South-West.

Yet figures such as these, while interesting, do not allow us 'to fully understand what youngsters are thinking and feeling' (to rephrase the *Evening Gazette* article). This is where the students' research comes in. It seems that the options available to young people – inadequate sexual advice and access to contraceptive products, abortion, or birth and motherhood – are all failing them in some way.

Hazel writes of her sister Sharon who had a child when she was sixteen. She reported not having felt 'ready' when, at fourteen, she first had sexual intercourse. A drunken night at a party introduced her to the world of sex, after which she experienced feelings of 'shame' and 'unease'. The only sex education class at school had, she said, been given by the music teacher. Instead of visiting her GP, Sharon used contraceptive pills provided by a friend who had received hers at a Family Planning Clinic (in other words she had no professional advice).

Hilda looked at the case of Heather, a friend she had known from the time she discovered her pregnancy when she was sixteen to her motherhood at seventeen. She wanted to investigate the reasons for Heather's decision to keep her child, a baby boy. A major theme in the interview was that Heather felt the decision was not really hers, but that of everyone else in her family. Her father, who came from a lower class background with a large family of many step-brothers and sisters, many of whom have themselves had children at a young age, reacted to the birth by going to the pub to celebrate and 'boast' about his achievement. Her family has been the main source of long-term support she has received, both in caring for the baby and financially. When she was sixteen she was not in the habit of going out in the evenings and did not feel she was missing anything when she first had the baby. Later on, when she saw her friends go out, she began to feel her loss.

For teenage mothers, the experience of giving birth does not always engender self-esteem. Doreen, now at university, writes of her own experience of giving birth as a teenage mother. 'You've been a bad, bad girl', said the midwife, 'and now this is what you get for your trouble'. This was twenty years ago, but how much has the 'culture' of obstetrics wards changed in the meantime?

Mary conducted research with Kate in order to look at the issue of housing choices in teenage pregnancy. She interviewed Kate at three key points: when she was pregnant (at seventeen) and living with her mother, when she was living in temporary accommodation, and finally after she had moved into her council home. Kate left further education prematurely to start work in her boyfriend's father's haulage business. When she discovered she was pregnant she found herself not only on her own but unemployed, which was when she returned home to live with her mother. However, owing to difficulties in their relationship while Kate was still with the father of the baby, and severe overcrowding in her mother's council flat (shared with two younger children), she had to move out. Unable to rent private accommodation she was left with no alternative but to apply for council housing. She was advised that to get housed more quickly she would have to declare herself homeless. This meant she would be placed in a 'hostel' until suitable housing was available. Mary found that the hostel was 'damp, dark, dirty, unfriendly, an unhealthy environment for a young inexperienced mother with a new-born baby'. Researchers have suggested that local authorities use such hostels to act as a deterrent to young girls who, it is claimed, contemplate pregnancy in order to receive council housing. Pushed into this position, they have to accept the first offer of housing made to them. As a result, young mothers are regularly housed in the areas suffering most from social deprivation, the areas with the fastest turnover and vacancy rates. Kate mentions that, if she had had a choice, she would never have taken council accommodation. 'They put us in houses which aren't fit for anyone else, no one else would be desperate enough to take them. They give us barely enough money to feed and clothe a baby, never mind the mother. They expect us to raise delinquents.'

One student speaks of the experience of a friend who had a child when she was fourteen. Moralism is writ large in her account. She had the child before the end of the fourth year of her secondary education, and had to return to finish her schooling. 'The teachers and a lot of the kids from the private estates wrote me off. I had made a mistake and was in every way going to pay for it for the rest of my life. They looked at me as though I was dirt, I could see the contempt in their eyes and hear it in their voices. They treat me as a nobody, one of life's down and outs.'

Abortion also poses problems. Melanie writes: 'I am aware and have knowledge of a number of women who have had abortions yet have suffered psychological and emotional effects. Not particularly from the terminations themselves, but more from the discrimination and disapproval reactions amongst the hospital staff and their own practitioners.' She interviewed in depth a woman, Emma, who had found herself pregnant after being assaulted by a male friend at a party when she was eighteen. Although her GP was supportive, she found the second, consultant signatory to the abortion very abrupt: 'He made me consider that it may have been my own fault for being in this position when I knew that I had not instigated anything. Different conversations began to roam around in my head that I could have with the consultant to try, and for some reason to gain, his approval, or something to at least tell me I was doing what I considered to be the right thing.' The consultant giving a scan 'was quite rough when handling me and did not turn the screen showing the foetus away at any point, she turned it deliberately towards me'. She was then told by a nurse that the other patients on her ward were in there for different reasons, and that she was the only one having a termination. However, talking to her fellow patients later in the day, she found that they were all in the same situation and realised that she was on a ward for women who wanted terminations. Emma understood that the nurse was probably trying to be nice and lied to her so that she could think that no one would know why she was there. However, the result was she was afraid to let people know what she was doing there and secluded herself from the rest of the ward by pulling the screen round her bed while she waited for the RU486 pill to do its work. She felt that, had she known the truth, it would have helped her to talk to the other patients on the ward rather than isolate herself and become more depressed as a result.

Sarah writes of a friend from a middle-class Irish Catholic background who became pregnant shortly after her arrival at university, aged eighteen. She was left feeling an outsider in her own community, whose predominantly anti-abortion values she originally supported and even fought for. She felt that those who were once her allies were now her enemies.

What is to be done?

It doesn't have to be like this. Some scholars have looked at Maori systems of 'open adoption' (e.g. Mullender, 1991; Rockel and Ryburn, 1988) that can be compared with Simpson's work (1994) on the 'unclear family' in the way that both reveal the flexible and innovative ways in which different peoples deal with the raising of children in complex circumstances. For example, 'in some cultures, it is clear that parenting at a youthful age is accepted and incorporated into everyday life' (Moore and Rosenthal, 1993:164). The combination of 'moral panic' with 'social problem' makes for poor solutions, and pushes health professionals (notoriously bad at combining with social services and other multidisciplinary teams) who might otherwise have a role in dealing with such a 'social problem' to adopt a 'head in the sand' approach. Our research indicates that it is not helpful to start with the premise that teenage pregnancy is a 'problem' that requires moralisation. For a start, 'teenagers' are not a homogenous group, and only for some do 'unwanted pregnancies' result in 'unwanted births'. There is also a feeling that, where national policy is inappropriate or fails, local involvement and interaction is the only way forward. This is not to say that teenagers should just be left to get on with it. Ways in which teenagers learn about sex (particularly boys) are currently solitary, fraught and haphazard (Walker, 1994; 1997). Peer education techniques are becoming increasingly used nationally as a means of breaking down the stigma that goes with adult moralising about teenage sexual activity (Health Education Authority, 1993). There is also a need to provide avenues for those who can to return to education at a later stage in their lives, along with effective care and support for their children: indeed, at UDSC we have a number of students who have been in just such a situation.

A final point. Some of the key figures for the possible prevention of unwanted pregnancies, teachers responsible for personal and social development in schools and colleges, are hamstrung by confusion and anxiety over how far, according to government regulations, sex education can go. For example, the Health Education Authority (1992) found only 12 per cent of teenagers in the North had had lessons at school concerning homosexuality, compared to 19 per cent in the South-West. It would appear there is as much variation between (and within?) schools and education authorities as between regions. A study by second-year students of the policies of two school districts, one in Teesside and the other in County Durham, showed provision for the continuing education of teenage mothers to be varied and patchy. We must also remember that by no means all teenagers are in full-time education, and that if effective sex education is the goal, other venues must be sought for its dissemination (Bury, 1984).

There is certainly a lot of innovation and innovative thinking taking place amongst educators and health professionals on

Teesside (such as the APAUSE,'Added Power and Understanding in Sex Education', study – Rees et al., 1998). However, there is also a lot going on nationally and internationally, and one of the objects of our research must be to identify initiatives and illustrate effective practice. Even where educationalists try to get round the policy hindrances and practical problems that surround the provision of services they are hampered by public moralising. In a conversation with a local newspaper reporter, it was put to me that giving sex education and contraceptive advice merely encourages sexual activity in the young. Yet at a local Further Education college one of my colleagues on this project recalls giving a lesson on condoms to a group of boys and telling them, to their apparent surprise, that they could get condoms free. Information leads to empowerment, and group activity to confidence. The boys went off that lunchtime to the Family Planning Clinic, only to be chased out of the building by a painter and decorator who was working there while the clinic was closed for lunch.

CHAPTER 12

THE REPRODUCTIVE HEALTH OF REFUGEES: LESSONS BEYOND THE INTERNATIONAL CONFERENCE ON POPULATION AND DEVELOPMENT

Colette Harris and Ines Smyth

Introduction

Reproductive health is intimately entwined with many of the worlds most controversial themes: population control, sexuality, the position of women and their rights, the right to abortion, violence against women, sex work, female genital mutilation, sexually transmitted diseases and HIV/AIDS. They all present considerable challenges in conceptual terms as well as in terms of policies and social provisioning. When added to another major critical theme, refugees and their care, the subject of reproductive health becomes truly complex.

Refugees are by definition survivors who use their personal and material resources to escape danger, persecution and fear. They are also very vulnerable to threats to their physical wellbeing, identity and at times their survival as a group (religious, ethnic etc.). Such vulnerability should be understood in the context of the increase in global economic, social and environmental insecurity that characterises recent decades (Baud and Smyth, 1997).

According to Pearson, the key elements of this 'new world disorder' are armed conflict, military actions and the disappearance of old state structures, all of which have profound implications for biological reproduction (Pearson, 1997:12).

The vulnerability of populations affected by conflict or environmental disasters was stressed at the International Conference on Population and Development (ICPD) held in Cairo in 1994, especially in terms of their high mortality and morbidity rates. More broadly the ICPD and its Program of Action have been instruments through which a consensus on the importance of reproductive health and rights, including that of refugees and internally displaced people, was reached.

From this consensus position, the international relief community has made a concerted effort in the last few years to work on the issue of reproductive health services in refugee situations. Both the UN agencies and international NGOs have been implementing reproductive health services in many parts of the world, as well as trying to systematise the way in which services are delivered to refugee communities.[1]

This chapter argues that the international community is bringing some of the language and concerns of the ICPD Programme of Action into the initiative mentioned above. However, the notion of reproductive health may, we argue, offer little support to the development and implementation of interventions in this field unless other important considerations become integral parts of these programmes and policies.

The chapter identifies the structural constraints that prevent policies and interventions from benefiting from the critical insights of feminist and anthropological approaches. The most important are related to the policies and practices of multilateral and bilateral donors. Among the policies the most critical are the persistence of Malthusian concerns and the personal attitudes and capacities of senior policy-makers and implementers. Among the practices are the limited involvement of local people and organisations, the poor understanding of staff and the conditions under which they are employed. The danger associated with these problems is that the international organisations responsible for

1. Among recent initiatives are the establishment of an inter-agency working group (IAWG) and through the publication of a field manual, outlining practices to be followed by the relief organisations. Another development has been the UNHCR's guidelines on the provision of services in reproductive health for refugees.

reproductive health services in refugee situations may repeat the mistakes and abuses of past family-planning programmes.

Finally, the chapter argues that because interest in the reproductive health and rights of refugees is relatively recent, and because of the difficulties of carrying out research at field level in certain situations, there is comparatively little research and literature on the subject. For the same reason, this paper is speculative. Rather than assessing existing programmes, it is intended to be a reminder of the lessons that can be learned from sources beyond the ICPD.

Reproductive Health and refugee populations

Data concerning the number of refugees in the world are notoriously unreliable. What is certain is that refugees are becoming more numerous. In the last few years displacement through conflicts and major natural disasters has escalated, as have the populations forced to move by deliberate government policies. The International Federation of Red Cross and Red Crescent Societies reports (1996) that in 1985 there were 22 million refugees and internally displaced people, and that by 1995 their number had increased to 37 million. In 1998 alone, well over a million people in Central America, Bangladesh, Central Asia and parts of Africa lost their homes in floods. Large numbers of refugees from Kosovo and East Timor have moved to neighbouring countries under extremely difficult conditions. It is impossible to assess how many of these people will be able to rebuild their homes and communities in the near future, and how many will continue to rely on relief agencies for help. Very long-term refugee camps now exist in a number of countries. Palestinians have been in camps for over forty years, Afghans for almost twenty. There are increasingly large populations in Africa joining them.

There are also large numbers of people who have been displaced but remain within the borders of their country of origin – at least 24 million according to one estimate (Wulf, 1994). Internally Displaced People often become refugees for the same reasons, and in the same circumstances, as those who have crossed national boundaries. However, the distinction in terminology means that they receive little recognition and help at international level and thus, at times, may be substantially worse off than 'legitimate' refugees.

The existence and care of these refugee populations presents considerable dilemmas, largely arising from the circumstances of extreme poverty, destitution and insecurity in which most have to live, and the large numbers involved. Further dilemmas stem from the fact that displacement is considered a temporary situation and the long-term solution is assumed to be repatriation to the place of origin or as near to it as possible. While a 'voluntary, safe return to their own countries' (Keen, 1992) may well be the best solution to the refugees' problems, it is not always possible. Thus, this position fails to acknowledge the fact that refugees represent a new type of population, not a temporary condition.

It is, therefore, undeniable that a sizeable proportion of the world's population exists in a political vacuum, outside the 'normal' life of any country, stripped of political and rights and alienated from viable economic opportunities and from access to social provisioning. This type of existence is not limited to refugees in the South but also applies all too frequently to those who seek asylum in the North. For large numbers of refugees virtually the only services available, including healthcare, are those supplied by the aid organisations: either in the first stages of emergency evacuation, or in the succeeding stages which may continue for a very long time.

The psychological as well as the physical conditions in which refugees live may mean that they have greater need for healthcare and good nourishment than the average citizens either of the country of origin or the host country. At present the provision of health care for refugees is a long way from adequate and this is especially true where reproductive health services are concerned.

The lack of adequate food, shelter and clean water, and the great stress that often occurs in refugee situations, may be seriously damaging to the reproductive health of the population, both male and female. Here it should be remembered that women and children comprise a large proportion of the refugee and displaced population, at least in some contexts, and are the sections of that population with the largest healthcare needs. The conditions under which flight and resettlement take place undeniably hold greater dangers for women because of their disadvantaged position in gendered relations and their role in biological reproduction. Their ability to conceive, carry successful pregnancies to term and give birth to healthy babies, as well as their capacity to have sexual relations and lead reproductive lives free of violence and abuse, may all be affected. The situation may be further exacerbated by the breakdown of the kinship ties or community networks on which women relied near and after giving birth or in times of illness. Similarly, women's traditional resources for contraception, abortion and the like may be lost to them. Refugee situations are, in addition, often marked by violence against women, including rape and forced sex in order to gain access to protection or the means of survival for themselves and their dependents. The possible consequences in terms of sexually transmitted diseases, HIV/AIDS and unwanted and dangerous pregnancies need not be spelled out.

As already mentioned, there is scant information on the reproductive health and needs of refugees, whether women or men. It is often stated that at least 75 per cent of the world's refugee and displaced people are women and girls (Bandarage, 1997), and that of these 20 per cent are of reproductive age and 25 per cent are expectant mothers (Davidson and Lush, 1995). The reproductive health risks to which they are exposed are well known, but accurate information on the consequences is lacking. An idea can, however, be gained from indirect statistical data. For example, the fact that maternal mortality in the countries between which refugees mostly move is up to 200 times higher than in western nations (Poore, 1995). Anecdotal evidence is sometimes used to claim very high fertility for women in refugee populations, but hard evidence for such a conclusion is often absent. In view of all these problems, the recent interest in the reproductive health of refugees is timely.

Lessons from Cairo and beyond

For several decades, feminists and other advocates working in the field of health and women's rights have been discussing issues related to reproductive health. The result has been a body of literature that has rehearsed many of the practical, theoretical, ethical and political dilemmas concerning reproductive health.

This body of literature can be divided into two related categories of material and analysis. Both could be of great use in the attempts to develop policies that take into account the specific circumstances of refugees, especially women. The first have come out of the international health movement and are directly related to aspects of reproductive health. The second have emerged from the discipline of anthropology and, to a lesser extent, sociology and are related to issues of cultural specificity and ways of working with local populations, though not necessarily directly related to questions of reproductive health.

Feminist insights into reproductive health

As stated earlier, the Plan of Action of the ICPD has provided a major impetus to interest in the reproductive health of refugees, and is also the source of the basic principles that should guide the provision of services. It is unanimously recognised that many of the positions taken by the Plan of Action are the result of the long-term influence of the work of feminist activists, academics and health workers (Lassonde, 1997).

A broader understanding of reproductive health

Among the most fundamental critical insights from feminist health advocates has been that reproductive rights are not limited to birth control, nor to birth control plus mother and child health and sexually transmitted diseases/HIV/AIDS. The concept encompasses many other aspects of health and well-being, including abortion rights, gynaecological health (including menstruation), issues of infertility (which may be a greater problem for some populations than the need for birth control), and sexual health (as well as violence). This expansion of the notion of reproductive health is a direct consequence of the critical stance that feminist and other health advocates have long taken in relation to population control programmes (Garcia Moreno and Claro, 1994). Such programmes, they maintain, have focused on fertility reduction as the solution to what policy makers perceive as the most pressing global problem: that of population growth, especially among the poor in developing countries. Sometimes they have added a concern for the containment of the growing pandemic of AIDS. Both these areas have lent themselves to the coercive treatment of populations (Hartmann, 1987).

Another essential critique put forward by feminists is that reproductive health cannot be addressed merely as a medical matter. It cannot be separated from the conditions of poverty and insecurity in which many men and women in developing countries live. Such conditions often dictate reproductive and fertility behaviour, but they also determine access to adequate nutrition, sanitation and health services. This understanding also helps locate broader population issues in the context of economic growth and development. As Sen states: '...the population issue must be defined as the right to determine and make reproductive decisions in the context of fulfilling secure livelihoods, basic needs (including reproductive health) and political participation' (Sen, 1994).

Also central to feminist analysis is the idea that problems of reproductive health are related to gender-based power relations, which systematically disadvantage women and girls. This thesis has several components. One is that in most societies women gain social status and position through their reproductive functions, so that their reproductive health has considerable repercussions for their overall existence (Gupta, 1996). At the same time, in many cases and locations women enjoy little control over their reproductive behaviour and its outcome. In fact, women's sexuality and procreative functions are generally at the centre of far-reaching cultural norms. As a consequence, if and when to marry, with whom and when to have sexual relations, and when and how many children they have, are in many societies matters controlled by spouses, other senior household members (mothers-in-law for example), religious leaders and policy makers (Berer, 1994). In particular, unmarried adolescent girls tend to be the focus of strict controls to guarantee not merely their virginity but also a spotless reputation.

The emphasis of feminist health advocates on women and their reproductive health and rights does not mean that women are the only focus in these debates. It has been recognised for some time that men and adolescents of both sexes also have reproductive needs. Furthermore, these issues are not only the concern of people of reproductive age. Both older men and post-menopausal women have reproductive health needs that should be acknowledged and taken into consideration.

Birth control and other medical provisions

Many of the relevant debates have concentrated largely on issues of birth control/family planning, as these were the major focus of the international community in the pre-Cairo era. Many studies have recorded the abusive character of fertility-control programmes (Dixon-Mueller, 1993). Women in general, as well as minority groups under-represented in governments, have been all too often targeted for specific fertility-reduction programmes, including forced sterilisation (Hartmann, 1987). At the same time, large numbers of people who might wish to use modern contraception do not have adequate access to affordable methods of their choice.

Coercive programmes have been shown to be very often ineffective, and even counterproductive. Research has indicated that countries with the strongest population policies are not necessarily those that show the greatest reduction in fertility (for example, India). Also, couples using modern methods of contraception do not necessarily have fewer children than those using traditional methods such as abstinence and breastfeeding (e.g. for practices among the Yoruba, see Pearce, 1995). The abusive practices of population control policies have often made women less willing to use contraceptives (Ravindran, 1993; Hartmann, 1993). Therefore, groups of people who have been targeted by very forceful population control programmes may be especially wary of contact with modern medicine and its practitioners, including modern methods of birth control.

The technology of these methods has also been a topic of heated debates, particularly on the problems associated with hormonal and with provider-dependent long-acting contraceptives such as Norplant, Depo-Provera and, more recently, vaccines (Hardon and Hayes, 1998). The latter are attractive to international providers and governments for their properties of effectiveness and ease of delivery (Sen and Snow, 1994). On the other hand, many women have experienced negative side effects from long-acting hormonal contraceptives, including increased bleeding, headaches, weight-loss or gain, and even infertility (Panos, 1994). Barrier methods, especially the female condom and the diaphragm, are insufficiently available, in great part because western providers believe them to be unacceptable to local populations, and because they do not consider them effective enough, although HIV/AIDS has lead to a re-evaluation of this position.

An important aspect of these debates, and the area in which there has been the most 'consensus', is the need to provide high quality programmes. Since Cairo the idea that these should not be limited to family planning but include a wide range of reproductive health services is gradually becoming accepted. Furthermore, in relation to such services the concept of quality of care is often mentioned. This encompasses various components, the most important of which are: choice of method; technical competence and good interpersonal skills of providers; full and informed consent in the choice of contraceptives, and appropriate constellations of services including mechanisms for follow-up (Bruce, 1990).

Cultural differences

As stated earlier, other insights that would be beneficial to policies and interventions targeting the reproductive health of refugees and displaced persons derive from anthropological traditions. In particular, much can be learned from the work of feminist anthropologists and others who have been concerned with the need to acknowledge the cultural specificity of reproductive practices and beliefs and, as a consequence, the importance of sensitivity to cultural differences and needs at the micro-level.

Such analysts have shown that all too often it is assumed that all groups of women and men have similar reproductive health needs. Individual country or culture group studies have shown this to be untrue. Reproduction is an area particularly subject to cultural differences. In order for services to be relevant and acceptable it is vital to situate reproductive health within people's real experience (Petchesky, 1998).

The tendency towards cultural generalisation is often unhelpful and even dangerous (Smith, 1998). Such generalisations are often made in relation to religion and reproductive health. This tends particularly to be applied to Muslim populations, where a simplistic link between religion, women's subordination and fertility is assumed. Any such relation is far from proven. It has been shown that religion is not necessarily a determining factor in the acceptance of contraceptives. For example, in Pakistan 77.6 per cent of those surveyed in a USAID study said that they had not taken religion into consideration (Siddiqi quoted in Correa and Reichman, 1994:32). The indigenous cultural environment together with the socio-economic and political circumstances of Muslims – as in the case of people professing other religions – are the main determinants of their reproductive behaviour, not their religion (see, for instance, criticisms of such approaches by Makhlouf, 1991; 1992; 1994).

For (feminist) health advocates, recognising the diversity of cultural attitudes to reproduction (as to other aspects of social life) is not synonymous with taking a relativist position that believes all cultural practices to be acceptable (Gasper, 1996). On the contrary, they stress that, within given cultures, reproduction is an area where women, and other subordinate groups, are often oppressed and silenced.

In practice this means that great cultural understanding and sensitivity are necessary both in order to assess needs, and in the provision of reproductive health services. Such sensitivity is necessary to allow grassroot Southern women (but also boys, girls and even men) to have a voice in all services provided for them, including those pertaining to reproductive behaviour and health. Furthermore, talking to the more educated male (or even female) leaders, and others who present themselves as knowing and speaking for their communities, does not provide an adequate or full picture of the overall situation. The least educated and vocal minority ethnic and cultural groupings must be consulted directly in order to ensure that interventions meet their needs, and are effective.

A discourse which emphasises the legitimacy of specific cultural practice is also compatible with advocating the need for women to mobilise themselves to achieve increased reproductive rights (Petchesky, 1998:5–6). Reproductive health interventions should include ways through which women may in some cases be supported to understand what their rights are in this respect. For instance, a literacy course run in a rural area of Senegal introduced its female students to notions of reproductive rights. The students themselves subsequently thought out the implications of what they had learnt for the practice of female genital mutilation common in their communities. After some weeks of discussion among themselves, the women returned to the class and declared that hitherto they had not realised they had a right to do anything about such practices. They decided that from then on they would oppose female genital mutilation in their villages (personal communication from Bertrade Mbom, CUNY).

While the need to incorporate local views and perspectives is recognised by all, in practice it remains difficult to realise. Here we use a study by Kathina (1998) on the Women Victims of Violence (WVV) programme in Dadaab camp, Kenya, to reflect on the difficulty of combining in practice a concern for the issues raised by women and health advocates with a true consideration for cultural differences.

Kathina's discussion makes it clear that the programme in many ways attempted to address the needs of women refugees, and the concerns often raised by feminist health advocates. However, several aspects of the programme were based on pre-conceived and often Eurocentric views. The programme was based on the realisation that violence against women is high in refugee camps and puts them at significant risk.[2] However, because a needs assessment was carried out in a superficial manner, it did not take into account the daily experiences of the most vulnerable women, but made assumptions about the nature of violence as well as the behaviour of women. Key assumptions were that the perpetrators of violence were necessarily 'outsiders' and that women spent their time exclusively within the (safe) confines of the camp. This bears considerable resemblance to the commonly held notion that women are safe within the private sphere, away from the dangers of the public domain (Sciortino and Smyth, 1997). Thus, it was considered sufficient to build a fence around the camp to keep the violent (and violence) out. Both the fact that much of the violence came from within the camp, and that many attacks took place during women's daily forages outside the camp for firewood, were ignored.

Another problem was that the WVV programme seemed to have limited sensitivity to local cultures in the way it dealt with the women who had experienced rape. The western-trained relief workers wished the women concerned to admit openly to having

2. This is in itself a major step in the right direction as violence against women in refugee camps had previously been considered either insignificant or else an inevitable concomitant of the situation, and one which it would be pointless to tackle.

been raped so that they could receive counselling. In the culture of the Somali women concerned, rape is a disgrace that marks a woman for life and makes it impossible for her to be accepted in her own community. Even her natal family cannot be seen to support her afterwards. In such circumstances women may prefer to keep their experiences secret. Women who acknowledge their situation publicly expose themselves to rejection by their families and communities and to the unwanted sexual attention of men. Therefore, many of the women concerned felt they could no longer continue to live in Africa where everyone knew of their plight; so they applied to emigrate to the west. The programme officers were not sympathetic to this problem, seeing it as a mere ploy to gain refugee status in a western country.

The WVV is a programme that, in its choice of focus, displays considerable sympathy for the issues that are a concern of women and health advocates, namely sexual violence in refugee situations. Nevertheless, it seems to have been very limited in its capacity to make significant improvements in refugee women's lives, and in fact it may have caused additional damage. In this, the programme is probably far from unique. Unfortunately, as mentioned earlier, to date we have very few studies of other similar programmes so that much of our discussion inevitably remains speculative.

Foreseeable obstacles

Policy makers and practitioners involved in the delivery of services to refugee populations have in principle accepted the recommendations of the ICPD Plan of Action, the central ideas of which are contained in the notion of reproductive health, summarised earlier.

According to Lassonde (1997), the advantage of the notion of reproductive health is that it is sufficiently flexible to allow the priorities and approaches of different – and differing – groups to be taken into account. However, Lassonde also stresses that there is a fundamental limitation: the fact that reproductive health '... is more a consensus-oriented idea than a standard-setting definition stipulating how programmes can be structured' (1997:22). In this section, we will highlight factors that, in combination with this limitation, may prevent the major providers from learning the insights of women and health advocates, and preclude the implementation of reproductive health programmes which truly reflect the needs and perceptions of different groups among the refugees themselves.

It should be said that it is not easy to incorporate the sorts of lessons learned from (feminist) research into the actual programmes carried out in refugee situations. There are many reasons for this. The sheer scale and urgency of the problems, and especially the large numbers of people affected, often make them appear overwhelming. It also makes it difficult to work at the micro-level in a way that responds to the needs of so many diverse individuals and small groups.

Policies and principles

A factor which may militate against learning from the insights summarised earlier is that the multilateral and bilateral donors who fund most activities aimed at providing services to refugee populations may have agendas which differ greatly from their stated objectives. Behind a language that claims commitment to the well-being of refugees, including their reproductive health, may hide other priorities. These may be geopolitical and stability concerns, Malthusian concerns with the growth of specific groups of people perceived to be unproductive, dependent and/or politically volatile, or concerns with limiting the spread of disease, especially among these same groups of people who are viewed as irresponsible.

Malthusian views, and those who hold them, are particularly inimical to migrant and refugee populations who are blamed for environmental destruction, security and social problems. As Bandarage stresses 'Malthusian calls to halt migration into the rich North overlook the roots of the refugee problem situated in global political and economic structures' (1997:271).

Another factor concerns the personal capacities of policy makers and implementers. No doubt a large number of middle- and upper-level UN officials involved both at policy and decision-making levels and in practical work have a genuine commitment to improving the conditions under which refugees and other displaced people live. They may also have skills and expertise in technical and managerial fields but suffer from a lack of knowledge and understanding of crucial aspects of women's health, and of anthropological information and gender and development issues. This applies also to staff working in NGOs.

In other words, there would appear to be a double dislocation within the international relief community: on the one hand between the policies stated at headquarters and in public pronouncements, and the projects actually carried out on the ground; on the other hand between individuals working in relief agencies, genuinely trying to propagate helpful and positive approaches to refugee welfare, and their ability to realise such approaches in practice.

But such dislocations only account for some of the reasons that may prevent providers from meeting the needs of refugees. Many of the approaches to practical development interventions dominant among international organisations tend to be technocratic and to lack a holistic approach (Sen and Grown, 1988). Reproductive health, as we have already pointed out, cannot be separated from other aspects of life. Research has shown that the attempt to deal with each aspect of refugee life separately is making it impossible to provide services that adequately correspond to needs. However, the international community has so far persisted in seeing such situations as susceptible to technical solutions. Here the discussion in Wulf (1994:34–5) of the likelihood that the provision of a largely grain-based diet to meat-eating, milk-drinking nomads within the camps has resulted in greatly increased levels of pre-eclampsia, is very relevant.

Above all, the lack of sensitive, ongoing, and serious consultation of the mass of refugees, especially the most vulnerable – which include not only women but also children of both sexes – makes it impossible to tailor programmes to fit their needs.

Practices

At the level of programme and projects a major problem is presented by the lack of appropriate information and training on the part of the project implementers. As stated earlier, the subject of reproductive health among refugee populations is closely related to some of the most complex and controversial cultural practices within all societies (Lee, 1993). This means that extremely accurate information and sensitivity are necessary when dealing with the provision of reproductive health services.

The staff of many agencies may not be equipped with specialised knowledge of reproductive health to ensure this. Even medical staff, otherwise interested and experienced, may not be equipped with specialised knowledge of reproductive health. Medical organisations may have limitations in resources, and so be able only to send a certain number of medical staff into relief operations. In this situation they may decide that the presence of a public health expert is more important than that of personnel with knowledge of reproductive health.

The length of contracts of staff working in relief programmes often means there is little opportunity to acquire the additional skills necessary to work effectively in such situations: relevant languages, a cultural understanding of the locality, and gender-awareness. The time constraints typical of emergency situations are blamed for this situation. The lack of continuity in programmes, and poor dissemination of relevant information and experience aggravate the difficulties.

Both UN agencies and NGOs are likely to suffer from such problems, although the staff of the latter may well have greater sensitivity to the issues involved. Local organisations and individuals are not, however, immune to these problems. They are more likely to have a better knowledge of customs, languages and needs. But they may have little chance of influencing programmes in which they are engaged because of hierarchies often present in aid work which prevent local views and priorities from determining policies.

Possible solutions

The obstacles just outlined are not all surmountable by changes in tactics on the part of agencies and field workers. Some would require the total restructuring of the international aid community and its relationships with donors. However, there is much that could be done to improve the situation by concentrating on those problems more amenable to solution.

Participatory principles

What the feminist and anthropological insights summarised above point to is the need for reproductive health programmes to respond directly to the needs and perspectives of the refugees themselves, especially women (but also men, children and others of non-reproductive ages) and thus to be based on a sound knowledge and understanding of cultural beliefs and practices. Such an approach may well reveal totally different requirements from those generally accepted. For instance, it may be that many refugee women are much more concerned about infertility and its causes than with controlling their fertility through contraception. Some populations may find abortion totally irrelevant or even abhorrent, others expect abortion services as a matter of right.

The abundance of methodologies which have been devised for participatory and gender-sensitive planning could be put to use in working with refugees on designing their own programmes. These methodologies can help ensure the participation of representatives of all groups involved. This includes women, children (or at least adolescents), old people, ethnic minorities, male and female representatives of all tribal and other minority groups concerned.

Such methodologies can only work if they are supported by knowledge and understanding. Major cultural and power differentials between various sub-groups of people may exist within apparently homogenous cultural groupings. Furthermore, such sub-groups may be in conflict with each other in the country of origin – even on opposite sides of a civil war. The resulting potential for conflict within settlements needs to be taken into account in all aspects of planning.

The understanding and use of such methodologies could have helped avoid the errors of the WVV programme. Consulting local women would have revealed the various loci of the violence that might have led to a different solution than that adopted. Similarly, an understanding of the rigidity of local cultural attitudes towards rape could have led to an attempt to help keep women's affairs private. Including local staff at decision-making levels may help to reveal such attitudes more efficiently than an exclusive use of international staff (see below).

Implementation of programmes

Many of the programmes and projects aimed at providing reproductive health services for refugees would benefit from being implemented in collaboration with, or at least with the advice of, women and refugee organisations. The co-operation of local NGOs, either in joint programmes or through financing such organisations would also be a step towards ensuring closer attention to local details. Among the advantages offered by these agencies is their ability to work closer to communities and with a better understanding of local cultures and needs than large international or governmental institutions. This approach can also improve the sustainability of programmes as the local NGOs will still be there when an externally initiated programme is completed.

It is also important to learn from existing innovative programmes and, when appropriate transfer their lessons to other situations. One such programme is that sponsored by the University of Zimbabwe (University of Zimbabwe Project Support Group Reproductive Rights and Health Partnerships) with community organisations in Southern Africa 1997. This provides contraceptives and information on birth control with minimum costs to huge numbers by means of local grass-roots organisations all over the country.

It was pointed out earlier that some problems are an outcome of a lack of understanding and suitable background among relevant staff. Thus it would be beneficial if staff with experience of participatory methodologies would be recruited. Anthropologists – especially those trained in the more sensitive methodologies, such as feminist anthropology – would be an invaluable source of knowledge and advice. Staff drawn from the population served, especially in higher positions, would provide much in the way of local knowledge and insight. On the other hand it is important to be sensitive to local politics and to avoid privileging certain cultural, religious or ethnic groups. The recruitment of female staff does not necessarily render programmes more sensitive to the needs of female refugees, but it can facilitate communication with refugee women (especially on sensitive topics) as well as offering them employment opportunities.

Conclusion

In this chapter we have identified a number of obstacles to the translation into effective action of the many lessons that emerge from feminist and anthropological approaches to reproductive health and rights. We also pointed out that the scarcity of research and accurate information on the reproductive health of displaced people, and of existing policies and programmes, limits our understanding of both.

We have suggested that the adoption of participatory methodologies, collaboration with and direct involvement of refugee institutions and individuals, improvements in skills and understanding, and even changes in recruitment practices would all facilitate the implementation of services that reflect the genuine needs of the beneficiaries. These changes would go some way to counterbalance the vulnerability of displaced people, by enabling them to contribute more directly to interventions affecting their reproductive health.

A more fundamental change is, however, necessary. As mentioned earlier, reproductive health is a consensus notion, and one that does not allow for the setting of standards in practices. This may make it easy for organisations involved in humanitarian interventions to carry out activities that do not necessarily match their language. A crucial step towards programmes that effectively address the many reproductive health needs and problems of refugee populations is that such organisations should be more explicit in their purpose and coherent in their practices, and thus more accountable to those they claim to serve. It is this accountability which, again, would make refugees and internally displaced people less vulnerable, not only in matters concerning their reproductive health but in all processes and decisions which affect their lives.

Bibliography

Abu-Lughod, L. (1990), 'Shifting Politics in Bedouin Love Poetry', in C. Lutz and L. Abu-Lughod (eds), *Language and the Politics of Emotion*, Cambridge: Cambridge University Press.

Adams, A. (1993), 'Food Insecurity in Mali: Exploring the Role of the Moral Economy', *IDS Bulletin*, 24:4, 41–51.

Adadevoh, B. K. (1974), 'Summary of Proceedings', in B. K. Adadevoh (ed.), *Subfertility and Infertility in Africa*, Ibadan: Caxton Press.

Adekunle, A. O. and O. A. Ladipo (1992), 'Reproductive Tract Infections in Nigeria: Challenges for a Fragile Health Infrastructure', in A. Germain, K. K. Holmes, P. Piot and J. N. Wasserheit (eds), *Reproductive Tract Infections*, New York: Plenum Press.

Adetoro, O. O. and E. W. Ebomoyi (1991), 'The Prevalence of Infertility in a Rural Nigerian Community', *African Journal of Medicine and Medical Sciences* 20 (1): 23–7.

Ahern, Emily M. (1973), *The Cult of the Dead in a Chinese Village*, Stanford: Stanford University Press.

Alan Guttmacher Institute (1998), *Into a New World: Young Women's Sexual and Reproductive Lives*, New York: The Alan Guttmacher Institute.

——— (1997), *Risks and Realities of Early Childbearing Worldwide: Issues in Brief*, New York: The Alan Guttmacher Institute.

Alemnji, G. A. and K. D. Thomas (1997), 'Socio-biological Status of Nigerian Males with Primary and Secondary Infertility', *East African Medical Journal*, 74:8, 519–52.

Alexander, L. (1979), 'Clinical Anthropology: Morals and Methods', *Medical Anthropology*, 3, 61–107.

Allen, T. (1989), 'Violence and Moral Knowledge: Observing Social Trauma in Sudan and Uganda', *Cambridge Anthropology*, 13:2, 45–66.

Anarfi, J. K. (1993), 'Sexuality, Migration and AIDS in Ghana: A Socio-Behavioural Study', in J. Caldwell et al. (eds), *Sexual Networking and HIV / AIDS in West Africa. Health Transition Review*, supplement to vol. 3, 45–67.

——— (1997), 'Vulnerability to Sexually Transmitted Disease: Street Children in Accra', *Health Transition Review*, supplement to vol. 7: 281–306.

Aral, S. and W. Cates (1983), 'The Increasing Concern With Infertility. Why Now?', *JAMA*, 250: 2327–31.

Armstrong, A. (1994), 'School and Sadza Custody and the Best Interests of the Child in Zimbabwe', in P. Alston (ed.), *The Best Interests of the Child: Reconciling Culture and Human Rights*, Oxford: Clarendon Press.

Armstrong, D. (1998), 'Bodies of Knowledge/ Knowledge of Bodies', in C. Jones and R. Porter (eds), *Reassessing Foucault: Power, Medicine and the Body*, Routledge: London, 17–27.

Asia Partnership for Human Development (1992), *Awake 2*, Manila: Asia Partnership for Human Development.

Asia Watch (1993), *A Modern Form of Slavery: Trafficking of Burmese Women and Girls into Brothels in Thailand*, New York: Human Rights Watch.

Bakouan, D., B. Bazie, J. Millogo and P. Ouedraogo (1991), 'Recherche sur les maladies sexuellement transmissibles dans les zones de Beïga et de Tassmakat (Province de l'Oudalan)', Ouagadougou: PSB-PB/Ministère de la Santé.

Baker, H. R. D. (1979), *Chinese Family and Kinship*, London and Basingstoke: Macmillan Press.

Baker, R. (1998), 'Runaway Street Children in Nepal: Social Competence Away From Home', in I. Hutchby and J. Moran-Ellis (eds), *Children and Social Competence, Arenas of Action*, London and Washington: The Falmer Press, 46–63.

Baker, R. and C. Panter-Brick (2000), 'A Comparative Perspective on Children's 'Careers' and Abandonment in Nepal', in C. Panter-Brick. and M. T. Smith (eds), *Abandoned Children*, Cambridge: Cambridge University Press.

Baldo, M., P. Aggleton and G. Slutkin (1993), 'Does Sex Education Lead to Earlier or Increased Sexual Activity in Youth?', *Proceedings of the IXth International Conference on AIDS* Berlin 6–10 June 1993 (Abstract PO-DO2–3444).

Bandarage, A. (1997), *Women, Population and Global Crisis*, London: Zed Books.

Barker, G. and S. Rich (1992), 'Influences on Adolescent Sexuality in Nigeria and Kenya: Findings from Recent Focus-Group Discussions', *Studies in Family Planning* 23:3,199–210.

Barnard. A. (1994), 'Rules and Prohibitions: the Form and Content of Human Kinship', in Tim Ingold (ed.), *Companion to the Encyclopedia of Anthropology: Humanity, Culture and Social Life*, London: Routledge, 785.

Barnett, E. et al. (1995), *Health and HIV/AIDS Education in Primary and Secondary Schools in Africa and Asia*, London: Overseas Development Administration and Liverpool: The Liverpool School of Tropical Medicine.

Barongo, L. et al. (1992), 'The Epidemiology of HIV-1 Infection in Urban Areas, Road-Side Settlements and Rural Villages in Mwanza Region, Tanzania', *AIDS*, 6:12, 1521–28.

Barral, H. (1977), *Les Populations nomades de l'Oudalan et leur espace pastorale*, Paris: ORSTOM.

Basu, A. (1997), 'The New International Population Movement: A Framework for a Constructive Critique', *Health Transition Review*, vol. 7 (Supplement 4), 7–32.

Baud, I. and I. Smyth (eds), (1997), *Searching for Security: Women's Responses to Economic Transformations*, London, Routledge.

Beattie. J. H. M. (1964), 'Kinship and Social Anthropology', *Man*, 101–3.

Behrman, J. and J. Knowles (1998), 'Population and Reproductive Health: An Economic Framework for Policy Evaluation', *Population and Development Review*, 24:4, 697–737.

Belaunde, L. E. (1994), 'Parrots and Oropendolas: The Aesthetics of Gender Relations Amongst the Airo-Pai of Western Amazonia', *Journal de la Société des Américanistes*, 80, 95–111.

——— (1997) 'Looking After Your Woman: Contraception Amongst the Airo-Pai (Secoya) of Western Amazonia', *Anthropology and Medicine*, 4: 2,131–44.

——— (2000), 'The Fear of Anger and the Convivial Self Amongst the Airo-Pai of Amazonian Peru', in J. Overing and A. Passes (eds), *The Anthropology of Love and Anger: The Aesthetics of Conviviality in Native Amazonia*, London and New York: Routledge, 209–20.

Bellier, I. (1991), *El Temblor y le Luna. Ensayo Sobre las Relaciones entre las Mujeres y los Hombres Mai Huna*, Quito: Abya-Yala.

Bentley, G. R., T. Goldberg and G. Jasineka (1993), 'The Fertility of Agricultural and Non-Agricultural Traditional Societies', *Population Studies*, 47:2, 269–81.

Berer, M. (1994), 'Motherhood, Fatherhood and Fertility: For Women Who Do and Women Who Don't Have Children', *Reproductive Health Matters*, 4, 6–11.

Berglund, S., J. Liljestrand, F. de Maria Marin, N. Salgado and E. Zelaya (1997), 'The Background of Adolescent Pregnancies in Nicaragua: A Qualitative Approach', *Social Science and Medicine*, 44:1, 1–12.

Berlin, E. A. (1995), 'Aspects of Fertility Regulation Among the Aguaruna Jivaro of Peru', in L. Newman (ed.), *Women's Medicine: A Cross-Cultural Study of Indigenous Fertility Regulation*, New Brunswick: Rutgers University Press, 125–46.

Bernus, E., (1988), 'Seasonality, Fluctuations and Food Supplies', in I. de Garine and G. A. Harrison (eds), *Coping with Uncertainty in Food Supply*, Oxford: Oxford University Press, 318–36.

——— (1991), *Touaregs nigeriens: Unité culturelle et diversité d'un peuple pasteur*, Paris: ORSTOM.

Betzig, L. (1988), 'Mating and Parenting in Darwinian Perspective', in L. Betzig, M. Borgerhoff Mulder and P. Turke (eds), *Human Reproductive Behaviour: a Darwinian Perspective*, Cambridge: Cambridge University Press, 3–20.

Bezmalinovic, B., W. Skidmore DuFlon and A. Hirschmann (1997), *Guatemala City Women: Empowering a Vulnerable Group to Prevent HIV Transmission*, Washington DC: International Center for Research on Women.

Bhat, R. (1993), 'The Private-Public Mix in Healthcare in India', *Health Policy and Planning*, 8 (1): 43–56.

Birdthistle, I. and C. Vince-Whitman (1997), *Reproductive Health Programs for Young Adults: School-Based Programs*, Washington DC: FOCUS on Young Adults, Pathfinder International.

Blake, J. (1998), 'Fertility Control and the Problem of Voluntarism', in P. Demeny and G. McNicoll (eds), *Population and Development*, London: Earthscan, 112–20.

Blanc, A. and A. Way (1998), 'Sexual Behavior and Contraceptive Knowledge and Use Among Adolescents in Developing Countries', *Studies in Family Planning* 29:2, 106–16.

Blanc-Szanton, C. (1985), 'Gender and Inter-Generational Resource Allocations: Thai and Sino-Thai Households in Central Thailand', in L. Dube and R. Parliwala (eds), *Structures and Strategies: Women, Work and Family in Asia*, New Delhi: Sage, 79–102.

Blanchet, T. (1996), *Lost Innocence, Stolen Childhoods*, Dhaka: The University Press Ltd.

Bledsoe, C. and U. Isuigo-Abanihe (1989), 'Strategies of Child Fosterage Among Mende Grannies in Sierra Leone', in R. J. Lesthaeghe (ed.), *Reproduction and Social Organization in Sub-Saharan Africa*, Berkeley: University of California Press, 442–74.

Bledsoe, C. and B. Cohen (eds) (1993), *Social Dynamics of Adolescent Fertility in Sub-Saharan Africa*, Washington D.C.: National Academy Press.

Bongaarts, J. (1978), 'A Framework for Analysing the Proximate Determinants of Fertility', *Population and Development Review*, 4:1, 105–32.

——— (1981), 'The Impact on Fertility of Traditional and Changing Child-Spacing Practices', *Population and Development Review*, 4, 105–32.

——— (1982), 'The Fertility-Inhibiting Effects of the Intermediate Fertility Variables', *Studies in Family Planning*, 13:6, 179–89.

Bongaarts, J. and R. G. Potter, (1983), *Fertility, Biology and Behaviour: An Analysis of Proximate Determinants*, London: Academic Press Inc.

Bongaarts, J. and J. Bruce (1995), 'The Causes of Unmet Need for Contraception and the Social Content of Services', *Studies in Family Planning*, 26:2, 57–75.

Bongaarts, J. and B. Cohen (1998), 'Introduction and Overview', *Studies in Family Planning*, 29:2 (special edition on Adolescent Reproductive Behavior in the Developing World), 99–105.

Boohene, E., J. Tsodzai, K. Hardee-Cleaveland, S. Weir and B. Janowitz (1991), 'Fertility and Contraceptive Use Among Young Adults in Harare, Zimbabwe', *Studies in Family Planning*, 22:4, 264–71.

Bourdieu, P, (1977), *Outline of a Theory of Practice*,Cambridge: Cambridge University Press.

Borland, M., A. Laybourn, M. Hill and J. Brown (1998), *Middle Childhood, the Perspectives of Children and Parents*, London and Philadelphia: Jessica Kingsley Publishers.

Boyden, J. (1997), 'Childhood and the Policy Makers: a Comparative Perspective on the Globalisation of Childhood' in A. James and A.

Prout (eds), *Constructing and Reconstructing Childhood; Contemporary Issues in the Sociological Study of Childhood*, London, New York and Philadelphia: The Falmer Press, 190–230.

Boyden, J. and S. Gibbs (1997), *Children of War: Responses to Psycho-Social Distress in Cambodia*, Geneva: The United Nations Research Institute for Social Development.

Boyer, D. and D. Fine (1992), 'Sexual Abuse as a Factor in Adolescent Pregnancy and Child Maltreatment', *Family Planning Perspectives*, 24:1, 4–10.

Brandon, A. J. (1990), 'Marriage Dissolution, Remarriage and Child-bearing in West Africa: A Comparative Study of Côte d'Ivoire, Ghana and Nigeria', PhD thesis, University of Pennsylvania.

Briggs, Jean L. (1986), 'Expecting the Unexpected: Canadian Inuit Training for an Experimental Lifestyle', paper presented at the Fourth International Conference on Hunting and Gathering Societies, Ontario, Canada.

Brown, J., F. Coeytaux, R. Chipoma, V. Manda and D. Muntemba (1987), 'Characteristics of Contraceptive Acceptors in Lusaka, Zambia', *Studies in Family Planning*, 18:2, 96–102.

Bruce, J. (1990), 'Fundamental Elements of the Quality of Care: a Simple Framework', *Studies in Family Planning*, 21, 61–75.

Brunham, R. C. and J. E. Embree, (1992), 'Sexually Transmitted Diseases: Current and Future Dimensions of the Problem in the Third World', in A. Germain, K. K. Holmes and P. Piot (eds), *Reproductive Tract Infections: Global Impact and Priorities for Women's Reproductive Health*, New York: Plenum Press, 35–58.

Brydon, L. (1979), 'Women at Work: Some Changes in Family Structure in Amedzofe-Avatime, Ghana', *Africa* 49:2, 97–111.

Buckley, A. (1985), *Yoruba Medicine*, Cambridge: Cambridge University Press.

Buckley, T. and A. Gottlieb (1988), *Blood Magic: The Anthropology of Menstruation*, Berkeley: University of California.

Bunster, X. and E. Chaney (1985), *Sellers and Servants: Working Women in Lima, Peru*, New York: Praeger.

Burghes, L. and M. Brown (1995), *Single Lone Mothers: Problems, Prospects and Policies*, London: Family Policy Studies Centre.

Burman, E. (1994), *Deconstructing Developmental Psychology*, London and New York: Routledge.

Bury, J. (1984), *Teenage Pregnancy in Britain*, London: The Birth Control Trust.

Buvinic, M. (1998), 'The Costs of Adolescent Childbearing: Evidence from Chile, Barbados, Guatemala and Mexico', *Studies in Family Planning*, 29:2, 201–9.

Caldwell, J. C. (1976), *The Socio-Economic Explanation of High Fertility*, Canberra: Australian National University.

Caldwell, J. C. and P. Caldwell (1983), 'The Demographic Evidence for the Incidence and Cause of Abnormally Low Fertility in Tropical Africa', *World Health Statistics Quarterly*, 36:1, 2–21.

——— (1987), 'The Function of Child-Spacing in Traditional Societies and the Direction of Change', *Current Anthropology*, 28, 235–43.

Campbell, K. L. and J. W. Wood, (1988), 'Fertility in Traditional Societies', in P. Diggory, S. Toper and M. Potts (eds), *Natural Human Fertility: Social and Biological Mechanisms*, London: Macmillan in association with the Eugenics Society, 39–69.

Caputo, V. (1995), 'Anthropology's Silent "Others": A Consideration of Some Conceptual and Methodological Issues for the Study of Youth and Children's Cultures', in V. Amit-Talai and H. Wulff (eds), *Youth Cultures, A Cross-Cultural Perspective*, London and New York: Routledge, 19–42.

Carr, D. (1997), *Female Genital Cutting: Findings from the DHS Program*, Calverton MD: Macro International.

Carrier, J. (1992), 'Emerging Alienation in Production: A Maussian History', *Man*, 27:539–58.

Carter, A. (1995), 'Agency and Fertility: For an Ethnography of Practice', in S. Greenhalgh (ed.), *Situating Fertility: Anthropology and Demographic Inquiry*, Cambridge: Cambridge University Press.

Casanova, J. (1998), 'La Misión Jesuita Colonial entre los Airo Pai (Secoya) y los Asentamientos Indígenas', *Investigaciones Sociales*, 2: 2, 25–38.

Cash, K. and B. Anasuchatkul (1995), *Experimental Educational Interventions for AIDS Prevention Among Northern Thai Single Migratory Factory Workers*, Washington DC: International Centre for Research on Women (ICRW).

Center for Population Options (1992), *Adolescents and Unsafe Abortion in Developing Countries*, Washington DC: Center for Population Options.

Centre for the Protection of Children's Rights (1991), *The Trafficking of Children for Prostitution in Thailand*, Bangkok: Centre for the Protection of Children's Rights.

Cheung, P., A. P. S. Hungin, J. Verrill, A. J. Russell and H. Smith (1997), 'Are the Health of the Nation's Targets Attainable? Postal Survey of General Practitioners' Views', *British Medical Journal*, 314: 1250–1.

Children's Defense Fund (1986), *Trends in Teen Births: Data Sheet*, Washington, DC: The Children's Defense Fund.

——— (1988), 'Adolescent Pregnancy Prevention: Prenatal Care Campaign', in *The Health of America's Children: Maternal and Child Health Data Book*, Washington, DC: The Children's Defense Fund.

Chisholm, J. S. (1996), 'Learning "Respect for Everything": Navaho Images of Development', in P. C. Hwang, M. E. Lamb and I. E. Sigel (eds), *Images of Childhood*, Mahwah, New Jersey: Lawrence Erlbaum Associates, 167–84.

Cipolletti, M. S. (1988) *Aipë Koka. La Palabra de los Antiguos. Tradición Oral Siona-Secoya*, Quito: Abay-Yala.

Claude, J., M. Grouzis and P. Milleville (1991), *Un Espace Sahelien: La Mare d'Oursi, Burkina Faso*, Paris: ORSTOM.

Cleveland, D. A. (1991), 'Migration in West Africa: A Savanna Village Perspective', *Africa* 61:2, 222–46.

Cohen, S. (1996), *Research to Improve Implementation and Effectiveness of School Health Programs*, Report prepared for WHO. Newton, MA: Education Development Centre, Inc.

Cole, M. (1992), 'Culture in Development', in M. H. Bornstein, and M. E. Lamb (eds), *Developmental Psycholgy: An Advanced Textbook*, Hillside, New Jersey: Erlbaum, 73–124.

Comaroff, J. and J. Comaroff (1999), 'Notes on the Political Economy of Youth', unpublished paper prepared for 'Understanding Exclusion, Creating Value: African Youth in a Global Era', Social Science Research Council [USA] Conference, Cape Town 30–31 July.

Cooper, G. (1998), 'British Teenagers Lead the World in their Sexual Activity – Why?' *Independent*, 16 May, 23.

Cordell, D. D., J. W. Gregory and V. Piché (1996), *Hoe and Wage: A Social History of a Circular Migration System in West Africa*, London: Westview Press.

Cornwall, A. (1996), 'For Money, Children and Peace: Everyday Struggles in Changing Times in Ado-Odo, S. W. Nigeria', PhD thesis: University of London.

Correa, S. and R. Reichman (1994), *Population and Reproductive Rights: Feminist Perspectives from the South*, London and New Jersey: Zed Books.

Corteen, K. and P. Scraton (1997), 'Prolonging "Childhood", Manufacturing "Innocence" and Regulating Sexuality', in Phil Scraton (ed.), *Childhood in Crisis?* London and Bristol, Pennsylvania: UCL Press, 76–100.

Crandon-Malamud, L. (1991), *From the Fat of Our Souls; Social Change, Political Process, and Medical Pluralism in Bolivia*, Berkeley: University of California Press.

Cunningham, H. (1991), *Children of the Poor*, Oxford: Basil Blackwell.

——— (1995), *Children and Childhood in Western Society since 1500*, London and New York: Longman.

Curtis, S. and K. Neitzel (1996), *Contraceptive Knowledge, Use, and Sources*, Calverton MD: Macro International (DHS Comparative Studies No. 19).

David, N. and D. Voas (1981), 'Societal Causes of Infertility and Population Decline Among the Settled Fulani of North Cameroon', *Man*, 16:4, 644–64.

David, R. (1995), *Changing Places? Women, Resource Management and Migration in the Sahel*, London: SOS Sahel.

Davidson, S. and L. Lush (1995), 'What is Reproductive Health Care?', in *Refugee Participation Network*, no. 20, 4–8.

Davies, S. (1996), *Adaptable Livelihoods: Coping with Food Insecurity in the Malian Sahel*, London: Macmillan.

Dawes, A. and D. Donald (eds), (1994), *Childhood and Adversity; Psychological Perspectives from South African Research*, Capetown and Johannesburg: David Philip.

Dawes, A. and D. David (1994), 'Understanding the Psychological Consequences of Adversity', in A. Dawes and D. Donald (eds), *Childhood and Adversity; Psychological Perspectives from South African Research*, Capetown and Johannesburg: David Philip, 1–27.

Day, S. (1994), 'What Counts as Rape? Physical Assault and Broken Contracts: Contrasting Views of Rape among London Sex Workers', in P. Harvey and P. Gow (eds), *Sex and Violence: Issues in Representation and Experience*, London: Routledge, 172–89.

—— (1996), 'The Law and the Market: Rhetorics of Exclusion and Inclusion Among London Prostitutes', in O. Harris (ed.), *Inside and Outside the Law*, London: Routledge, 75–97.

De Bruijn, M. and H. Van Dijk, (1995), *Arid Ways*, Amsterdam: Thesis Publishers.

De Bruyn, M. (1992) 'Women and AIDS in Developing Countries', *Social Science and Medicine*, 34:3, 249–62.

Demeny, P. (1985), 'Bucharest, Mexico City and Beyond', *Population and Development Review*, 11:1, 99–106.

——— (1988), 'Social Science and Population Policy', *Population and Development Review*, 14:3, 451–79.

DFID (Department for International Development), (1997), *Report on DFID Sponsored Research Workshop on Healthcare in Unstable Situations*, London: Centre for International Child Health, Institute of Child Health.

Diggins, J. (1994), *The Promise of Pragmatism: Modernism and the Crisis of Knowledge and Authority*. Chicago: University of Chicago Press.

Dissanayake, W. (1996), *Narratives of Agency: Self-Making in China, India and Japan*, Minnesota: University of Minnesota Press.

Dixon-Mueller, B. (1993), *Population Policy and Women's Rights: Transforming Reproductive Choice*, Westpoint: Praeger.

Douglas, M. (1966), *Purity and Danger: An Analysis of Concepts of Pollution and Taboo*, London: Routledge and Kegan Paul.

ECPAT. (1992), *Newsletter Number 5*, Bangkok: ECPAT.

Ekejiuba, F. (1995), 'Down to Fundamentals: Women-Centred Hearth-Holds in Rural West Africa', in D. Fahy Bryceson (ed.), *Women Wielding the Hoe*, Oxford: Berg, 47–62.

Ellis, R. (1997), 'A Taste for Movement: An Exploration of the Social Ethics of the Tsimanes of Lowland Bolivia', PhD thesis: University of St. Andrews.

Ellison, P. T. (1995), 'Understanding Natural Variation in Human Ovarian Function', in R. I. M. Dunbar (ed.), *Human Reproductive Decisions: Biological and Social Perspectives*, St Martin's Press/Galton Institute, 22–51.

Ennew, J. (1986), *The Sexual Exploitation of Children*, Cambridge: Polity Press.

Ennew, J. and B. Milne (1989), *The Next Generation – Lives of Third World Children*, London: Zed Books.

Ennew, J., K. Gopal, J. Heeran, H. Montgomery (1996a), 'The Commercial Sexual Exploitation of Children: Background Papers and Annotated Bibliography for the World Congress on the Commercial Sexual Exploitation of Children', Oslo: Childwatch.

——— (1996b), 'Children and Prostitution; How Can We Measure and Monitor the Commercial Sexual Exploitation of Children?', mimeo, Cambridge and Oslo: UNICEF, Centre for Family Research, University of Cambridge and Childwatch International.

Erulkar, A. and B. Mensch (1997), *Youth Centres in Kenya: Evaluation of the Family Planning Association of Kenya Programme*, New York and Nairobi: The Population Council.

Erwin, J. (1993), 'Reproductive Tract Infections Among Women in Ado-Ekiti, Nigeria: Symptoms Recognition, Perceived Causes and Treatment Choices', *Health Transition Review*, 3: Supplementary Issue, 135–49.

Family Welfare Society (1986), *An Exploratory Study on Parents' Choice and Satisfaction on Childminding in Hong Kong*, Hong Kong.

Fapohunda, E. (1988), 'The Non-pooling Household: A Challenge to Theory', in D. Dwyer and J. Bruce (eds), *A Home Divided*, Stanford: Stanford University Press.

Farmer, P. (1992), *AIDS and Accusation: Haiti and the Geography of Blame*, Los Angeles: University of California Press.

Findley, S. E. (1989), 'Choosing Between African and French Destinations; The Role of Family and Community Factors in Migration in the Senegal River Valley' Bamako: CERPOD Working Paper.

——— (1994), 'Does Drought Increase Migration? A Study of Migration from Rural Mali During the 1983–1985 Drought', *International Migration Review* 28:3, 539–53.

Finkle, J. and B. Crane (1985), 'Ideology and Politics at Mexico City: The United States at the 1984 International Conference on Population', *Population and Development Review*, 11:1, 1–28.

Ford, N. and S. Saiprasert (1993), 'Destinations Unknown: The Gender Construction and Changing Nature of the Sexual Lifestyle of Thai Youth', Paper presented at the Fifth International Conference on Thai Studies – SOAS, University of London.

Fordham, G. (1995), 'Whisky, Women and Song: Men, Alcohol and AIDS in Northern Thailand', *Australian Journal of Anthropology*, 6:3, 154–77.

Foucault, M. (1976), *The Birth of the Clinic: An Archaeology of Medical Perception*, Tr. Sheridan Smith, London: Routledge.

——— (1980), *Power/Knowledge: Selected Interviews and Other Writings 1972–1977*, London: Harvester Press.

——— (1990), *The History of Sexuality, Volume One: An Introduction*, London: Allen Lane (originally published 1976).

Fox, N. (1997), 'Is There Life After Foucault? Texts, Frames and Differends', in A. Petersen and R. Bunton (eds), *Foucault, Health and Medicine*, London: Routledge, 31–50.

Francombe, C. (1986), *Abortion Practice in Britain and the United States*, London: Allen and Unwin.

Frank, O. (1983), 'Infertility in Sub-Saharan Africa: Estimates and Implications', *Population and Development Review* 9:1, 137–44.

Franklin. S. and H. Ragone (eds), (1998), *Reproducing Reproduction: Kinship, Power and Technological Innovation*, Philadelphia: University of Pennsylvania Press.

Fyfe, A. (1989), *Child Labour*, Cambridge: Polity Press.

Gage, A. (1998), 'Sexual Activity and Contraceptive Use: The Components of the Decision-Making Process', *Studies in Family Planning* 29:2, 154–166.

Gage-Brandon, A. and D. Meekers (1993), 'Sex, Contraception and Childbearing Before Marriage in Sub-Saharan Africa', *International Family Planning Perspectives*, 19:1, 14–18, 33.

Gallais, J. (1975), *Pasteurs et Paysans du Gourma*, Paris: CNRS.

——— (1984), *Hommes du Sahel: Espaces-Temps et Pouvoir: Le Delta Intérieur du Niger 1960–1980*, Paris: Flammarion.

Garbarino, J. (1999), 'Psychology's Contribution to the Study of Refugees', seminar paper, Refugee Studies Programme, University of Oxford, Oxford, November.

Garcia Moreno, C. and A. Claro (1994), 'Challenges From the Women's Health Movement: Women's Rights Versus Population Control', in G. Sen, A. Germain and L. Chen (eds), *Population Policies Reconsidered: Health, Empowerment and Rights*, Cambridge MA: Harvard University Press, 47–61.

Garenne, M., M. Madison, B. Zanzou, J. Aka and R. Dogore, (1995), *Conséquences Démographiques du SIDA en Abidjan 1986–1992'* Paris: CEPED.

Gasper, D. (1996), 'Culture and Development Ethics: Needs, Women's Rights and Western Theories', *Development and Change*, 27, 628–59.

Germain, A. (1997) 'Addressing the Demographic Imperative Through Health, Empowerment and Rights: ICPD Implementation in Bangladesh', *Health Transition Review*, vol. 7 (Supplement 4), 33–6.

Germain, A., S. Nowrojee and H. H. Pyne (1994), 'Setting a New Agenda: Sexual and Reproductive Health and Rights', in G. Sen, A. Germain and L. Chen (eds) *Population Policies Reconsidered: Health, Empowerment and Rights*, Cambridge MA: Harvard University Press, 27–46.

Giddens, A. (1984), *The Constitution of Society: Outline of the Theory of Structuration*, Cambridge: Polity Press.

Gillham, B. (1997), *The Facts About Teenage Pregnancies*, London: Cassell.

Ginsburg, F. and R. Rapp (1991), 'The Politics of Reproduction', *Annual Review of Anthropology*, 20.

——— (1995a), 'Rethinking Demography, Biology and Social Policy', in F. Ginsburg and R. Rapp (eds), *Conceiving a New World Order: The Global Politics of Reproduction*, Berkeley: University of California Press, 159–61.

——— (1995b), (eds), *Conceiving a New World Order: The Global Politics of Reproduction*, Berkeley: University of California Press, 159–61.

Given, J. (1998), 'A Local Anthropology of Exclusion', in I. R. Edgar and A. Russell (eds), *The Anthropology of Welfare*, London: Routledge, 161–82.

Good, B. (1994), *Medicine, Rationality and Experience*, Cambridge: Cambridge University Press.

Goody, E. N. (1982), Parenthood and Social Reproduction: Fostering and Occupational Roles in West Africa, Cambridge: Cambridge University Press.

Gordon, L. (1997), 'Teenage Pregnancy and Out-Of-Wedlock Birth: Morals, Moralism, Experts', in A. M. Brandt and P. Rozin (eds), *Morality and Health*, London: Routledge, 251–70.

Gorgen, R., B. Maier, and H. Diesfeld (1993), 'Problems Related to Schoolgirl Pregnancies in Burkina Faso', *Studies in Family Planning* 24:5, 283–94.

Government of India (1987), *Jaipur District Gazetteer*, Jaipur: Government Publications.

——— (1995), *National Family Health Survey 1992–3: Rajasthan*, Udaipur: Population Research Centre and Bombay: International Institute for Population Sciences.

——— (1995), *National Family Health Survey 1992–93: India*, Bombay: International Institute for Population Sciences.

Gould, W. T. S. (1994), 'Circular Migration and Rural Fertility in Sub-Saharan Africa', paper presented at the BSPS Conference, Durham.

Govindasamy, P. et al. (1993), *High Risk Births and Maternity Care*, Colombia Md: Macro International (Demographic and Health Surveys Comparative Studies, No. 8).

Gow, P. (1991), *Of Mixed Blood: Kinship and History in Peruvian Amazonia*, Oxford: Oxford University Press.

Graham, W., W. Brass and R. Snow (1988), 'Indirect Estimation of Maternal Mortality: The Sisterhood Method', CPS Research Paper 88–1, London: LSHTM, April.

Gray, R. (1993) 'The Impact of Health and Nutrition on Natural Fertility' in R. Bulatao and R. Lee (eds), *Determinants of Fertility in Developing Countries*, New York: Academic Press, 139–62.

Greenaway, C. (1998), 'Hungry Earth and Vengeful Stars: Soul Loss and Identity in the Peruvian Andes', *Social Science and Medicine*, 47:8, 993–1004.

Greenhalgh, S. (1990), 'Toward a Political Economy of Fertility: Anthropological Perspectives', *Population and Development Review* 16:1, 85–106.

——— (1995), 'Anthropology Theorizes Reproduction: Integrating Practice, Political Economic, and Feminist Perspectives' in S. Greenhalgh (ed.), *Situating Fertility: Anthropology and Demographic Inquiry*, Cambridge: Cambridge University Press, 3–28.

——— (ed.), (1995), *Situating Fertility: Anthropology and Demographic Enquiry*, Cambridge: Cambridge University Press.

——— (1996), 'The Social Construction of Population Science: An Intellectual, Institutional, and Political History of Twentieth Century Demography', *Comparative Studies in Society and History* 38:1, 26–66.

Griffin, C. (1993), *Representations of Youth: The Study of Youth and Adolescence in Britain and America*, Cambridge: Polity Press.

Grunseit, A. (1997), *Impact of HIV and Sexual Health Education on the Sexual Behaviour of Young People: A Review Update*, Geneva: Joint United Nations Programme on AIDS (UNAIDS).

Grunseit, A. and S. Kippax (1993), *Effects of Sex Education on Young People's Sexual Behaviour*, Geneva: World Health Organisation, Global Programme on AIDS.

Guilmoto, C. Z. (1998), 'Institutions and Migrations. Short-Term Versus Long-Term Moves in Rural West Africa, *Population Studies* 52:1, 85–103.

Gupta, J. A. (1996), 'New Freedoms, New Dependencies: New Reproductive Technologies, Women's Health and Autonomy', PhD thesis, University of Leiden.

Guyer, J. I. (1981), 'Household and Community in African Studies', *African Studies Review*, XXIV:2/3, 87–137.

——— (1994), 'Lineal Identities and Lateral Networks: the Logic of Polyandrous Motherhood', in C. Bledsoe and G. Pison (eds), *Nuptiality in Sub-Saharan Africa: Contemporary Anthropological and Demographic Perspectives*, Oxford: Clarendon.

Guyer, J. I. and Pauline Peters (1987), 'Introduction', in *Conceptualising the Household: Issues of Theory and Policy in Africa*, in Jane I. Guyer and Pauline Peters (eds), *Development and Change* 18 (2): 197–214.

Haffner, D. and E. Goldfarb (1997), 'But Does It Work? Improving Evaluations of Sexuality Education', *Siecus Report*, 25:6.

Hajnal, J. (1953), 'Age at Marriage and Proportions Never Marrying', *Population Studies*, 7.

Hall, C. M. (1992), 'Sex Tourism in South-East Asia', in D. Harrison (ed.), *Tourism and the Less Developed Countries*, London: Bellhaven, 64–74.

Hammel, E. A. (1990), 'A Theory of Culture for Demography', *Population and Development Review*, 16:3, 455–85.

Hampshire, K. and S. C. Randall, (1999), 'Seasonal Labour Migration Strategies in the Sahel: Coping with Poverty or Optimising Security?', *International Journal of Population Geography* 5, 367–85.

——— (2000), 'Pastoralists, Agropastoralists and Migrants: Interactions Between Fertility and Mobility in Northern Burkina Faso', *Population Studies*, 54 (3), 247–62.

Hanks, J. (1964), *Maternity and its Rituals in Bang Chan*, Data Paper 51, South-East Asia Programme, Ithaca: Ithaca University Press.

Harcourt. W. A. (1997), 'An Analysis of Reproductive Health: Myths, Resistance and New Knowledge', in W. A. Harcourt (ed.), *Power, Reproduction and Gender: The International Transfer of Knowledge*, London: Zed Books, 8–34.

——— (1999), 'Reproductive Health and Rights and the Quest for Social Justice', *Development*, 42:1, 7–10.

Hardman, C. (1973), 'Can There Be an Anthropology of Children?' *Journal of the Anthropological Society of Oxford*, 4, 1, 85–99.

Hardon, A. and E. Hayes (eds) (1998), *Reproductive Rights in Practice: A Feminist Report on Quality of Care*, London: Zed Books Ltd.

Hartmann, B. (1987), *Reproductive Rights and Wrongs: The Global Politics of Population Control and Contraceptive Choice*, New York: Harper Row.

——— (1993), 'The Present Politics of Population and Reproductive Rights', *Women's Global Network for Reproductive Rights Newsletter*, 43, 1–3.

Havanon, N. and W. Chairut (1985), *Nuptiality and the Family in Thailand*, Bangkok: Chulalongkorn University Press.

Hawkins, K. and N. Price (2000), *A Peer Ethnographic Tool for Social Appraisal and Monitoring of Sexual and Reproductive Health Programmes*, Swansea: Centre for Development Studies, University of Wales Swansea.

Health Education Authority (1992), *Today's Young Adults. 16–19 Year Olds Look at Diet, Alcohol, Smoking, Drugs and Sexual Behaviour. Report on the Survey Period March-May 1990*, London: Health Education Authority.

——— (1993), *Peers in Partnership: HIV/AIDS Education with Young People in the Community*, London: Health Education Authority.

Hempel, M. (1996), 'Reproductive Health and Rights: Origins of and Challenges to the ICPD Agenda', *Health Transition Review*, 6:1, 73–84.

Henin, R. A. (1968), 'Fertility Differences in the Sudan', *Population Studies*, 22:1, 147–64.

——— (1969), 'Patterns and Causes of Fertility Differentials in the Sudan', *Population Studies*, 23:2, 171–98.

Henry, L. (1961), 'Some Data on Natural Fertility', *Eugenics Quarterly*, 8:81–91.

Hern, W. (1994), 'Conocimiento y Uso de Anticonceptivos Herbales en una Comunidad Shipibo', *Amazonía Peruana*, 24, 143–60.

Heywood, S. (1998), 'Stop Tide of Teen Births', *Evening Gazette*, 20 November, 1.

Hiew, C. C. (1992), 'Endangered Families in Thailand: Third World Families Affected by Socio-economic Change', in G. Albee, L. A. Bond and T. V. Cook Monsey (eds), *Improving Children's Lives – Global Perspectives on Prevention*, New Delhi: Sage, 129–46.

Hinton, R. (2000), '"Seen but not Heard": Refugee Children and Models of Coping', in C. Panter-Brick and M. Smith (eds), *Abandoned Children*, Cambridge: Cambridge University Press, 199–212.

Hodgson, D. (1983), 'Demography as Social Science and Policy Science', *Population and Development Review*, 9:1, 1–34.

Hodgson, D. and S. Cotts Watkins (1997), 'Feminist and Neo-Malthusians: Past and Present Alliances', *Population and Development Review*, 23:3, 469–523.

Hong Kong Census and Statistics Department (1991), *Hong Kong 1991 Population Census Summary Results*, Hong Kong.

——— (1993), *Hong Kong Social and Economic Trends 1982–1992*, Hong Kong.

Holland, P. (1992), *What is a Child?* London: Virago.

Holmstrom, L. (ed.), (1990), *The Inner Courtyard: Stories by Indian Women*, London: Virago.

Hoyles, M. (ed.), (1989), *Changing Childhood*, London: Writers and Readers Publishing Co-operative.

Hubley, J. (1997), *School Health Promotion in Developing Countries: A Literature Review*, Leeds: Leeds Metropolitan University.

Hudson, F. and B. Ineichen (1991), *Taking it Lying Down: Sexuality and Teenage Motherhood*, Hong Kong: Macmillan Education.

Hughes, J. and A. McCauley (1998), 'Improving the Fit: Adolescents: Needs and Future Programmes for Sexual and Reproductive Health in Developing Countries', *Studies in Family Planning*, 29:2, 233–45.

Hung, Beatrice Kit-May (1983), 'Mother-Infant Interaction and the Infant's Social Development in the First Half Year of Life', M.Phil dissertation, University of Hong Kong.

Hutchby, I. and J. Moran-Ellis (1998), 'Situating Children's Social Competence', in Ian Hutchby and Jo Moran-Ellis (eds), *Children and Social Competence, Arenas of Action*, London and Washington: The Falmer Press, 7–26.

Iliffe, J. (1987), *The African Poor: A Comparative History*, Cambridge: Cambridge University Press.

Ingham, R. (1997), 'The Development of an Integrated Model of Sexual Conduct Amongst Young People', End of Award Report to the Economic and Social Research Council, Ref. H52425701495

Ingstad, B. (1994) 'The Grandmother and Household Viability in Botswana', in A. Adepoju and C. Oppong (eds), *Gender, Work and Population in Sub-Saharan Africa*, London: James Currey, 209–40.

Inhorn, M. (1994), *Quest for Conception: Gender, Infertility and Egyptian Medical Traditions*, Philadelphia: University of Pennsylvania Press.

INSD (1994), 'Analyse des resultats de l'enquête démographique 1991' Ouagadougou: INSD.

International Federation of Red Cross and Red Crescent Societies (1996), *World Disasters Report 1996*, Oxford: Oxford University Press.

International Planned Parenthood Federation (1994) *Understanding Adolescents*, London: International Planned Parenthood Federation.

Ireland, K. (1993), *Wish you Weren't Here*, London: Save the Children.

James, A., C. Jenks, and A. Prout (1998), *Theorizing Childhood*, Cambridge, UK: Polity Press.

Jeffrey, P., R. Jeffrey and A. Lyon (1987), *Labour Pains and Labour Power: Women and Childbearing in India*, London: Zed.

Jeffrey, R. and P. Jeffrey (1997), *Population, Gender and Politics: Demographic Change in Rural North India*, Cambridge: Cambridge University Press.

Jejheebhoy, S. (1997), 'Addressing Women's Reproductive Health Needs: Priorities for the Family Welfare Programme', *Economic and Political Weekly*, March 1–8, 475–84.

Johns Hopkins School of Public Health (1995) *Reaching Young People Worldwide: Lessons Learned from Communication Projects 1986–95*, Baltimore: Johns Hopkins School of Public Health (Centre for Communication Programs, Working Paper No. 2).

Johnson, A. M., J. Wadsworth, K. Wellings and J. Field (1994), *The National Survey of Sexual Attitudes and Lifestyles*, Oxford: Blackwell Scientific Publications.

Jolly, M. (1998), 'Colonial and Postcolonial Plots in Histories of Maternities and Modernities', in M. Jolly and R. Kalpana (eds), *Maternities and Modernities: Colonial and Postcolonial Experiences in Asia and the Pacific*, Cambridge: Cambridge University Press.

Jones, E. et al. (1985), 'Teenage Pregnancy in Developed Countries: Determinants and Policy Implications', *Family Planning Perspectives*. 17:2, 53–63.

Juarez, A. (1993), 'Gente Joven: Meeting Needs', *Planned Parenthood Challenges* 1993/2, 31–3.

Jutensen, A., S. Kapiga and H. van Asten (1993), 'Abortions in a Hospital Setting: Hidden Realities in Tanzania', *Newsletter of the Women's Global Network for Reproductive Rights*, 42, 21–2.

Kambou S., M. K. Shah and G. Nkhama (1998), 'For a Pencil: Sex and Adolescence in Peri-Urban Lusaka', in I. Guijt and M. K. Shah (eds), *The Myth of Community: Gender Issues in Participatory Development*, London: Intermediate Technology Publications, 110–20.

Karras, R. M. (1996), *Common Women: Prostitution and Sexuality in Medieval England*. Oxford: Oxford University Press.

Kathina, M. (1998), 'A Pilot Study of Refugee Camps in Kenya', unpublished paper for Research Project on Reproductive Health in Post-Crisis Situations in Africa, University of Amsterdam, NL.

Keen, D. (1992), *Refugees: Rationing the Right to Life*, London: Zed Books.

Keller, S. (1997), 'Pressures Influence Contraceptive Use', *Network* 17:3, 25–27.

Ketting, E. (1995), 'Meeting Young People's Sexual and Reproductive Health Needs Worldwide', *Planned Parenthood Challenges*, 1, 28–31.

Keyes, C. F. (1984), 'Mother or Mistress but Never a Monk', *American Ethnologist* 11: 2, 223–41.

Kielman, K. (1998), 'Barren Ground: Contesting Identities of Infertile Women in Pemba, Tanzania', in M. Lock and P. Kaufert (eds), *Pragmatic Women and Body Politics*, Cambridge: Cambridge University Press, 127–64

Kinoti, S., L. Gaffikin, J. Benson and L. Nicholson (1995), *Monograph of Complications of Unsafe Abortion in Africa*, Baltimore: Johns Hopkins Program of International Education in Reproductive Health.

Kirsch, A. T. (1985), 'Text and Context: Buddhist Sex Roles: The Culture of Gender Revisited', *American Ethnologist*, 12:2, 302–20.

Kitzinger, J. (1997), 'Who Are You Kidding? Children, Power and the Struggle Against Sexual Abuse', in A. James and A. Prout (eds), *Constructing and Reconstructing Childhood; Contemporary Issues in the Sociological Study of Childhood*, London, New York, Philadelphia: The Falmer Press, 157–83.

Kleinman, A. (1980), *Patients and Healers in the Context of Culture*, Berkeley: University of California Press.

Kligman, G. (1998), *The Politics of Duplicity: Controlling Reproduction in Ceausescu's Romania*, Berkeley: University of California Press.

Komin, S. (1991), *Psychology of the Thai People*, Bangkok: National Institute of Development Administration.

Konde-Lule, J., N. Sewankambo and M. Morris (1997), 'Adolescent Sexual Networking and HIV Transmission in Rural Uganda', *Health Transition Review*, Supplement to vol. 7, 89–100.

Koo, H., G. Dunteman, C. George, Y. Green and M. Vincent (1994), 'Reducing Adolescent Pregnancy through a School and Community Based Intervention: Denmark, South Carolina, Revisited', *Family Planning Perspectives*, 26: 5, 206–17.

Koompraphant, S. (1993), 'Sexual Exploitation and Child Prostitution in Thailand in Child Abuse and Neglect', in *Child Abuse and Neglect:*

Asian Perspectives: Conference Papers from Proceedings of Third Asian Conference on Child Abuse and Neglect, Kuala Lumpur: International Society for the Prevention of Child Abuse and Neglect (ISPCAN).

Koso-Thomas, O. (1992), *The Circumcision of Women: A Strategy for Eradication*, London: Zed Books.

Kulin, H. E. (1988), 'Adolescent Pregnancy in Africa: A Programmatic Focus', *Social Science and Medicine*, 26:7, 727–35.

La Fontaine, J. S. (1998), *Speak of the Devil: Tales of Satanic Abuse in Contemporary England*, Cambridge, New York, Melbourne: Cambridge University Press.

Lagrou, E. (1998), 'Cashinahua Cosmovision: A Perspectival Approach to Identity and Alterity', PhD thesis, University of St. Andrews.

Landon, K. (1939), *Siam in Transition: A Brief Survey of Cultural Trends in the Five Years since the Revolution of 1932*, Oxford: Oxford University Press.

Langdon, J. M. (1974), 'Siona Medical System: Belief and Behaviour', PhD thesis, Tulane University.

Laqueur, T. (1990), *Making Sex: Body and Gender from the Greeks to Freud*, Cambridge Mass: Harvard University Press.

Larme, A. (1998), 'Environment, Vulnerability and Gender in Andean Ethnomedicine', *Social Science and Medicine* 47:8, 1005–15.

Larsen, U. (1989), 'A Comparative Study of the Levels and Differentials of Sterility in Cameroon, Kenya and Sudan', in R. Lesthaeghe (ed.), *Reproduction and Social Organisation in Sub-Saharan Africa*, University of California Press, 167–211.

——— (1994), 'Sterility in Sub-Saharan Africa', *Population Studies* 48, 459–74.

Larsen, U. and J. Menken, (1989), 'Measuring Sterility from Incomplete Birth Histories', *Demography*, 26:2, 185–201.

——— (1991), 'Individual Level Sterility: A New Method of Estimation with Application to Sub-Saharan Africa', *Demography*, 28:2, 229–47.

Lassonde, L. (1997), *Coping with Population Challenges*, London: Earthscan Publications.

Lee, R. (1993), *Doing Research on Sensitive Topics*, London: Sage Publications.

Lock, M. and P. Kaufert (eds), (1998), *Pragmatic Women and Body Politics*, Cambridge Studies in Medical Anthropology no. 5, Cambridge: Cambridge University Press.

Lockwood, M. (1989), 'The Economics of Fertility and the Infertility of Economics: Theory and Demographic Reality', *Centro Studi 'Luca d'Agliano' Papers in Development Studies*, 12, Oxford and Torino: QEH.

——— (1995), 'Structure and Behaviour in the Social Demography of Africa', *Population and Development Review*, 21:1,1–32.

Loizos. P. and P. Heady (eds) (1999), *Conceiving Persons: Ethnographies of Procreation, Fertility and Growth*, London and New Brunswick, N.J.: The Athlone Press.

Lutkehaus, C. and Roscoe, O. (1995), *Gender Rituals: Female Initiation in Melanesia*, London: Routledge.

Lutz, C. (1988), *Unnatural Emotions: Everyday Sentiments on a Micronesian Atoll and Their Challenge to Western Theory*, Chicago: University of Chicago Press.

Lutz, C. and L. Abu-Lughod (eds), (1990), *The Language of Politics and Emotion*, Cambridge: Cambridge University Press.

Lynch, O. (ed.) (1990), *Divine Passions: The Social Construction of Emotion in India*, Berkeley: University of California Press.

Lyon, M. and S. Barbalet (1995), 'Society's Body: Emotion and the Somatisation of Social Theory', in T. Csordas (ed.), *Embodiment and Experience: The Existential Ground of Culture and Self*. Cambridge: Cambridge: Cambridge University Press.

McCauley, A. and C. Salter (1995), *Meeting the Needs of Young Adults*, Baltimore, Johns Hopkins School of Public Health, Population Information Program (Population Reports Series J, 41).

McDevitt, T. (1996), *Trends in Adolescent Fertility and Contraceptive Use in the Developing World*, Washington DC: United States Bureau of the Census, Population Studies Branch (IPC/95–1).

McFalls, J. A. and M. A. McFalls (1984), *Disease and Fertility*, London: Academic Press Inc.

Macfarlane, Alan (1986), *Marriage and Love in England: Modes of Reproduction 1300–1840*, Oxford: Blackwell.

McHoul, A. and W. Grace (1993), *A Foucault Primer, Discourse, Power and the Subject*, London: University College London Press.

McKaig, C., S. Mullen and R. Magnini (1996), *Reproductive Health Programs for Young People in Developing Countries: A Review of Evaluation Findings*, Washington DC: FOCUS on Young Adults, Pathfinder International.

McKintosh, A. and J. Finkle (1995), 'The Cairo Conference on Population and Development: A New Paradigm?', *Population and Development Review*, 21:2, 223–60.

McLaren, A. (1984), *Reproductive Rituals: the Perception of Fertility in England from the Sixteenth Century to the Nineteenth Century*, London: Methuen.

McNicoll, G. (1980), 'Institutional Determinants of Fertility Change', *Population and Development Review*, 6:3, 441–62.

——— (1992), 'The Agenda of Population Studies: A Commentary and Complaint', *Population and Development Review*, 18:3, 399–420.

Makhlouf, O. C. (1991), 'Women, Islam and Population: Is the Triangle Fateful?' Working Paper Series no. 6, Harvard: Harvard School of Public Health, Harvard Center for Population and Development Studies.

——— (1992), 'Islam, Women and Politics: The Demography of Arab Countries', *Population and Development Review*, 18:1.

——— (1994), 'Religious Doctrine, State Ideology, and Reproductive Options in Islam', in G. Sen and R. Snow (eds), *Power and Decision: The Social Control of Reproduction*, Cambridge, MA: Harvard University Press, Harvard Series on Population and International Health.

Maliki, A. B., C. White, L. Loutan and J. J. Swift, (1984), 'The WoDaaBe', in J. J. Swift (ed.), *Pastoral Development in Central Niger:*

Report of the Niger Range and Livestock Project, Niamey: Ministère du Developpement Rural and USAID, 255–529.

Martin, Diana (1991), 'Chinese Ghost Marriage', in H. Baker and S. Feuchtwang (eds), *An Old State in New Settings: Studies in the Social Anthropology of China in Memory of Maurice Freedman,* Oxford: JASO, 26–43.

——— (1994), 'Pregnancy and Childbirth Among the Chinese of Hong Kong', unpublished D.Phil. thesis, University of Oxford.

——— (1997) 'Motherhood in Hong Kong: The Working Mother and Child-Care in The Parent-Centred Hong Kong Family', in Grant Evans and Maria Tam Siu-mi (eds), *Hong Kong: The Anthropology of a Chinese Metropolis,* Richmond: Curzon Press, 198–219.

Martin, E. (1987), *The Woman in the Body: A Cultural Analysis of Reproduction.* Boston: Beacon Press.

Manning, W. (1990), 'Parenting Employed Teenagers', *Youth and Society,* 22:2, December, 184–200.

Mansurov, V. (1993), 'Child Work in Russia', unpublished report INTERDEP/CL/1993/1, 1993, Geneva: ILO.

Massey, D. and B. Mullman (1981), 'A Demonstration of the Effect of Seasonal Migration on Fertility', *Demography,* 21:4, 501–7.

Mayaram, S. (1997), 'Shamanism, Medical Pluralism and Intercommunity Relations: Spirit Possession, Exorcism and Women's Agency in a Rural Rajasthani Shrine', Institute of Development Studies, Jaipur, working paper no. 85.

Mayall, B. (ed.), (1994), 'Introduction', in *Children's Childhoods Observed and Experienced,* London and Washington: The Falmer Press, 1–12.

Meekers, D., A. Gage and L. Zhan (1995), 'Preparing Adolescents for Adulthood: Family Life Education and Pregnancy-Related School Expulsion in Kenya', *Population Research and Policy Review,* 14:1, 91–110.

Meheus, A., J. Reniers and M. Collet (1986), 'Determinants of Infertility in Africa', *African Journal of Sexually Transmitted Disease* 2/2: 31–6.

Mehta, R. (1976), 'From Purdah to Modernity', in, B. R. Nanda (ed.), *Indian Women: From Purdah to Modernity,* New Delhi: Vikas Publishing House.

Mensch, B., J. Bruce, and M. Greene (1999), *The Uncharted Passage: Girls' Adolescence in the Developing World,* New York: Population Council.

Mensch, B. and C. Lloyd (1998), 'Gender Differences in the Schooling Experiences of Adolescents in Low-Income Countries: The Case of Kenya', *Studies in Family Planning,* 29:2, 167–84.

Milleville, P. (1991), 'Les Systèmes de Culture, in J. Claude, M. Grouzis and P. Milleville (eds), *Un Espace Sahelien: La Mare d'Oursi, Burkina Faso,* Paris: ORSTOM, 143–55.

Mills, M. B. (1990), 'Moving Between Modernity and Tradition: The Case of Rural-Urban Migration from North-Eastern Thailand to Bangkok', *AUA American Studies* 2, 52–71.

Monimart, M. (1989), *Femmes du Sahel: La Désertification au Quotidien,* Paris: Karthala.

Montgomery, H. (1996), 'Public Vice and Private Virtue: Child Prostitution in Thailand', PhD thesis, University of Cambridge.

Moore, S. and D. Rosenthal (1993), *Sexuality in Adolescence*, London: Routledge.

Morokvasič M. (1981), 'Sexuality and the Control of Procreation', in K. Young, C. Wolkowitz and R. McCullagh (eds), *Of Marriage and the Market: Women's Subordination in International Perspective*, London: CSE Books, 127–143.

Morris, A., H. Giller, E. Szwed and H. Geach (1980), *Justice for Children*, London and Basingstoke: Macmillan.

Morsy, S. A. (1995), 'Deadly Reproduction Among Egyptian Women: Maternal Mortality and the Medicalization of Population Control', in F. Ginsburg and R. Rapp (eds), *Conceiving the New World Order: The Global Politics of Reproduction*, Berkeley: University of California Press, 162–76.

Morton-Williams, P. (1956), 'The Atinga Cult Among the South-Western Yoruba: a Sociological Analysis of a Witch-finding Movement', *Bulletin de l'Institut Français d'Afrique Noire*, 18 (Ser.B.):3–4, 315–34, Paris: Karthala.

Moss, J. C. (1994), 'From Family Planning and Maternal and Child Health Care to Reproductive Health', *Focus on Gender*, 2:2.

Muecke, M. A. (1981), 'Changes in Women's Status Associated with Modernization in Northern Thailand', in G. B. Hainsworth (ed.), *Women, Changing Social Structures and Cultural Continuity in South-East Asia*, Ottawa: University of Ottawa Press, 53–65.

——— (1984), 'Make Money Not Babies: Changing Status Markers of Northern Thai Women', *Asian Survey*, 24:4, 459–70.

——— (1992), 'Mother Sold Food, Daughter Sells Her Body – The Cultural Continuity of Prostitution', *Social Science and Medicine* 35: 7, 891–901.

Mulder, N. (1979), *Inside Thai Society – An Interpretation of Everyday Life*, Bangkok: Duang Kamol.

Mullender, A. (ed.) (1991), *Open Adoption: the Philosophy and the Practice*, London: British Agencies for Adoption and Fostering.

Muntabhorn, V. (1992), *Sale of Children: Report Submitted by the Special Rapporteur*, Document E/CN.4/1992/55, New York: United Nations.

Nash, J. (1979), *We Eat the Mines and the Mines Eat Us: Dependency and Exploitation in the Bolivian Tin Mines*, New York: Columbia University Press.

Noble, J., J. Cover and M. Yanagishita (1996), *The World's Youth 1996: A Special Focus on Reproductive Health*, Washington DC: The Population Reference Bureau.

Nsamenang, B. and A. Dawes (1998), 'Developmental Psychology as Political Psychology in Sub-Saharan Africa: The Challenge of Africanisation', *Applied Psychology: An International Review* 47 (1), 73–87.

Nunn, A., J. Kengaya-Kayondo, S. Malanda, A. Seely, and D. Mulder (1994), 'Risk Factors for HIV-1 Infection in Adults in a Rural Ugandan Community: A Population Study', *AIDS* 8:1, 81–6.

O'Grady, R. (1992), *The Child and the Tourist*, Bangkok: ECPAT.

——— (1994), *The Rape of the Innocent*, Bangkok: ECPAT.

Ogunbanjo, B. O., A. O. Osoba and J. Ochei (1989), 'Infective Factors of Male Infertility amongst Nigerians', *African Journal of Medical Sciences*, 18:1, 35–8.

Okonofua, F. E., K. A. Ako-Nai and M. D. Dighitoghi (1995), 'Lower Genital Tract Infections in Infertile Nigerian Women Compared with Controls', *Genitourinary Medicine*, 71:3, 163–8.

Okonofua, F. E., E. D. Harris, A. Odebiyi, T. Kane and R. Snow (1997a), 'The Social Meaning of Infertility in Southwest Nigeria', *Health Transition Review*, 7, 205–20.

Okonofua, F. E., R. C. Snow, G. A. Alemnji, A. Okoruwa and C. O. Ijaware (1997b), 'Serological and Clinical Correlates of Gonorrhoea and Syphilis in Fertile and Infertile Nigerian Women', *Genitourinary Medicine*, 73:3, 194–7.

Okonofua, F. E. and A. Ilumoka (eds), (1991), *Prevention of Morbidity and Mortality from Unsafe Abortion in Nigeria*, New York: Population Council.

Okonofua, F. E., A. Abejide, and R. Makanjuola (1992), 'Maternal Mortality in Ile-Ife, Nigeria: A Study of Risk Factors', *Studies in Family Planning*, 23:5, 319–24.

Okoth-Ogendo, H. W. O. (1989), 'The Effect of Migration on Family Structures in Sub-Saharan Africa', *International Migration*, 27:2, 309–17.

O'Laughlin, B. (1995), 'The Myth of the African Family in the World of Development', in D. Fahy Bryceson (ed.), *Women Wielding the Hoe*, Oxford: Berg, 63–91.

Oldenburg, V. (1990), 'Lifestyle as Resistance: The Case of the Courtesans of Lucknow, India', *Feminist Studies*, 16:259–87.

Oppong, C. and W. Bleek (1982), 'Economic Models and Having Children: Some Evidence from Kwahu, Ghana', *Africa*, 52:4, 15–33.

Overing, J. (1986), 'Men's Control Over Women? Catch 22 in Gender Analysis', *International Journal of Moral and Social Studies*, 1, 135–56.

Page, H. and R. Lesthaeghe (eds), (1981), *Child-Spacing in Tropical Africa: Traditions and Change*, London: Academic Press.

Painter, T. A. (1982), *Migration and AIDS in West Africa*, New York: CARE.

Paiva, V. (1993), 'Sexuality, Condom Use and Gender Norms Among Brazilian Teenagers', *Reproductive Health Matters*, 2, 98–109.

Palmer, C. (1998), 'Reproductive Health for Displaced Populations', in *Relief and Rehabilitation, Network*, Paper no. 24.

Panos, (1994), *Private Decisions, Public Debates: Women, Reproduction and Population*, London: Panos.

Parker, R. (1994), 'Sexual Cultures, HIV Transmission and AIDS Prevention', *AIDS* 8 (Supplement 1), S309–S314.

Patel, T. (1994), *Fertility Behavior: Population and Society in a Rajasthan Village*, Oxford: Oxford University Press.

Pauli, G. (1999), 'The Creation of Real Food and Real People: Gender Complementarity Among the Menkü of Central Brazil', PhD thesis, University of St. Andrews.

Payaguaje, F. (1990), *El Bebedor de Yajé*, Aguarico: Vicariato Apostolico de Aguarico.

Payne, L. (1998), *Rebuilding Communities in a Refugee Settlement: A Casebook from Uganda*, Oxford: Oxfam Publications.

Peacock, A. (1992), 'Access to Science Learning for Children in Rural Africa', unpublished paper presented at the World Conference on Research and Practice in Children's Rights, University of Essex, Colchester, September 8–11.

Pearce, T. (1995), 'Women's Reproductive Practices and Biomedicine: Cultural Conflicts and Transformations in Nigeria', in F. Ginsburg and R. Rapp (eds), *Conceiving the New World Order: The Global Politics of Reproduction*, Berkeley: University of California Press, 195–208.

Pearson, G. (1985), *Hooligan: a History of Respectable Fears*, London and Basingstoke: Macmillan Press.

Pearson, R. (1997), "Global Change and Insecurity:Are Women the Problem or the Solution? in I. Baud and I. Smyth (eds), *Searching for Security: Women's Responses to Economic Transformations* London, London, Routledge, 10–24.

Pearson, S., I. Diamond et al. (1996), *Promoting Young People's Sexual Health Services*, Report to the Health Education Authority by Brook Advisory Centres and Centre for Sexual Health Research (University of Southampton). London: Health Education Authority.

Pease, Catherine E. (1995), 'Remembering the Taste of Melons: Modern Chinese Stories of Childhood', in Anne Behnke Kinney (ed.), *Chinese Views of Childhood*, Honolulu: University of Hawaii Press.

Petchesky, R. P. and K. Judd (eds), (1998), *Negotiating Reproductive Rights: Women's Perspectives Across Countries and Cultures*, London: Zed Books.

Phoenix, A. (1991), *Young Mothers?* Cambridge: Polity Press.

Poore, P. (1995), 'Delivering Reproductive Health Care', *Refugee Participation Network*, 20, 16–20.

Portes, A. (1997), 'Neoliberalism and the Sociology of Development: Emerging Trends and Unanticipated Facts', *Population and Development Review* 23:2, 229–59.

Potter, J. (1976), *Thai Peasant Social Structure*, Chicago: Chicago University Press.

Potter, S. H. (1979), *Family Life in a Northern Thai Village: A Study of the Structural Significance of Women*, Berkeley: University of California Press.

Potter, S. H. and Jack M. Potter (1990), *China's Peasants: The Anthropology of a Revolution*, Cambridge: Cambridge University Press.

Preston-Whyte, E. (1994), 'Gender and the Lost Generation: The Dynamics of HIV Transmission among Black South African Teenagers in KwaZulu/Natal', *Health Transition Review*, 4 (supplement), 241–55.

Price, N. L. (1989) *Behind the Planter's Back: Lower Class Responses to Marginality in Bequia Island, St Vincent*, London: Macmillan Books.

——— (1996), 'The Changing Value of Children Among the Kikuyu of Central Province Kenya', *Africa* 66:3, 411–37.

—— (1997), *Uganda: Reproductive Health Sector Review*, London: Options Consultancy Services for the UK Department of International Development.

—— (1998), 'Institutional Determinants of Fertility in Gwembe Tonga Society', *Social Sciences in Health*, 4:1, 25–44.

Price, N. L. et al. (1993), 'Pre-Appraisal Studies for the Kenya Family Health Project', unpublished report, London: Overseas Development Administration.

Price, N. L. and N. H. Thomas (1999), 'Continuity and Change in the Gwembe Valley Tonga Family and their Relevance to Demography's Nucleation Thesis', *Africa*, 69:4, 510–34.

Pruitt, I. (1945), *A Daughter of Han: The Autobiography of a Chinese Working Woman*, Stanford: Stanford University Press.

Punch, S. (1998), 'Negotiating Independence: Children and Young People Growing up in Rural Bolivia', PhD thesis, University of Leeds.

Rabain, J. (1979), *L'Enfant du linage*, Paris: Payot.

Rabibhadana, A. (1985), 'Kinship, Marriage and the Thai Social System', in N. Havanon and W. Chairut (eds), *Nuptiality and the Family in Thailand*, Bangkok: Chulalongkorn University Press, 2–27.

Raffaelli, M. et al. (1993), 'Sexual Practices and Attitudes of Street Youth in Belo Horizonte, Brazil', *Social Science and Medicine* 37:5, 661–70.

Raheja, G. G. and A. G. Gold (1994), *Listen to the Heron's Words: Reimagining Gender and Kinship in Northern India*, Berkeley: University of California Press.

Rance, S. (1997), 'Safe Motherhood, Unsafe Abortion: A Reflection on the Impact of Discourse', *Reproductive Health Matters*, 9, 10–19.

Randall, S. C. (1984), 'The Demography of Three Sahelian Populations', PhD thesis, London School of Hygiene and Tropical Medicine.

Rao, A. (1998), *Autonomy: Life Cycle, Gender and Status Among Himalayan Pastoralists*, Oxford: Berghahn Books.

Ravindran, S. (1993), 'The Politics of Women, Population and Development in India', in *Reproductive Health Matters*, 8:3, 27–42.

Reddy, W. (1999), 'Emotional Liberty: Politics and History in the Anthropology of Emotions', in *Cultural Anthropology* 14 (2): 256–88, American Anthropological Association.

Rees, J., A. Mellanby and J. Tripp (1998), 'Peer-Led Sex Education in the Classroom', in J. Coleman and D. Roker (eds), *Teenage Sexuality: Health, Risk and Education*, Amsterdam: Harwood Academic, 137–61.

Reniers, A. J. and M. Collet (1986), 'Determinants of Infertility in Africa', *African Journal of Sexually Transmitted Disease*, 2/2, 31–6.

Renne, E. (1996), '"The Pregnancy that Doesn't Stay": The Practice and Perception of Abortion by Yoruba Women', *Social Science and Medicine*.

Retel-Laurentin, A. (1974), *Infecondité en Afrique Noire*, Paris: Masson et Cie.

—— (1979), *Causes de l'infécondité dans la Volta Noire*. Institut National d'Etudes Démographiques/CNRS. Travaux et Documents: Cahier no. 87. Presses Universitaires de France.

Reynolds-Whyte, S. (1998), *Questioning Misfortune*, Cambridge: Cambridge University Press.

Rival, L. (1998), 'Androgynous Parents and Guest Children: The Huaorani Couvade', *Man*, 4:4, 619–42.

Rivière, P. (1974), 'The Couvade: A Problem Reborn', *Man*, 9, 423–35.

Roberts, P. (1991), 'Researching the Household: Methodological and Empirical Issues', *IDS Bulletin* 22:1, 60–4.

Robertson. A. F. (1991), *Beyond the Family: the Social Organisation of Human Reproduction*, Cambridge: Polity Press.

Robinson, W. C. and W. Robinson (1997), 'The Economic Theory of Fertility over Three Decades', *Population Studies*, 51: 63–74.

Rockel, J. and M. Ryburn (1988), *Adoption Today: Change and Choice in New Zealand*, Auckland: Heinemann Reed.

Rogoff, B. (1990), *Apprenticeship in Thinking; Cognitive Development in Social Context*, New York, Oxford: Oxford University Press

Rosaldo, M. (1984), 'Towards an Anthropology of Self and Feeling', in R. Shweder and R. Levine (eds), *Culture Theory: Essays on Mind, Self and Emotion*, Cambridge: Cambridge University Press.

Rose, N. (1992), 'Governing the Enterprising Self', in P. Heelas and P. Morris (eds), *The Values of the Enterprise Culture: The Moral Debate*, London: Routledge, 141–64.

Roth, E. A. (1993), 'A Re-examination of Rendille Population Regulation', *American Anthropologist* 95:3, 597–611.

Rozario, S. (1998), 'The Dai and the Doctor: Discourses on Women's Reproductive Health in Rural Bangladesh', in M. Jolly and R. Kalpana (eds), *Maternities and Modernities: Colonial and Postcolonial Experiences in Asia and the Pacific*, Cambridge: Cambridge University Press, 144–76.

Ruddick, S. (1980), 'Maternal Thinking', *Feminist Studies* 6: 342–64.

Saavendra, M. (1996), 'Young People in Bogota, Colombia, Develop Their Own Strategies to Prevent Risky Sexual Behavior', *Siecus Report*, 24:3, cited in UNFPA (1997: 26).

Sai, F. (1997), 'The ICPD Programme of Action: Pious Hope or a Workable Guide?', *Health Transition Review*, 7:4 (supplement), 1–5.

Santow, G. and M. Bracher (1999), 'Explaining Trends in Teenage Childbearing in Sweden', *Studies in Family Planning*, 30:3, 169–82.

Sargeant, C. and T. Johnson, (1996), *Medical Anthropology: Contemporary Theory and Method*, London: Praeger.

Scheper-Hughes, N. (1992), *Death Without Weeping: The Violence of Everyday Life in Brazil*, Berkeley: University of California Press.

Schildkraut, E. (1973), 'The Fostering of Children in Urban Ghana: Problems of Ethnographic Analysis in a Multi-Cultural Context', *Urban Anthropology*, 2, 48–73.

——— (1978), 'Roles of Children in Urban Kano', in J. S. La Fontaine, (ed.), *Sex and Age as Principles of Social Differentiation*, London: Academic Press, 109–38.

Schneider, D. (1980), *American Kinship: A Cultural Account*. Chicago: Chicago University Press. (First edn, 1969).

Schneider, P. and J. Schneider (1995a), 'Coitus Interruptus and Family Respectability in Catholic Europe: A Sicilian Case Study', in F. Ginsburg and R. Rapp (eds), *Conceiving the New World Order: The Global Politics of Reproduction*, Berkeley: University of California Press, 177–92.

——— (1995b), 'High Fertility and Poverty in Sicily: Beyond the Culture vs. Rationality Debate', in S. Greenhalgh (ed.), *Situating Fertility: Anthropology and Demographic Inquiry*, Cambridge: Cambridge University Press, 179–201.

Schoepf, B. (1994), 'Action Research and Empowerment in Africa', in B. Schneider and N. Stoller (eds), *Women Resisting AIDS: Feminist Strategies for Empowerment*, Philadelphia: Temple University Press, 246–69.

Schrijvers, J. (1997), 'Internal Refugees in Sri Lanka: The Interplay of Ethnicity and Gender', *The European Journal of Development Research*, 9:2, 62–82.

Schuler, S. R., M. Choque and S. Rance (1994), 'Misinformation, Mistrust, and Mistreatment: Family Planning Among Bolivian Market Women', *Studies in Family Planning* 25:4, 211–21.

Sciortino, R. and I. Smyth (1997), 'The Triumph of Violence: The Denial of Domestic Violence in Java', *Austrian Journal of Development Studies*, 13:3, 299–319.

Scordas, T. (1994), *Embodiment and Experience: The Existential Grounds of Culture and Self*, Cambridge: Cambridge University Press.

Scott, J. (1993), 'Everyday Forms of Resistance', PRIME Occasional Paper Series, 15, Yokohama: International Peace Research Institute Meigaku, Meiji Gakuin University.

Sen, G. (1994), 'Development, Population, and the Environment: A Search for Balance', in G. Sen, A. Germain and L. Chen (eds), *Population Policies Reconsidered: Health, Empowerment and Rights*, Cambridge MA: Harvard University Press, 63–73.

Sen, G. and Grown, K. (1988), *Development, Crises and Alternative Visions*, London: Earthscan Publications.

Sen, G., A. Germain and L. C. Chen (1994), (eds), *Population Policies Reconsidered: Health, Empowerment and Rights*, Cambridge MA: Harvard University Press.

Sen, G. and R. Snow (1994), *Power and Decision: The Social Control of Reproduction*, Cambridge, MA: Harvard University Press.

Senderowitz, J. (1997a), *Reproductive Health Outreach Programmes for Young Adults*, Washington DC: FOCUS on Young Adults, Pathfinder International.

——— (1997b), *Health Facility Programs on Reproductive Health for Young Adults*, Washington DC: FOCUS on Young Adults, Pathfinder International.

——— (1999), *Making Reproductive Health Services Youth Friendly*, Washington DC: FOCUS on Young Adults, Pathfinder International.

——— and J. Paxman (1985), 'Adolescent Fertility: Worldwide Concerns', *Population Bulletin* 40:2.

Serpell, R. (1996), 'Cultural Models of Childhood in Indigenous Socialization and Formal Schooling in Zambia', in P. C. Hwang, M. E. Lamb and I. E. Sigel (eds), *Images of Childhood*, Mahwah, New Jersey: Lawrence Erlbaum Associates, Publishers, 129–42.

Shah, M., R. Zambezi and M. Simasiku (1999), *Listening to Young Voices: Facilitating Participatory Appraisals on Reproductive Health with Adolescents*, Washington DC: FOCUS on Young Adults, Pathfinder International.

Shahar, S. (1992), *Childhood in the Middle Ages*, London and New York: Routledge.

Shankar Sing, J. (1998), *Creating a New Consensus: The International Conference on Population and Development*, London: Earthscan Publications.

Sharpe, S. (1987), *Falling for Love: Teenage Mothers Talk*, London: Virago Press.

Shorter, E. (1982), *Women's Bodies*, New Brunswick: Transaction Publishers.

Shweder, R. and R. Levine (eds) (1984), *Culture Theory: Essays on Mind, Self and Emotion*, Cambridge: Cambridge University Press.

Siedlecky, S. (1984), 'Defusing a New Teenage Baby Boom', *Education News*, 18, 20–3.

Simmel, G. (1971), *Georg Simmel on Individuality and Social Forms: Selected Writings*, D. Levine (ed.), Chicago: University of Chicago Press.

Singh, S. (1998), 'Adolescent Childbearing in Developing Countries: A Global Review', *Studies in Family Planning*, 29:2, 117–36.

Singh, S. and R. Samara (1996), 'Early Marriage among Women in Developing Countries', *International Family Planning Perspectives*, 22:4, 148–75.

Sittitrai, W. and T. Brown (1994), *The Impact of HIV on Children in Thailand*, Bangkok: Thai Red Cross Society.

Simpson, R. (1994), 'Bringing the Unclear Family into Focus', *Man*, 29:4, 831–51.

Smith, S. (1998), 'Gender, Culture and Development: AGRA East Workshop Report', Hanoi: Oxfam.

Smith, T. (1993), 'Influence of Socio-Economic Factors on Attaining Target Rates for Reducing Teenage Pregnancies', *British Medical Journal*, 306, 1232–5.

Smyth, I. (1994), 'Population Policies: Official Responses to Feminist Critiques', *Discussion Paper 14*, London: London School of Economics (Centre for the Study of Global Governance).

Sommerville, J. (1982), *The Rise and Fall of Childhood*, New York: Sage Publications.

Stainton-Rogers, R. and W. Stainton-Rogers (1992), *Stories of Childhood: Shifting Agendas of Child Concern*, Hemel Hempstead: Harvester Wheatsheaf.

Stenning, D. (1958), 'Household Viability Among the Pastoral Fulani', in J. Goody (ed.), *The Development Cycle of Domestic Groups*, Cambridge: Cambridge University Press, 92–119.

Stone, L. (1977), *The Family, Sex and Marriage in England 1500–1800*, Harmondsworth: Penguin.

Stewart, L., A. Sebastiani, G. Delgado, and G. Lopez (1995), 'Dealing with Sexual Abuse in Adolescents', *Planned Parenthood Challenges* 1995:1, 17–20.

Stewart, T. and D. Richter (1995), 'Perceived Barriers to HIV Prevention among University Students in Freetown, Sierra Leone', *International Quarterly of Community Health Education* 15:3, 253–65.

Super, C. and S. Harkness (eds), (1996), *Parents' Cultural Belief Systems, Their Origins, Expressions and Consequences*, New York and London: The Guildford Press.

Swift, J. J. (1977), 'Sahelian Pastoralists: Underdevelopment, Desertification and Famine', *Annual Review of Anthropology*, 6, 457–78.

Tantiwiramanond, D. and S. Pandey, (1987), 'The Status and Role of Women in the Pre-Modern Period: A Historical and Cultural Perspective', *Sojourn*, 2:1, 125–47.

Thitsa, K. (1980), *Providence and Prostitution: Women in Buddhist Thailand*, London: Change International.

Thomas, N. H. (1991), 'Land, Fertility and the Population Establishment', *Population Studies*, XLV, 379–97.

Thomas, N. H. and N. L. Price (1999), 'The Role of Development in Global Fertility Decline', *Futures: The Journal of Forecasting, Planning and Policy* 31:8, 779–802.

Timaeus, I. and W. Graham (1989), 'Labour Circulation, Marriage and Fertility in Southern Africa', in R. J. Lesthaeghe (ed.), *Reproduction and Social Organisation in Sub-Saharan Africa*, University of California Press, 364–400.

Toubia, N. (1996), *Female Genital Mutilation: A Call for Global Action*, New York: Women Ink.

Tucker, S. (1986), 'The Canton Hospital and Medicine in Nineteenth Century China, 1835–1900', Ph.D., University of Indiana, University Microfilms International.

Turner, B. (1997), 'From Governmentality to Risk: Some Reflections on Foucault's Contribution to Medical Sociology', in A. Petersen and R. Bunton (eds), *Foucault, Health and Medicine*, London: Routledge, ix–xxi.

Uganda (1995), *1995 Demographic and Health Survey*, Calverton MD: Macro International.

UNAIDS (Joint United Nations Programme on AIDS) (1997), *Integrating HIV/STD Prevention in the School Setting*, Geneva: UNAIDS.

UNAIDS/WHO (1997), *Report of the Global HIV/AIDS Epidemic, December 1997*, Geneva: UNAIDS.

UNAIDS/WHO (1999), *Report of the Global HIV/AIDS Epidemic, December 1999*, Geneva: UNAIDS.

United Nations (1983), *Manual X: Indirect Techniques for Demographic Estimation*, New York: United Nations.

——— (1989), *Adolescent Reproductive Behavior: Evidence from Developing Countries*, Volume 11 of UN Population Studies (No.109/Add.1) New York: United Nations.

——— (1994), *Programme of Action of the International Conference on Population and Development (Cairo, 5–13 September 1994)*, New York: United

Nations (reprinted in *Population and Development Review*, 1995, 22:1, 22:2).

——— (1995), *Platform of Action of the Fourth World Conference on Women (Beijing, 4–15 September 1995)*, New York: United Nations.

——— (1997), *The Sex and Age Distribution of the World Populations: The 1996 Revision*, New York: United Nations, Population Division.

United Nations Children's Fund (UNICEF) (1997), *Youth Health For a Change: A UNICEF Notebook on Programming for Young People's Health and Development*, New York: United Nations Children's Fund.

United Nations Population Fund (UNFPA) (1997), *Thematic Evaluation of Adolescent Reproductive Health Programmes*, New York: United Nations Population Fund.

——— (1998), *The Sexual and Reproductive Health of Adolescents: A Review of UNFPA Assistance*, New York: United Nations Population Fund (UNFPA Technical Report No. 43).

Unnithan (Unnithan-Kumar), M. (1999), 'Households, Kinship and Access to Reproductive Healthcare among Rural Muslim Women in Jaipur', *Economic and Political Weekly*, Mar 6–13, Bombay: Hitkari House.

——— (2001), 'Reproductive Rights, Health and Emotion', Unpublished paper presented at ASA conference on 'Rights, Claims and Entitlements', Sussex, UK.

——— (forthcoming), 'Midwives among Others: Knowledges of Healing and the Politics of Emotions', in S. Rozario and G. Samuels (eds), *Daughters of Hariti: Birth and Female Healers in South and Southeast Asia*, London: Gordon and Breach.

van Esterik, P. (1996), 'Nurturance and Reciprocity in Thai Studies', in E. P. Durrenberger (ed.), *State, Power and Culture in Thailand*, Princeton: Princeton University Press.

Vasconcelos, A., A. Neto, A. Valenca et al. (1995), *Sexuality and AIDS Prevention among Adolescents from Low-Income Communities in Recife, Brazil*, Washington DC: International Centre for Research on Women (ICRW).

Vichit-Vadakan, J. (1990), 'Traditional and Changing Values in Thai and American Societies', *AUA American Studies* 2, 27–52.

Vickers, W. (1989), *Los Siona y Los Secoyas. Su Adaptación al Medio Ambiente Amazónico*, Quito: Abya-Yala.

Walker, B. (1994), *No-one to Talk With: Norfolk Young People's Conversations about Sex – a Basis for Peer Education*, Norwich: CARE/University of East Anglia.

——— (1997), 'You Learn it from Your Mates, Don't You?' Young People's Conversations about Sex as a Basis for Informal Peer Education', *Youth and Policy*, 57: 44–54.

Ward, B. E. (1985), *Through Other Eyes*. Hong Kong: Chinese University Press.

Ward, H. et al. (1993) 'Prostitution and Risk of HIV: Female Prostitutes in London', *British Medical Journal*, 307:356–8.

Ward, H., S. Day and J. Weber (1999), 'Risky Business: Health and Safety in the Sex Industry over a Nine-Year Period', *Sexually Transmitted Infections*, 75: 340–3.

Wartofsky, M. (1984), 'The Child's Construction of the World and the World's Construction of the Child', in F. S. Kessel and W. Siegel (eds), *The Child and Other Cultural Inventions*, New York: Praeger, 188–244.

Warwick, D. (1982), *Bitter Pills: Population Policies and Their Implementation in Eight Developing Countries*, Cambridge: Cambridge University Press.

Weatherley, R. A. (1987), 'Teenage Pregnancy, Professional Agendas, and Problem Definitions', *Journal of Sociology and Social Welfare* 14:2, 5–35.

Weeks, J. (1989), *Sex, Politics and Society: the Regulation of Sexuality since 1800* (2nd edn), London: Longman.

Weiss, E., D. Whelan and G. Gupta (1996) *Vulnerability and Opportunity: Adolescents and HIV/AIDS in the Developing World*, Washington DC: International Centre for Research on Women (ICRW).

Wikan, U. (1989), 'The Situation of the Girl Child in Bhutan', Unpublished report to UNICEF, Bhutan.

—— (1990), *Managing Turbulent Hearts: A Balinese Formula for Living*, Chicago: University of Chicago Press.

Willis, P. (1977), *Learning to Labour: How Working-Class Kids Get Working-Class Jobs*, Aldershot: Ashgate.

Wilson, E. (1998), *Concilience: The Unity of Knowledge*, New York: Alfred A. Knopf.

Wilson, S. H., T. P. Brown and R. G. Richards (1992), 'Teenage Conception and Contraception in the English Regions', *Journal of Public Health Medicine*, 14:1, 17–25.

Wolf, M. (1970), 'Child Training and the Chinese Family' in M. Freedman (ed.), *Family and Kinship in Chinese Society*, Stanford: Stanford University Press, 37–62.

—— (1972), *Women and the Family in Rural Taiwan*, Stanford: Stanford University Press.

—— (1985), *Revolution Postponed*, Stanford: Stanford University Press.

Wood, K., F. Maforah and R. Jewkes (1998), 'He Forced Me to Love Him: Putting Violence on Adolescent Sexual Health Agendas', *Social Science and Medicine*, 47:2, 233–42.

Woodhead, M. (1997), 'Psychology and the Cultural Construction of Children's Needs' in A. James, and A. Prout (eds), *Constructing and Reconstructing Childhood: Contemporary Issues in the Sociological Study of Childhood*, London, New York, Philadelphia: The Falmer Press, 63–84.

—— (1998), 'Is There a Place for Work in Child Development? Implications of Child Development Theory and Research for Interpretation of the UN Convention on the Rights of the Child, with Particular Reference to Article 32, on Children, Work and Exploitation', Stockholm: Rädda Barnen.

World Bank (1994), *A New Agenda for Women's Health and Nutrition*, Washington DC: The World Bank.

—— (1995), *World Development Report*, Oxford: Oxford University Press.

—— (1996), *World Development Report*, Oxford: Oxford University Press.

——— (1998), *Improving Reproductive Health: The Role of the World Bank*, Washington DC: The World Bank.

World Congress Against the Sexual Exploitation of Children (1996), *Declaration and Agenda for Action*, Stockholm: Host Committee for the World Congress Against the Sexual Exploitation of Children.

WHO/UNESCO/UNICEF (1992), *Comprehensive School Health Education: Suggested Guidelines for Action for Adolescent Health*, Geneva: World Health Organisation.

WHO/UNFPA/UNICEF (1989), *The Reproductive Health of Adolescents: A Strategy for Action*, Geneva: World Health Organisation.

World Health Organisation (WHO), (1986), *Young People's Health: A Challenge for Society. A Report of a WHO Study Group on Young People and 'Health for All by the Year 2000'*, Geneva: World Health Organisation (Technical Report Series 731).

——— (1991), *Infertility: A Tabulation of Available Data on the Prevalence of Primary and Secondary Fertility*, Geneva: MCH/FP programme, WHO.

——— (1993a), *The Health of Young People: A Challenge and a Promise*, Geneva: World Health Organisation, Adolescent Health and Development Programme.

——— (1993b), *The Narrative Research Method*, Geneva: World Health Organisation, Adolescent Health and Development Programme.

——— (1994a), *Mother-Baby Package: Implementing Safe Motherhood in Countries*, Geneva: World Health Organisation, Maternal and Safe Motherhood Programme, Division of Family Health.

——— (1994b), *Abortion: A Tabulation of Available Data on the Frequency and Mortality of Unsafe Abortion*, Geneva: World Health Organisation, Maternal and Safe Motherhood Programme, Division of Family Health.

——— (1994c), *Health, Population and Development. Position Paper Prepared for the International Conference on Population and Development, Cairo, 1994*, Geneva: World Health Organisation (WHO/FHE/94.1).

——— (1998), *The Second Decade: Improving Adolescent Health and Development*, Geneva: World Health Organisation (WHO/FRH/ADH/98.18).

World Health Organisation and United Nations Children's Fund (UNICEF) (1996), *A Picture of Health? A Review and Annotated Bibliography of the Health of Young People in Developing Countries*, Geneva: World Health Organisation.

Wulf, D. (1994), *Refugee Women and Reproductive Health Care*, New York: Women's Commission for Refugee Women and Children.

Wulff, H. (1995), 'Introduction: Introducing Youth Culture in its Own Right: The State of the Art and New Possibilities', in V. Amit-Talai and H. Wulff (eds), *Youth Cultures: A Cross-Cultural Perspective*, London and New York: Routledge, 1–18.

Yanagisako, S. and C. Delaney (eds), (1995), *Naturalizing Power: Essays in Feminist Cultural Analysis*. London: Routledge.

Yoddumnern-Attig, B., K. Richter, A. Soonthorndhada, C. Sethaput and A. Pramualratana (1994), *Changing Roles and Statuses of Women in Thailand: A Documentary Assessment*, Bangkok: Institute for Population and Social Research, Mahidol University.

Younghusband, E. (1981), *The Newest Profession: A Short History of Social Work*, London: IPC Business Press.

Youniss, J. and M. Yates (1994), 'Introduction: International Perspectives on the Roots of Civic Identity', in J. Yates and J. Youniss (eds), *Roots of Civic Identity, International Perspectives on Community Service and Activism in Youth*, Cambridge: Cambridge University Press, 1–15.

Zabin, L. and K. Kiragu (1998), 'The Health Consequences of Adolescent Sexual and Fertility Behavior in Sub-Saharan Africa', *Studies in Family Planning* 29:2, 210–32.

Zeitz, D. (1969), *Child Welfare: Services and Perspectives*, New York: John Wiley and Sons.

Zelizer, V. (1985), *Pricing the Priceless Child: The Changing Social Value of Children*, New York: Basic Books Inc.

Zelnik, M. and J. F. Kantner (1980), 'Sexual Activity, Contraceptive Use and Pregnancy among Metropolitan-Area Teenagers: 1971–80', *Family Planning Perspectives*, 12:5, 230–7.

Zelnik, M., J. F. Kantner and K. Ford (1981), *Sex and Pregnancy in Adolescence*, Beverley Hills: Sage.

Index

R

S